VIRGINS of VENICE

VIRGINS *of* VENICE

Broken Vows and Cloistered Lives

in the Renaissance Convent

MARY LAVEN

VIKING

VIKING
Published by the Penguin Group
Penguin Putnam Inc., 375 Hudson Street,
New York, New York 10014, U.S.A.
Penguin Books Ltd, 80 Strand,
London WC2R ORL, England
Penguin Books Australia Ltd, 250 Camberwell Road, Camberwell,
Victoria 3124, Australia
Penguin Books Canada Ltd, 10 Alcorn Avenue,
Toronto, Ontario, Canada M4V 3B2
Penguin Books India (P) Ltd, 11 Community Centre, Panchsheel Park,
New Delhi – 110 017, India
Penguin Books (N. Z.) Ltd, Cnr Rosedale and Airborne Roads, Albany,
Auckland, New Zealand
Penguin Books (South Africa) (Pty) Ltd, 24 Sturdee Avenue,
Rosebank, Johannesburg 2196, South Africa

Penguin Books Ltd, Registered Offices:
Harmondsworth, Middlesex, England

First American edition
Published in 2003 by Viking Penguin,
a member of Penguin Putnam Inc.

10 9 8 7 6 5 4 3 2 1

Illustration credits appear on pp. xi–xii.

LIBRARY OF CONGRESS CATALOGING-IN-PUBLICATION DATA
Laven, Mary, 1969–
    Virgins of Venice : broken vows and cloistered lives
in the Renaissance convent / Mary Laven.
        p.   cm.
    ISBN 0-670-03183-6
    1. Monastic and religious life of women—Italy—Venice—
History.   2. Venice (Italy)—Religious life and customs.   3. Venice
(Italy)—Church history.   4. Convents—Italy—Venice.   I. Title.
BX4220.I8 L38 2003
271'.9004531—dc21   2002034924

This book is printed on acid-free paper. ∞

Printed in the United States of America
Set in Bembo
Designed by Francesca Belanger

For Nubar and Pallina

Contents

List of Maps and Illustrations

MAPS AND PLANS

pp. ii–iii: View of the city of Venice by Matthaeus Merian, 1630. London, the British Library, Maps 22670 (3) 1630. (Photo: British Library)

p. xiii: The Venetian Lagoon.

pp. xiv–xv: Plan of the city of Venice and the lagoon by Pietro Forlani, 1566, showing convents of Venice and Murano at that time. Venice, Museo Correr. (Photo: Museo Correr)

p. 13: Sixteenth-century plan of the church of San Servolo. Venice, Archivio di Stato, *Miscellanea Mappe* 57, DS 25/16, positivo 66. (Photo: Archivio di Stato)

INSERT ILLUSTRATIONS

1. The Convent of Sant'Alvise in Cannaregio. (Photo: author)

2. Surviving arch at Santa Maria delle Vergini. (Photo: Osvaldo Böhm, Venice)

3 & 4. Title pages of decrees regulating the behavior of visitors and prostitutes in the ambit of convents. Venice, Archivio di Stato, *PSM, B.* 269. (Photo: Archivio di Stato)

5. Gabriel Bella, *The Clothing Ceremony of a Nun at San Lorenzo* (before 1782). Venice, Fondazione Querini Stampalia. (Photo: Scala)

6. Roundel at the Miracoli. (Photo: Osvaldo Böhm, Venice)

7. Titian, *Portrait of Caterina Cornaro* (1542). Florence, Uffizi. (Photo: Scala)

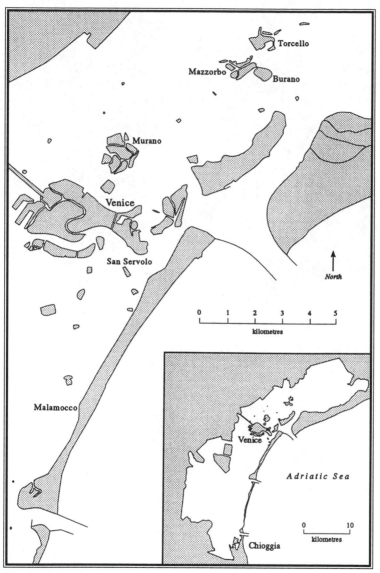

The Venetian Lagoon

The City of Venice and the Lagoon (1566), showing the convents of
Venice and Murano

KEY

Castello
1. Sant'Anna
2. Santa Maria delle Vergini (Le Vergini)
3. San Daniel
4. San Iseppo
5. San Sepolcro
6. Santa Maria della Celestia (La Celestia)
7. San Giorgio dei Greci
8. San Lorenzo
9. San Zaccaria
10. San Giovanni

Lateran
11. Santa Maria dei Miracoli
12. Santa Giustina (also parish church)

Cannaregio
13. Santa Caterina
14. Sant'Alvise
15. San Girolamo
16. Corpus Domini
17. Santa Lucia (also parish church)

San Marco
18. San Rocco e Santa Margarita

Santa Croce
19. Santa Chiara
20. Sant'Andrea de Zirada
21. Santa Maria Maggiore
22. Santa Croce di Venezia (also parish church)

Introduction

AKE A WALK into Cannaregio, the northwestern district of Venice, which is now dominated by the railway terminus. From the Strada Nova to the Lista de Spagna, a busy shopping route leads east and west to and from the station, following the curve of the Grand Canal. But cut north, and you will quickly find yourself in a quiet part of town, divided up by long, straight canals running in parallel, flanked by spacious pavements, or *fondamente*. Signs will lead you to a densely inhabited square, encircled by canals, whose crumbling buildings veer awkwardly up to the skies. This is the Ghetto Nuovo, the new ghetto.

Among Venice's many claims to fame, the invention of the original ghetto is perhaps the most ambivalent. In the Middle Ages, it was the site of the city's metal foundries; *geto* (foundry) came from the verb *getar* (to pour). Then, in 1516, following the relocation of the foundries to the opposite side of Venice, the government decreed that the city's Jewish population, "at present living in different parishes within our city," should be forced to reside within the disused *geto*.[1] The associations around the word would be irrevocably altered.

The island of the Ghetto Nuovo adapted well to its new function of segregating the Jews. (Its only drawback was that it was insufficiently large to house all of Venice's burgeoning Jewish population because the core of so-called *tedeschi,* from Italy and the German-speaking lands, was augmented by traders from Iberia and the Near East; hence the continued extension of the buildings upward.)[2] Just two bridges linked the ghetto to the rest of the city, and these were sealed off with gates. High walls were built to close off houses overlooking the surrounding canals, and all points of access to the water were blocked up. The gates to the ghetto were kept by Christian guards, who were salaried at the expense of the Jewish community. They ensured the observation of the nightly curfew, which lasted from dusk until dawn. Two patrol boats—also financed by the Jews—circled the island day and night. During daylight hours, the new inhabitants of the ghetto were allowed to go out into the city to ply their invaluable trades: lending money, selling secondhand clothes, and purveying medical services to those rich enough to pay for them. But when outside the ghetto the Jews were required to wear yellow hats, signaling to Christians to keep apart.[3]

If you strike out of the ghetto to the north, across the bridge that has long been ungated, and continue to walk toward the edge of the city, you will soon come to the convent of Sant'Alvise, the site of a very different enclosed community. The church announces itself by its solemn brick façade; a modest portico features the sculpted image of Saint Louis of Toulouse, the dedicatee of the convent. ("Louis" has mutated through the Italian "Luigi" to the characteristically Venetian "Alvise.") It is said that in 1388 the French saint appeared in a dream to the noblewoman Antonia Venier—a cousin of the doge, no less—commanding her to found a convent in his name. Venier duly obliged, bringing together a group of pious women under her leadership to follow the Rule of Saint Augustine. By the early fifteenth century, the nuns of Sant'Alvise were already flourishing, and, following a major benefaction by Pope Martin V, their wooden buildings were reconstructed in stony Gothic. In keeping with the convent's lofty origins, the nuns came almost exclusively from the families of the Venetian nobility.

One of the few Venetian nunneries that has retained its original function into the twenty-first century, Sant'Alvise is today inhabited by a small community of women belonging to the Canossian Institute of the Daughters of Charity, a religious order founded in the nineteenth century and devoted to medical care and education. Swamped by the buildings of the old convent, once home to over a hundred nuns, the current occupants let out the empty cells to young women studying in Venice away from home. As part of a modern order pursuing charitable activities across the world, the Canossian sisters lead a comparatively uncloistered life. But inside the church there survive some unsettling reminders of an older regime.

On entering the church, you find yourself at once overshadowed by the wood-beamed underside of the nuns' choir. Suspended upon two columns, this imposing structure connected directly with the nuns' living quarters. To the choir they would come, at regular intervals throughout the day and night, to hear mass and hold their own services out of sight of the public. They were shielded from view by a high wall, rising almost to the ceiling of the church; at head height a series of rectangular openings, secured with wrought-iron grates and shrouded with thick curtains, enabled the invisible women to hear and to be heard. During the offices, the church would have been filled with the eerie sound of their disembodied voices.[4] The veiled windows continue along the south side of the church, following the line of a corridor that joins the choir to the rest of the convent. Beneath them, toward the high altar, there survives the communion window, also veiled and grated, where the nuns would have queued up once a month or thereabouts to receive the sacraments from the hands of the priest—

an intensely dramatic moment when Christ's body was passed to the hidden community through a slit in the curtains.

Blind windows, concealed corridors, forbidding walls—these are the vestiges of a forgotten world. They were the concrete mechanisms by which nuns were once kept secluded and isolated from contact with the rest of society, and their function was symbolic as well as practical. The architecture cries out, "Keep your distance; do not touch"—a little like the veil of a Muslim woman, or the yellow hat of the Venetian Jew. So the aristocratic nuns of Sant'Alvise had something in common with their neighbors in the ghetto. And the origins of that overlap lie at the beginning of the sixteenth century. For at the very time when the Jews first came to live on an island in Cannaregio, the convents of Venice faced a concerted campaign of reform that would seek to subject all the city's nuns to compulsory enclosure—the principle that aspired to sever women in religious institutions from all contact with the outside world. This was no mere coincidence, for the segregation of the Jews and the enclosure of the nuns typified a certain style of discipline and order anxiously pursued by the Venetian authorities at the time. Other groups experienced similar treatment: In the same period, the government passed new laws insisting on the restriction of prostitution to a defined area, and foreign merchants were increasingly forced to reside within their own ethnic groups.[5] Thus the city was to be parceled up into zones. The blood of Venice was to be kept clean of foreign bodies. Vice was to be contained and virtue shielded. These campaigns of segregation and purification were motivated by insecurity—the profound insecurity of an ancient city-state which, at the height of its glory, seemed to some observers to be on the point of collapse.

By the standards of the preindustrial world, Venice was a massive metropolis. The capital of a republic extending from the Adriatic coast to within a few miles of Milan, its overseas dominions included the islands of Zakinthos, Cephalonia, Corfu, Crete and Cyprus, as well as large swaths of Dalmatia. Despite the sporadic ravages of plague, the city's population—exceeding 150,000 at its highest point—remained throughout the sixteenth and seventeenth centuries among the top ten in Europe. The wealth of Venice was built on trade with the East; for centuries, spices, dyes and other luxury goods had been brought to the city to be sold across Italy and Northern Europe. The docks and markets were thronged with foreign merchants, and the smells of local fish mingled with the exotic scents of nutmeg, cinnamon and ginger. Manufacturing also played an important role in the Venetian economy. The city's weavers turned out over 20,000 pieces of woolen cloth a year, and there were more than 2,000 silk looms in operation. Other local industries included the production and refinement of soap, sugar, wax and leather. The glass factories on Murano were already famous by the sixteenth century, and the republic's shipyard, the Arsenal (situated on the eastern edge of the city), was one of the new wonders of the world, its gates opening to 2,000 employees every day.

These commercial and industrial achievements provided the backdrop to the artistic and intellectual activities that marked the final brilliant phase of the republic's Renaissance. At the start of the sixteenth century, Carpaccio, Giorgione and Bellini were at work on the decoration of the Doge's Palace, and the printing presses of Aldus Manutius were dazzling the whole of Europe with their products. During the course of the century, massive programs of building and redevelopment were led by architects such as Palladio and Sansovino, while patrons competed to commission portraits and religious paintings from the hands of Titian and Tintoretto. Early in the seventeenth century, Claudio Monteverdi was introducing audiences to opera for the first time. And work was soon to begin on the church of the Salute, the architectural jewel by Longhena, which dominates to this day the entrance to the Grand Canal.

But despite these displays of growth and prosperity, Venetian society was experiencing a crisis of confidence. By the beginning of the sixteenth century, the republic's expansionist aspirations had made it an object of hatred and envy throughout Italy and beyond. Its bitterest enemy was the warrior pope, Julius II (in office 1503–13), whose pride could tolerate neither Venice's claims to independence in matters ecclesiastical, nor its occupation of papal lands in the Romagna (the area south of the republic, stretching from Bologna to the Adriatic coast). Invoking all his powers as a temporal and spiritual leader, Pope Julius first sponsored the League of Cambrai, an alliance concluded at the end of 1508 that united the major states of Italy and Europe against Venice. Then, on April 27, 1509, he pronounced an interdict upon the republic, banning its subjects from receiving the sacraments of the church and preventing its clergy from administering them. Here began a century of escalating conflict between Venice and Rome.

Opposed by the combined forces of Spain, France, the Holy Roman Empire and the papacy, Venetian troops suffered a crushing military defeat on May 14, 1509, at Agnadello, on the far western edge of the republic's empire. What was left of the vanquished army retreated to the safety of the lagoon, and the cities of the mainland dominions rapidly fell to the enemy. Only the capital city and a small portion of land to its north remained in Venetian hands. As Machiavelli, the contemporary Florentine political theorist observed, "If their city had not been surrounded by the waters, we should have beheld her end."[6] This traumatic and humiliating event appeared to mark the demise of the ancient maritime republic as a European force. But, despite the fact that it had been denuded of almost all its mainland territories, the city-state, with the help of its wealth and skillful diplomacy, managed to cling to its precious independence and to piece its empire together again in the years that followed. Still, events in the rest of Italy presented a terrifying reminder of what might yet happen, as every other corner of the peninsula was falling under the yoke of Spain.

Agnadello occurred as the Venetian state was coming to terms with the impact of new trade routes, which had jolted the Rialto from the center of the global economy. (News of the arrival of the first cargo of pepper at Lisbon in 1501 for some spelled the beginning of the end for the Venetian state.)[7] Partly as a result of this, the city's reputation for tolerance and liberality was increasingly tainted by claims from within and without that it was decadent and corrupt. Reacting to the growing uncertainties of commerce, many nobles retreated from a life of merchant enterprise to one of idleness and luxury. The ruling class of the republic, those men who by dint of their birth wore the robes of government and sat on the Great Council, became renowned for their gambling and their violence. Meanwhile, Venetian noblewomen attracted censure for their extravagant way of dressing, for their makeup and their high-heeled clogs. Foreign authors marveled at the "20,000 courtesans" who walked the streets, and at the presence of Jews and "infidels," who threatened to outnumber Christians. These ostentatious profanities were countered by a desperate piety. Public processions, acts of corporate devotion, redemptive masses and charitable benefactions proliferated in an effort to regain God's favor and forgiveness.

The convents of Venice—communities of women whose lives and bodies were consecrated to Christ—contributed ambiguously to this mood of spiritual anxiety. There had been nuns in the lagoon area since 640, the year in which the Benedictine community of San Giovanni Evangelista was founded on the island of Torcello. The earliest phase of expansion gave rise not just to the ancient and famous houses of San Zaccaria and San Lorenzo—founded in the ninth century, in the heart of Venice—but to a whole host of forgotten communities scattered throughout the lagoon. As convents on the more remote and swampy islands, blighted by malaria and indiscipline, were closed down, new communities grew up in the city itself. Contributing to the process of urban development, these mostly took root in the outer neighborhoods, or *sestieri,* of Castello (east), Cannaregio and Santa Croce (west), Dorsoduro and the Giudecca (south); there was just one convent in the *sestiere* of San Marco, and none at all in San Polo, the central *sestiere* incorporating the Rialto trading zone.[8] For it was on the edge of the city, often on land artificially reclaimed from the lagoon, that the swelling population of nuns found space to establish their many buildings, cloisters, courtyards and gardens.[9] By the middle of the seventeenth century, Venice could boast no fewer than fifty nunneries—thirty-three in the city itself and seventeen in the lagoon, concentrated on the islands of Murano, Burano, Mazzorbo and Torcello—accommodating well over three thousand nuns.[10]

On the one hand, these virgin colonies were construed as bastions of chastity and prayer, a precious spiritual resource that served to counterbalance the worldliness of the laity. On the other, they were perceived as places of vice and indiscipline, a spiritual liability that put the salvation of the whole republic in jeopardy. In the wake of Agnadello, the diarist Girolamo Priuli wrote that the city's nunneries were public bordellos, and the nuns public whores. He blamed the "most grave sins of these whoring nuns" (along with the nefarious deeds of "sodomites") for bringing about the ruin of the Venetian state.[11] Priuli, like many of his contemporaries, saw religious reform as essential if the city was to escape God's wrath. He condemned his fellow noblemen, in their capacity as the city's governors, for stopping short of imposing rigorous reforms upon their kinswomen in the convents.

Criticisms such as these evidently touched a nerve. For, at the time Priuli was writing, the Venetian authorities were on the point of initiating the most intense phase of reforms that the city's nunneries had ever undergone. In June 1509, the Senate passed the first in a new series of laws against those who violated the sacred boundaries of the convent. For those who dared to enter a nunnery without license or who were complicit in a nun's departure from the cloister, the penalties now ranged from imprisonment to perpetual exile. Meanwhile, the patriarch—the head of the Venetian church—was preparing to launch his own set of reforming measures against a target group of convents, which included the ancient houses of Le Vergini, La Celestia and San Zaccaria, all well-known for their aristocratic character and for their relaxed discipline. The most significant development in this ongoing crusade was the establishment, in 1521, of the *provveditori sopra monasteri,* a new state magistracy with special responsibility for affairs relating to the city's convents. The three noblemen who served as the convent magistrates, together with their staff of assistants and informers, rapidly turned their attention to policing the convent walls. It fell to them to enforce the new laws that aspired to obliterate all contact—from the most innocent and inconspicuous to the flagrantly sexual—between the city's nuns and the outside world.

In its drive to impose order and discipline on the city's nunneries, Venice was ahead of the game. In the early sixteenth century, the perceived corruption of the religious orders had been a major factor in precipitating the Protestant Reformation, which had torn the fabric of Christendom apart.

Protestant pamphlets had exhorted parents to liberate their daughters from the cloister (and from the sexual wiles of the predatory male clergy). This sort of propaganda was highly damaging to the credibility of Catholicism. But the Counter-Reformation—the process of internal reform and regeneration undertaken by the old church in response to the Reformation—was slow in rebutting it. Not until the 1560s did the Council of Trent, the great reforming council of the Catholic Church, set about devising a coherent policy for regulating the conduct of monks and nuns. The council decreed that all nunneries should be subject to compulsory enclosure, and its decision was reaffirmed by Pope Pius V's bull *Circa pastoralis* in 1566. This was a rare instance of a papal ruling with which the republic of Venice, notorious for its disobedience to Rome and its cynical approach to the politics of religion, could happily be in accord. After all, it had imposed enclosure almost sixty years earlier and had enforced it zealously, motivated if not by purely spiritual concerns then by a determination to protect the city's convents from scandal and ill repute.

But this unusual convergence of interests did not constitute a rapprochement between Venice and the Holy See. And in the early seventeenth century, relations between the two powers hit an all-time low. For the second time in less than a century, in the spring of 1606, the republic of Venice was placed under papal interdict and its subjects denied the sacraments. Once again, the conflict was fueled by a combination of issues in which spiritual and secular concerns were complexly intertwined. At the heart of the argument was the question of where the authority of the state ended and where that of the church began. Take, for example, ecclesiastical personnel. To what extent were the clergy—priests, monks, friars and nuns—subject to the power of the state? Could they be called upon to pay taxes to the republic? Were they exempt from criminal prosecution? Comparable jurisdictional issues related to the laity. Should a bigamist be tried by a secular or ecclesiastical court? What about a bookseller purveying heretical texts? Then there were the principles governing foreign policy. Was a Catholic state bound to take sides against infidels and heretics, even when its political and economic interests dictated otherwise? What level of toleration was it permissible to grant to Jewish or Muslim immigrants? These were hoary old chestnuts, debated not only in Venice but also throughout Europe and the New World.

The disputes over these questions were, however, rendered all the more intense thanks to the geographical proximity of the Venetian and papal territories, which played as important a part in precipitating this interdict as that pronounced by Julius II in the previous century. In relation to Venice, the pope was not just a spiritual leader; he was the temporal ruler of a neighboring power. In the run-up to the 1606 interdict, Pope Clement VIII (in office 1592–1605) sought to challenge the Venetian monopoly of Adriatic trade, and to establish the ports of Ancona and Goro, situated in his own territory, as rival entrepôts. The Venetians, meanwhile, attempted to put paid to the pope's schemes by undertaking complex engineering works in the Po Valley. They planned to cut a canal to reroute the river, thereby remedying flooding in Venice's southern territories. But the republic's actions would have another, not undesirable, consequence—they would disable Goro by turning the papal port into a muddy marsh. At the bottom of all the squabbles over jurisdiction, there smouldered a trade war.[12]

Another factor propelling events toward a second interdict was the renewed militancy of the Counter-Reformation church. This was clearly illustrated in the row over the appointment of the Venetian patriarch. In the name of improving standards, the Council of Trent had ruled that all bishops or their equivalents should have a degree in either theology or canon law (the law of the church). To these conditions, in 1592, Clement VIII added the requirement that all prospective Italian bishops come to Rome to be examined in divinity before the pope and a panel of cardinals. Such a ruling was anathema to the Venetians, who guarded their right to control ecclesiastical appointments jealously. On January 26, 1600, after ten years of energetic service, Patriarch Lorenzo Priuli breathed his last, and the Venetian Senate duly elected Matteo Zane to the post. Of Zane's expertise and experience in the world of international diplomacy there could be no doubt: He had served the republic as ambassador to Urbino, Piedmont, Spain, Austria and Constantinople. His theological qualifications were, however, nonexistent, and there were serious doubts as to whether he would be able to leap through the required hoops in Rome. After a year and a half of frenzied negotiations (and, one imagines, some closet cramming) a compromise emerged, and Zane headed off to Rome in order "to receive the honors which it pleased His Holiness to bestow upon him"—this was how the Venetians chose to word their concession. The pope contented himself with pitching questions at Zane's level, and both sides claimed victory.

A façade of cooperation had been maintained, but only just. The real crunch came when Cardinal Camillo Borghese was elected as Pope Paul V in 1605. An expert in canon law, Paul was determined from the outset to exact submission from those who trespassed on papal authority. Unfortunately, Venice had become more determined than ever to limit the pope's power. The government was now dominated by a party known as the *giovani* (youths, though they were far from being universally youthful), committed to defending "the liberty of the republic." In January 1605, preeminent *giovane* Leonardo

Donà was elected doge, much to the horror of the papacy. The story went that Donà had once met the young Cardinal Borghese when in Rome on a diplomatic mission. Borghese had said to the Venetian, "If I were pope, I would excommunicate you." Donà had replied, "If I were doge, I would laugh at your excommunication." These were to prove prophetic words.[13]

The Venetian response to Paul V's interdict was brazen. The government banned the circulation of the papal decree on pain of death. The majority of the clergy remained loyal to the republic and continued to administer the sacraments. Meanwhile, the cause of Venetian liberty—justified in the writings of Paolo Sarpi, propagandist supreme—became a rallying cry for states throughout Europe that wished to assert their independence from the Holy See. Print was just one of the weapons deployed in the propaganda war waged by the city of Venice. The government also sponsored theatrical rites of devotion in order to convey political messages to its subjects and to foreign observers. Most spectacular were the celebrations for Corpus Christi in May 1606. The Feast of the Body of Christ, occurring eleven days after Pentecost, was always a high point of the Venetians' devotional year, but its focus on the Eucharist—that precious sacrament the pope had attempted to withhold—made it the perfect occasion for a display of defiance. As the immense procession snaked its way round Piazza San Marco, several floats rammed home the republic's points. The most inflammatory float was sponsored by a group of local friars: It displayed a collapsing church supported by the doge, assisted by Saints Dominic and Francis (representing the religious orders). On either side of the church stood friars brandishing swords, inscribed with the motto *Viva il dose* ("Long live the doge.")[14]

In the event, this interdict lasted for nearly a year, eventually being brought to an end through the diplomatic mediation of Henry IV, king of France. But the war of words it had spawned lasted far longer. And for as long as this war raged, Venice was once again at the forefront of European politics, enjoying an international reputation as an island of republican liberty.

It is in the light of Venice's vexed history—its wavering status on the world stage, its determination to assert control over the local church—that we must understand the almost obsessional concern with subjecting the city's nunneries to enclosure. That is not to say that Venetian nuns were merely pawns in a game of international power politics, victims of forces beyond their control. The nun's relationship with the enclosed convent in which she lived out her days was more complex than that. To begin to think about the experience of life in the nunnery, we might turn to a fragment of evidence from the convent of Santa Maria delle Vergini, on the opposite side of the city from Sant'Alvise. Formerly one of the oldest and grandest of the city's nunneries, all that remains of Le Vergini now is the tracery of a neo-Gothic arch (once the main entrance to the convent church), which has been incorporated into a wall of the Arsenal. Beneath the arch, a plaque reads:

MDLVII ADI II MAZO

SPES ET AMOR GRATO

CARCERE NOS RETINENT

S.M. DELE VERZENE

"Hope and love keep us in this pleasant prison." The date of the plaque is May 2, 1557, so it was erected some years before the Council of Trent had begun to turn its attentions to the reform of nunneries. The activities of the Venetian secular and spiritual authorities had already turned the convent into a place of incarceration, albeit (from whose point of view?) a pleasant one.

That image of the "pleasant prison" encapsulates paradoxes that continue to dominate our thinking about the convent. On the one hand, nuns have been presented as helpless victims—victims of cruel parents, of tyrannical abbesses, of lascivious priests and of their own lusts and vanities. On the other, they have been cast as powerful women, whose separation from the domestic sphere presented opportunities rather than constraints. The former view belongs to an old tradition, sustained over centuries by moralists, satirists and—occasionally—pornographers. It is an outsider's view, to be found principally in the writings of male authors. The latter perspective is more recent, and has been nurtured above all within the sphere of feminist historiography. It is also an outsider's view.

As nuns have emerged as a feminist issue, we have been invited to see the venerable institution of the convent as a precious space of female independence and individualism. Not only did the religious life offer women a certain dignity, casting them as brides of Christ, but it could also offer practical possibilities for the wielding of power and the fulfilment of personal aspirations, possibilities not accessible to wives and mothers. Centuries before laywomen got the vote, nuns were regularly called to the chapter, where they would place their ballots in the box, electing one another to office, and participating in key decisions regarding the convent's future. The same women might be called upon to act, on the convent's behalf, as landowners, employers and administrators. Some nuns were empowered by educational advancement and creativity, others by their spiritual lives. Nuns' identities have been revealed in all their rich variety, running the gamut from rebellious saint to visionary lesbian.[15]

One scholar neatly sums up this way of thinking about nunneries when she writes (recalling Virginia Woolf's famous phrase), "for centuries, most of the women who . . . had a 'room of their own' found it in the cloister."[16] But the utopian vision of the nunnery presented by some feminist writers rides roughshod over the complexities articulated in that sixteenth-century motif of "the pleasant prison." Within the context of the campaign to reduce convents to compulsory enclosure—an initiative that was often hostile to women and derived from male authorities—there seems little cause for celebration. And yet, if one approaches the documentary evidence produced in this era of discipline and reform with the expectation of finding a uniform story of oppression, there will be surprises in store. For the records of prelates and magistrates, which provide the densest and most fascinating source of insights into the ways in which nuns encountered the reforms, testify to the ongoing struggle of religious women to exercise agency in the new, harsher climate of the sixteenth and seventeenth centuries.

This is the irony: Embedded in the records forged by male officials, acting on behalf of the institutions of church and state, are the lost voices of women in convents. At a time when nuns were denied access to pen and ink, and when their opportunities for communicating with the outside world were strictly limited, a visit from the patriarch or from the *provveditori* offered these women a rare chance to set forward their own responses to the convent life. In the course of their prosecutions, the convent magistrates interrogated thousands of witnesses—convent employees, priests, neighbors, nuns' friends and relatives—anyone, in short, who was in any way connected with the nunneries. These diverse accounts have survived in careful transcriptions, preserving the peculiarities of the local dialect, and registering the variations in language that reflected status and education. Every case sheds new light on the lives of nuns in the age of reform. Enclosure sought to keep out the curious. And yet, it is through the records of its implementation that we are granted entry to the convents of Venice.

VIRGINS *of* VENICE

1. Behind Closed Doors

To the sound of the organ, a procession of clerics files into the church, ushered in Cardinal Francesco Vendramin, successor to Matteo Zane as patriarch of Venice. Hidden from view in the choir, ninety-six nuns wait in anticipation while the priests celebrate mass below. Just one week ago, the women of San Zaccaria learned that their convent was to be subject to a new patriarchal visitation.

The abbess, Suor Andriana Gradenigo, and her deputies had hurriedly prepared the necessary documentation: the financial accounts of the convent, a register of all the nuns, noting their family names and ages, and a list of the priests who served in the church. We can be sure that they also toured the convent's extensive premises, quickly taking in the refectory, workroom, gardens and cloisters, as well as the dozens of private cells occupied by the aristocratic nuns, and sought to remove any obvious evidence of poor order. But seven days were scarcely enough time to accomplish major reforms, and in surveying the buildings, the convent superiors must have recalled with discomfort the instructions Patriarch Priuli had issued thirteen years earlier, which had somehow never been effected.[1]

Now, in October 1609, San Zaccaria had been selected as the first convent to be inspected by the patriarch in a series of "pastoral visitations," which would take the best part of ten years to complete. Like Lorenzo Priuli, who had performed his own thorough inspection of the convents during the years

1592 to 1596, Vendramin took his duties as shepherd to the city's nuns most seriously. After mass, he made his way to the chapter, the room in which all the professed members of the community met regularly to discuss the business affairs of the convent. Occupying the abbess's throne, the cardinal preached to the nuns on "the heavenly dignity of being Christ's brides." There then followed the *visita oculare,* a full visual inspection of the convent church and living quarters, which ranged from checking the grates on the windows and the bolts on the doors to conducting a book-by-book examination of the library. Once Vendramin and his men had taken in as much as they could with their eyes, they prepared to continue their investigations using their ears. Every one of the nuns came before the patriarch in order to answer questions regarding life in the convent and, as often as not, to air grievances against one another.[2]

The cacophony of tale telling that emerges from these records is ironic, for if there was a single issue that dominated the patriarch's questions, it was the maintenance of the common life. Enshrined in the three self-denying vows of poverty, chastity and obedience, this was the principle governing every detail of the monastic existence. The nun was supposed to live a life unencumbered by property, ambition and personal ties, and to love each and every one of her sisters equally. She was expected to eat from the common table in the refectory, to take her garments from the convent clothes store, to work alongside her sisters in the workroom and, of course, to participate in all the communal acts of worship. And yet, in reality, this ideal of community was honored chiefly in the breach. Time and again, the prelates who visited the convents found nuns asserting their individual and familial interests and fashioning their identities in willful opposition to the common life.

What would the patriarch have encountered once he had passed through the heavy gates of a Venetian convent? Judging from repeated remarks in the visitation records, it seems that his senses may first have been assailed by chickens. This in itself was not a matter of complaint. Just as convents had orchards and gardens in which fruit and vegetables were cultivated for the nuns' consumption, so they were encouraged to keep poultry in order to supply the community with eggs. The demand ran high, especially on Wednesdays and Saturdays, which were commonly fast days, but not fish days, when nuns were supplied with two eggs in the morning and a third in the evening, as an alternative to meat.[3] Thus a community of one hundred nuns would need to garner at the very least six hundred eggs every week.

It was the manner in which the chickens were kept, rather than the chickens per se, that attracted the criticisms of the patriarch. At several convents, hens were to be found wandering around upstairs in the dormitory.[4] An anonymous letter from a nun at Sant'Andrea de Zirada in 1609 complained that she could not proceed through the convent without walking in chicken shit.[5] Vendramin's concern, however, was not hygiene but property. For the birds that strutted through the living quarters of the convent belonged to individual nuns. The point was clearly made by the patriarch in 1610, following his visitation to the convent of Ogni Santi, when he instructed the abbess to have slaughtered all chickens kept on an individual basis and ensure that the meat was consumed communally in the "public refectory."[6] For the same reasons, nuns were not allowed to keep "either bitches or dogs" as pets.[7] At San Biagio e Cataldo in 1593, the women were given twenty-four hours to get rid of their dogs; as for "birds, doves, hens and other poultry," kept privately for profit or as pets, these were to be put into common use within three days.[8]

The issue of chicken ownership encapsulated the struggle between individuality and community that marked every aspect of the convent life. The patriarch would have seen the very same struggle being played out in the physical appearance of the nuns. The rules governing the dress and appearance of women in convents aimed at a modest and somber uniformity. Patriarch Vendramin exhorted the Sant'Andrea nuns to eschew fine and colored fabrics, especially silks; to wear a long wimple and a high-cut habit; and to cover their shoulders and breast with abundant veils. Their hair was, of course, to be cropped short, and "locks on the temples, and curls on the head" were expressly forbidden. Only flat shoes were allowed. The overclothes and underclothes of all the nuns were to be identical.[9] In writing this detailed set of prohibitions and instructions, Vendramin was reacting to the transgressions he had witnessed at that convent. Elsewhere, he chastised nuns for wearing low-cut dresses and commented on their locks, curls and frizzes as "inventions of the devil."[10]

Through their self-adornment and engagement with fashion (elaborate coiffures, gold jewelry, silk stockings, lace and those notorious high-heeled clogs for which the gentlewomen of Renaissance Venice were renowned), nuns expressed their opposition to the ideal of uniformity invoked by the prelates who inspected them. For some, the thrill of dressing up was intensified when they gained access to a mirror, or even a pane of glass, which allowed them the forbidden luxury of seeing their own images.[11] Although the patriarch and his men urged the nuns to adopt a more modest style of dress, they were probably resigned to the fact that these women treasured their every item of clothing as an expression of personal identity and material status, and those who could afford to do otherwise would rarely consent to dress from the communal wardrobe. Many of these women had, after all, grown up in palaces; they came from the highest ranks of Venetian society. Small wonder that they took pleasure in the trappings of wealth and that they shared in their lay sisters' propensity for sumptuous self-adornment.[12] When visiting San Biagio e Cataldo, Patriarch Priuli satisfied himself with instructing the nuns to use the *vestiario* (clothes store) as a repository for the garments of deceased nuns, thereby prohibiting items from being passed between nuns as personal bequests. But he acknowledged the perceived right of the women to have their clothes tailor-made from their own supplies of cloth.[13] In contravention of the vow of poverty, personal possessions were an institutional reality, and an accepted fact of convent life.

The convention whereby nuns were allowed to have their own possessions and dispose of their own financial resources was neatly worked into the rules governing convents. Thus Patriarch Vendramin told the women of Sant'Andrea:

> Since the nuns are prevented by their vow of poverty from having property, they are exhorted to follow the convention of other convents, that is to place their money in the safekeeping of the Mother Prioress . . . requesting that she put it aside until such occasion arises that they need to buy clothes . . . And they shall have only the use, not the dominion of such money.[14]

By such reasoning, nuns' spending habits were legitimized. It was common for noble nuns to receive from their relatives extensive annual allowances, which would be placed in the hands of the convent superior but made readily available for their "needs" and "necessities."[15]

The patriarch would also have been struck by evidence of personal property in the nuns' cells, which were viewed by many as private apartments to be furnished and adorned at their own expense. At Sant'Andrea in 1596, Patriarch Priuli urged the convent superiors to carry out unannounced inspections of the cells at least four times a year, and to search inside the chests, cupboards and desks of each to ensure that there was nothing in the way of "books, clothes, writings, dishonest paintings, dogs, birds, nor other animals" that did not conform to the rule.[16] Again, the list of prohibitions gives us a fair indication of what might in fact be found in a nun's cell.[17] The vow of poverty was contravened yet more brazenly when nuns saw fit to bequeath such fripperies to one another in their wills. Indeed, at San Daniel in 1604 the patriarchal visitors reported that the nuns made legacies not just of their clothes and furnishings, but of the cells themselves.[18]

The private space of the cell posed fundamental contradictions to the communal ideal. Modesty required that every nun sleep alone, but the patriarchal authorities feared what might go on behind closed doors. Consequently, they insisted upon the removal of locks and bolts from cell doors and the burning of candles all night long throughout the sleeping quarters. As a further precaution, older nuns were appointed to check every cell after the night bell had rung.[19] And yet the complaint was frequently made that nuns were sharing cells, a practice frowned upon not only because of the sexual temptations involved, but also because it constituted a violation of the common life. Conversely, the nuns of Corpus Domini were reprimanded for occupying more than one cell each.[20] At Spirito Santo, nuns attracted criticism not only for their sleeping arrangements, but also for sewing and reading in groups of three or four in their cells.[21]

The one private act within the cell that was sanctioned was prayer, but—as Patriarch Zane complained of the nuns of San Daniel—the time that was set aside for private devotions was too often given over to the pursuit of profit. For, in clear contravention of the ideals of poverty and community, nuns sewed and embroidered clothes, handkerchiefs and other accessories, which they sold outside the convent through intermediaries for personal gain.[22] Such enterprises were sometimes combined with leisure and hospitality. Nuns kept personal supplies of food and wine (including leftovers taken from the refectory) in their chests and store cupboards to share among their friends.[23]

The nun's cell offered a place of retreat from the common life. As well as being a repository of personal possessions, it was often the venue of selective sociability and a site for self-interested business activity. But the more public areas of the convent were also colonized by particular interest groups. The gardens of a nunnery were sometimes subdivided into a patch-work of individual plots in which nuns tended their own vegetables.[24] And, despite repeated prohibitions, the parlors—where nuns received visitors from the outside world—were frequently the scene of private parties and family get-togethers. Even those members of the community who deigned to work in the convent workroom and eat in the refectory were apt to sit with their close friends and blood relations rather than adhere to the prescribed order of seniority.[25] And groups of nuns who worked together—whether cooking in the kitchens, operating the looms or guarding the doors—often turned the place of their labor into a center for sociability where they ate, drank and made merry. At San Zaccaria the principal location of such "banquets" was the convent laundry.[26]

Above all, convents were united and disunited along family lines. Nuns ate and slept with their sisters, cousins or aunts, and looked for chances to further their families' interests in the outside world. The custom of sending noble girls from the age of seven to board in the convents where their aunts were nuns reinforced the bonds of family and lineage that cut across the religious community.[27]

Touring a convent in late Renaissance Venice, and speaking with its inmates, the patriarch and his assistant clergy became aware of a morass of alternative groupings and networks based on kinship, friendship, occupation and status. Such associations challenged the fundamental principles of convent life. Yet the institution itself was not without its formal hierarchies and divisions, and these could also be the source of tensions and enmities within the cloistered world.

To begin with, the convent population was made up of two distinct categories: *monache da coro,* or choir nuns, and *converse,* comparable to what we today call lay sisters. Technically, the difference between the two derived from the kind of vows they took. Choir nuns took full, solemn vows and progressed from the status of the novice to be first professed and then consecrated, whereas *converse* took simple vows once only.[28] But if the technical distinction was somewhat subtle, the social distinction between the two groups was blindingly obvious. *Converse* were the social inferiors of choir nuns, and they were treated as such within the convent. They did not bring great wealth to the community, but they did bring their labor. It fell to them to carry out the menial chores, and they were excluded from privileges and power. The rationale behind this system was that the presence of *converse* liberated the choir nuns from the more mundane duties of convent life to enable them to devote themselves to the rigors of piety. But the custom whereby *converse* were employed by noble nuns as personal servants told another story.[29] Choir nuns were not embarrassed to complain to the patriarchal authorities when the *converse* failed to act with sufficient deference or behaved "as if they were like us."[30]

Only choir nuns were eligible to become members of the chapter, the governing body of the convent, and to hold personal offices within the nunnery. Each office, known as an *obedientia,* had a term of one or two years, and selections had to be confirmed by the patriarch or his deputy.[31] During his visitation of Santa Maria Maggiore in 1594, Patriarch Priuli approved the appointments of over fifty nuns to posts ranging from gardeners and spicers through nurses and bookkeepers to sacristans and choir mistresses.[32] The list suggests the variety of careers available to women in convents, but also points to an unequal distribution of power. Some positions, such as those of novice mistress (in charge of schooling the new nuns) or gatekeeper, were senior to others, such as those of loom worker and baker. The most influential officeholders were the six or more *discrete* (discreet ones) or *madri di consiglio* (mothers of counsel), selected from among "the oldest and most prudent nuns."[33] These elderly sages constituted the ruling elite of the nunnery, but their supremacy did not go unquestioned. Frequent were the complaints noted by the patriarchal visitors that "the young nuns do not pay that respect which is due to their seniors."[34]

At the very top of the convent hierarchy was the abbess or, in certain houses, the prioress.[35] Her role was to oversee all aspects of conventual life, from economic affairs to discipline and devotion. Although all important business had to pass before the chapter, and certain offices had particular administrative duties, overall responsibility for managing the nunnery's resources fell to the abbess. Patriarch Priuli advised the abbess of Sant'Andrea de Zirada in 1596 thus: "You must make every effort to ensure that the nuns are provided for in health and sickness, and that the money, income and expenses of the convent are managed in accordance with our orders."[36] Above all, the abbess had to prevent the economic crises that could plunge a nunnery into ruin: "She must endeavour to ensure that the nuns do not suffer on account of negligent governance, or meanness, but must prudently supply their needs according to the resources of the convent."[37]

Patriarchal visitors did not hesitate to question nuns about those in charge of the convent, particularly regarding disciplinary matters. Interestingly, the nuns' complaints (and there were many) were less often against autocratic superiors than against weak ones. During the visitation of San Maffio di Mazzorbo in 1564, the remarks of Suor Brodata Minio were typical: "The abbess is but little obeyed, especially by the young nuns." This abbess failed to instill the respect owing to her, not only as head of the convent but also as a noblewoman. Suor Paula di Albori attached the blame to two renegade nuns, "who have treated the abbess as if she were a servant, and not a gentlewoman." Finally, Suor Andriana Basadona had this insight to offer: "She is obeyed in so far as she knows how to command, but the poor woman does not know how to command, and she is therefore little obeyed!"[38] Such accusations were common, suggesting that inversions of authority were both frequent and troubling. Choir nuns from the noble house of Le Vergini reported that "the abbess does not know how to exact obedience from the *converse*, who for the last five or six years have behaved as if they were choir nuns."[39] The inadequacies of the abbess had combined with the presumptuousness of the *converse* to turn the hierarchy on its head.

But what of the abbess's role as "head of spiritual government"? On this matter, the reports of the patriarchal visitors have rather less to say. It was, perhaps, inevitable that the abbess's authority over matters spiritual would be a pale reflection of that enjoyed by the superior of a male religious house. Excluded from the priesthood, nuns were reliant on the spiritual services of men to provide them with confession, communion and sermons. The abbess had merely to shepherd her sisters into the choir to fulfill their devotional obligations with the required regularity. But the comparative silence regarding the abbess's qualities as spiritual mentor to the other nuns reflects the more general concern of the Catholic Church to control, rather than to nurture, the religiosity of women. Mindful of Protestant attacks on Catholic "superstition," the authorities of the church were fearful of any departure from the spiritual norm. Following the Council of Trent, tales of the miraculous were vetted with increasing stringency, and the process of canonization was tightened up. Women—religious and lay—who claimed to have had visions or mystical experiences were frequently brought before the courts of the Inquisition, charged with "feigned sanctity."[40]

Regular, orderly, inconspicuous—this was the style of piety fostered by the authorities overseeing the convents. The nuns' devotional regimen was an exacting one. The day's monastic offices began in the middle of the night with Matins and continued at two-to-three-hour intervals until bedtime: Prime, Terce, Sext, None, Vespers and Compline. It was the vocation of the choir nuns to attend all of these services and to "stand, sit, face the front, kneel, incline the head, and make every reverent gesture according to the correct procedure and due order of the office." As mechanical as these motions might seem, the nuns were warned that their prayers would count for nothing if spoken only with the tongue, and that they must be accompanied by devotion from the heart.[41] The intensity of their religious observances took its toll physically. In 1638, the community of San Zaccaria petitioned Rome, complaining that the nuns were suffering from recurrent sickness as a result of their having to get up in the middle of the night to recite offices. The officials in Rome responded sympathetically and conceded that in future they could say Matins either in the evening or in the morning after an uninterrupted night's sleep.[42]

On the whole, however, prelates exhorted women in convents to an ever more strenuous life of piety. The full schedule of communal prayer was supplemented by private prayer and meditation. Nuns were supposed to fling themselves onto their knees as soon as they got out of bed and to thank God for having preserved them from the devil throughout the night. Before going to bed in the evening, they were expected to examine their consciences lest they had offended the Lord during the day.[43] In between, they were urged to engage in "continuous meditations" upon the glories of the virginal state.[44] Confession and communion remained relatively infrequent obligations. The Council of Trent required nuns to take communion and to confess just once a month, though "the good and pious custom" of taking the sacraments more frequently was sanctioned.[45] By contrast, penitential activity featured more prominently in the devotions of nuns. A visitation report, addressed to the nuns of Sant'Andrea by Patriarch Priuli, urged the women to "render the spirit more ready for devotion" by mortifying the flesh. To this end, Priuli proposed that the nuns fast and whip themselves, and he encouraged them to participate in meetings of the *capitolo delle colpe*—literally, "the chapter of faults"—at least once a week.[46] These were community gatherings at which individual nuns were expected to come forward and confess their sins, "not excusing their own defects, but heaping accusations and blame upon themselves"; it was then the role of the abbess or prioress to mete out penances.[47]

These were the standard elements in the religious timetable of Venetian nuns, the habitual observances that were supposed to regulate every nun's daily life. Of course, things did

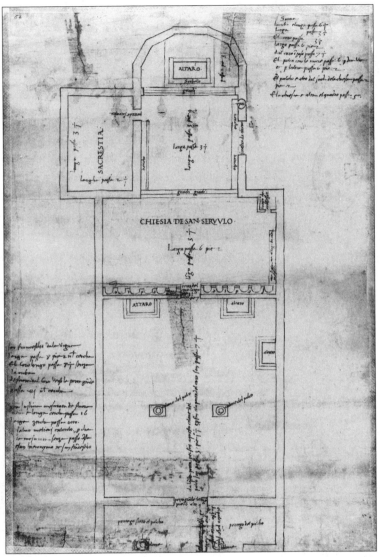

Sixteenth-century plan of San Servolo, showing the typical design of
a convent church. On the right hand side near the high altar is the
fenestra da comunicar, through which the nuns took communion; next
to it is a *roda,* or wheel, which allowed things to be passed between
the nunnery and the church without human contact. The pillars in
the nave supported the nuns' choir.

not always proceed according to the rule book. Visitation reports provide ample evidence of offices being neglected or of penances being dodged. At Santa Croce della Giudecca, the nuns concealed their laxity behind the barriers of enclosure. So concerned was the patriarch about their failure to attend sermons that he ordered a small window in the nuns' choir to be kept open so that the preacher could judge the size of his audience within; the nuns, however, were to be shrouded in darkness so that their anonymity could be maintained while their heads were counted.[48]

Unsurprisingly, perhaps, the testing rituals of the *capitolo delle colpe* were not always adopted with enthusiasm. At San Rocco e Santa Margarita, the nuns met to disclose their sins but once a year; at Santa Giustina, the sessions occurred nominally once a week, but in practice the nuns shied away from making their confessions before the community.[49]

For the most part, however, the evidence suggests that nuns fulfilled their spiritual obligations. Typical is the response of one nun at San Biagio e Cataldo, when asked about her observances: "I confess and take communion with all the other nuns, and I hear mass once a day; I say my prayers at the prescribed hours."[50] The life of the nun was dominated by religious routine. Even meals and practical employment took place to the sound of holy readings.

Fearful of excess, prelates did their best to root out additional stimulants to the nuns' spiritual imagination. Suspicious of the emotive power of Baroque music, they forbade the nuns from singing elaborate anthems and from playing musical instruments. It was preferable for the women to speak rather than to sing the liturgy, but in convents where singing was customary, only plainchant should emanate from the nuns' choir.[51] Access to painting and sculpture—perhaps the most powerful media of Counter-Reformation piety—was severely restricted. The artistic treasures that we may see today in the surviving churches of convents—for example, the sublime Bellini altarpiece of the Virgin and Saints at San Zaccaria or Alessandro Vittoria's statue of John the Baptist poised on the edge of the font at the same church—would rarely if ever have been seen by the nuns, who were excluded from the public part of the building.[52] Not that this stopped prelates from insisting that paintings in convent churches should conform to "pious decorum and sacred beauty," avoiding "scandalous rich colours and profane ornaments."[53] But the most significant art for nuns was that situated within the confines of the enclosed convent—in the refectory, in the choir, in the corridors of the nunnery.[54] While convents commissioned artists from the city to supply images to adorn their enclosed quarters, nuns were themselves sometimes engaged in providing artwork for their communities. Sadly, a photograph is all that remains of an embroidered altar frontal, a meticulous reproduction of Tintoretto's *Crucifixion* in the Scuola Grande di San Rocco. The frontal was sewn by two of the artist's daughters, Ottavia and Perina, for the church of the convent of Sant'Anna, where they were nuns in the early seventeenth century. In laboring over their copy of the masterpiece, the two nuns paid tribute not just to their Lord God, but also to their father, who had died in 1594.[55]

Nuns' access to books was also closely controlled. The inspection of the convent library was an essential part of the patriarchal visitation. Patriarch Priuli took with him two priests specially appointed for the purpose. Their job was to read and censor every book in the convent, inscribing the acceptable volumes with their signatures, and removing the unacceptable.[56] Few could have remained. Saint Ambrose on virginity, Jean Gerson's *Imitation of Christ* and *Lives of the Saints* were among the few books permitted in the libraries of Venetian convents. Reading aloud, in the refectory or workroom, was a ceaseless discipline. Bishop Antonio Grimani of Torcello, who had responsibility for the twenty or so convents on the lagoon islands, prescribed a cycle consisting of three books: a chapter of a "spiritual book," a chapter of the rule (Saint Benedict, Saint Francis or Saint Augustine, depending on the order of the community), and a chapter of the bishop's own diocesan regulations for nuns. As soon as one of the volumes was complete, the nuns were obliged to go back to the beginning and start again.[57] Sermons, too, were designed to control rather than to inspire. Reinforcing the agenda of the reformers, they focused on the merits of discipline and obedience, peace and union, poverty, virginity and contempt for the world; preachers were advised to steer clear of "high, subtle and philosophical questions," and "to accommodate their sermons to the intelligence and state of their listeners."[58]

How most nuns responded to this unappetizing diet of spiritual instruction we do not know. Occasionally, noble nuns expressed their dissatisfaction with the clergy who served them and demanded access to more inspiring or better-qualified confessors.[59] Others were simply bored by the regimen. Indeed, the exhortations of the church authorities to the nuns "not to chat nor laugh nor behave scandalously in the choir" sometimes suggest that they were fighting a losing battle.[60]

Chattering and laughing in the choir might suggest mere indiscipline, but it could also be seen as a rebellion against the humdrum routines of the convent. That some nuns desired more, not less, from the religious life—a more intense and personal relationship with God—is demonstrated by one extraordinary tale of a nun who attempted to break free. Suor Gratiosa Raspi escaped from the Franciscan convent of San Sepolcro in 1618. She paid a boatman to supply her with an outfit of men's clothes and row her from the convent (which was situated on the Riva degli Schiavoni not far from San Marco) to the mainland. Her plan was to enter a friary at Rua, near Padua, where she hoped she would be able to lead a more austere way of life. Once discovered, Suor Gratiosa was returned to her convent, where she was interviewed by the patriarch's vicar or deputy. This is her own account of why she ran away:

> Inspired, as I believed, by the majesty of God . . . I left the convent with the intention of becoming a friar at Rua, where I would live in chaste and pure service to God, pursuing the most austere way of life, believing that this mortification of the body would be pleasing to the Lord and of service to him. . . . This thought came to me having read that Saint Marina and Saint Eufrosina had each led a life in a monastery of friars. And it was my idea that if this plan could not be achieved, then I would join the female community of capuchins in Padua or some other place, wherever I could go.

Suor Gratiosa's plan belonged to a holy tradition, of which she was well aware. Both the saints mentioned by her did indeed serve God under the habits of monks. Eighth-century Saint Marina (of Bythinian origins) was, moreover, a cross-dressing model of local significance, since her relics were transferred to Venice in 1230. Gratiosa's choice of religious houses—the Camaldolese hermitage at Monte di Rua or, failing that, the Capuchins (a reformed offshoot of the Franciscan order)—signaled an awareness of where to find the top Counter-Reformation monastic communities in the Padua region. For an enclosed nun, she was surprisingly well informed about the outside world.[61]

Gratiosa's plan was thought out and executed with care. She slipped out of the convent unseen, carrying with her a crucifix, the office of the Madonna, two unnamed "spiritual books," a hair shirt, and her "discipline" (or flail). She also had money to purchase clothes from the boatman who rowed her out of Venice. But her disguise was not foolproof, and the suspicion of a fellow traveler was aroused when he heard her moaning from exhaustion: "Poor me, wretched me"—"*Poverina mi, meschina mi*"—the feminine endings of the adjectives she used gave her game away!

Gratiosa was at pains to stress that "it was never her intention to return to the world, either to get married or to live in any other manner"; and further, that "she would rather die a thousand times than leave the convent to such a wicked end." Her actions were the result of spiritual, not worldly motives. Her quest, which she now perceived as foolhardy, had been for a more rigorous penitential regimen. She confessed that she had made a "very great error," and that she now knew "as a result of her past mistakes, that *this* is my vocation."

Suor Gratiosa's case was a one-off. Others may have shared her aspirations, but they did not act with her daring, and their stories have not come to light. But the tale of her escape is important in suggesting how a nun's dissatisfaction with the conventual existence could manifest itself even in the spiritual realm. The monotony of the nuns' daily observances—like the rules that governed their dress and diet—was intended to subordinate the individual to the common life. As with every other effort to standardize nuns' conduct, it met with resistance.

In a variety of more subtle ways, the nuns of Venice sought to reshape their devotions according to their own needs and interests. The chores and obligations of daily life were offset by a whole host of special occasions, which broke up and brought variety to the year. Nuns were acutely attuned to the rhythms of the liturgical calendar, its feasts and its fasts.[62] So important was food to the religious life of the convent that business contracts were drawn up to ensure the provision of the correct festive fare throughout the year. According to a tenancy agreement of 1614 for the lease of a farm on the mainland, belonging to the convent of San Bernardo in Murano, Agnolo Fratisoi was obliged to make his basic annual payment of twenty-five *stara* (circa 2082 liters) of fine-quality wheat on the feast of Saint Peter (June twenty-ninth). On the same day, he had to supply the nuns with a pair of fat pullets. The next payment was due on the feast of Saint Michael (September twenty-ninth): twelve *mastelli* (*c.* 900 liters) of good wine. For All Saints Day (November first), the nuns demanded a goose, "a fine live bird, big and fat." At Christmastime, a large pig (weighing one hundred local pounds) and two fat capons were required; and at Carnival, a pair of black hens. A final payment of one hundred eggs was due at Easter.[63]

Adapting the injunction to receive the sacraments on a monthly basis—a routine that held little meaning—nuns preferred to link their confession and communion to particular feast days. One nun at San Biagio e Cataldo reported that the nuns confessed and took communion twelve times a year, "that is, on all the feasts of the Madonna, as well as that of All Saints, the beginning of Advent, and the beginning of Lent." The nun went on to modify this statement, adding that her community did not receive the sacraments on the feast of the "February Madonna" (the Purification of the Virgin, or Candlemas, on February second), preferring to delay communion until the following day, which was the convent's own feast commemorating the early Christian martyr San Biagio (or Saint Blaise).[64] On these holy days, it was customary for nuns to give their father confessor, in recognition of his services, a gift of food—

a basket of figs or some fresh eggs.[65] Other special occasions, such as the days on which nuns took and reiterated their holy vows, also prompted gift giving. One nun revealed that she had presented the confessor with six gifts to mark the occasion on which she had taken her final vows—a pair of white doves (living), presented in a basket lined with scented carnations; a box containing four men's collars; an *agnus dei* (missal) bound in crimson satin embroidered in gold; a basket of biscuits; a pair of chickens; and, finally, a confection of marzipan given together with six handkerchiefs.[66]

These moments of joy and festivity, expressed through celebratory gifts and meals, were counterbalanced by periods of fasting and remorse. Just as the week was punctuated by symbolic fast days (Wednesday, Friday, Saturday), so the year was broken up by Lent and Advent, extended periods of fasting and self-mortification. According to another nun at San Biagio e Cataldo, "every night during Lent, we assemble in the dark in the new dormitory, and we whip ourselves; and during Advent we do the same, twice a week."[67] The rituals of flagellation provided an important occasion for releasing tensions within the enclosed community. Experiences such as these had whetted Suor Gratiosa's appetite for a more rigorous penitential regimen.

The patriarchs who visited the convents of late Renaissance Venice saw lives caught between renunciation and self-indulgence, monotony and flashes of high color. While touring cells furnished with fine rugs and embroidered linen, opening up chests of clothes and jewels, or cupboards replete with food and wine, the visitation teams were appalled by the luxury enjoyed by some nuns. But such impressions of opulence sat alongside reports of institutional hardship, insufficient funds, food shortages, poor wine, draughts and damp.[68]

In December 1594, during the visitation of Santa Chiara, Patriarch Priuli experienced the discomforts of the nunnery firsthand. So indisposed was the patriarch, because of the extreme cold and bitter wind that prevailed in the convent buildings, that he was forced to abandon the visitation and take to his bed. Returning after Christmas, the visitors noted that the choir—to which the nuns were required to go during the night as well as the day—was "very cold and windy," and they proposed that the nuns' seats should be raised above the draughts.[69] In the minds of the patriarchal visitors, the extravagance of the individual and the impoverishment of the community were closely linked. If the nuns of Santa Chiara could not afford the costs of adequately roofing their buildings, this was the result of profligacy and waste. Indeed, the same visitation report, which told of the dire physical condition of the convent, complained that the nuns were squandering the resources of the community through their excessive gifts of cakes and doughnuts.[70]

The visitations of the Venetian nunneries resulted in detailed lists of "disorders" and "orders"—accounts of what was wrong with the nuns' conduct, followed by instructions for rectifying these abuses. The documents testify to the reforming zeal of the patriarchs in this age of discipline, but they also reveal the density of transgression that they faced. The reiteration of the same "disorders" from one patriarch to the next—vain choir nuns, disrespectful *converse,* chickens in the dormitories—underlines the perennial failure of the visitation as a means of reform. The nuns knew that the authorities would not come back for another decade or so; so in the meantime, they would carry on much as they had done before. Perhaps the visitors had most to suspect when the nuns appeared to greet their commands with compliance. Following the visitation of San Zaccaria in 1596, the patriarch got wind of the fact that "some of the young nuns, who had tamed their hairstyles for the visitation, went back to adorning themselves after the visitation."[71] No sooner had the doors slammed behind the patriarch than the nuns returned to their old ways.

The persistence of these somewhat tawdry abuses must have been a source of perpetual disillusionment for Counter-Reformation zealots like the Cardinal Patriarchs Priuli and Vendramin. And yet they knew that at the root of all the indiscipline lay a wrong far more serious, one for which the nuns themselves were not responsible. For no amount of reforming energy could turn the convents of Venice into well-run communities of obedient nuns when those same institutions were filled with women who had no calling to the religious life.

2. Becoming a Nun

A girl lies prostrate, her lips touching the stone floor. A black cloth is thrown over her, and lighted candles are placed at her feet and at her head. Up above her, the litanies are being sung. All the signs suggest that she is dead. She is a witness at her own funeral. From within her bier she accompanies the singing with tears and sobs, sacrificing all her senses to suffering and pain.[1]

THESE CHILLING WORDS were written toward the middle of the seventeenth century by a nun at the Venetian convent of Sant'Anna: Elena Cassandra Tarabotti, better known by her religious name, Arcangela. Tarabotti considered herself the victim of a "forced vocation." Rather than being called to the religious life, she had been compelled to become a nun against her will, in accordance with the interests of her family. Her destiny had been determined by two circumstances that lay entirely beyond her control—she was the eldest of six daughters, and she was lame. Since her parents could not possibly afford to provide all their daughters with marriage dowries, they concentrated their efforts on finding good husbands for their younger daughters, who were free from physical disabilities—a strategy that also allowed the family to buy time while the all-important dowries were raised. Over three decades after her consignment to the convent, as she neared her fiftieth year, Tarabotti wrote against the kind of treatment she had received in a diatribe that she entitled *Inferno monacale* (*The Nun's Hell*). This anguished work bears testimony to the misery of the unwilling nun. And, highly rhetorical though the *Inferno* undoubtedly is, the paradoxical "forced vocations" against which Tarabotti inveighed were a socioeconomic fact that, centuries later, historians have not disputed. Tarabotti was one of thousands of women who—having kissed the stony ground and made the irrevocable vows of poverty, chastity and obedience—passed through the doors of the nunnery never to return to the outside world.

Becoming a nun was a sacrificial rite. That much was made clear by the liturgies of the ceremonies at which women took or renewed their religious vows, the rituals of clothing, profession and consecration. These were the three main events in the passage of a nun's life, events which in some ways paralleled the progression of the laywoman from nubile adolescence through betrothal to marriage, for women who embarked on the religious life took Christ as their spiritual husband. Like secular brides, they wore robes of white. As in the marriage ceremony, the climax of profession and consecration was the placing of the ring upon the woman's finger. Taking the nun's right hand, the patriarch—for it was he who officiated—proclaimed:

> I marry you to Jesus Christ, son of the Father Almighty, your protector. Accept therefore this ring of faith as a sign from the Holy Spirit that you are called to be the wife of God.[2]

But whereas the marriage of a young woman might involve a good deal of reorientation, by forcing her to recommence life at the center of a new household and family, the nun's vows committed her to an even sharper uprooting. "Forget your people, and your father's home" was the injunction that newly accepted novices received at their clothing. Casting off their lay garments, the incomers allowed their hair to be cut short before taking the veil; then they made the physical transition from the public church to the enclosed convent.[3]

Who were these women, and what motivated them to enter the convent? These were questions that contemporary observers answered without hesitation. Patriarch Giovanni Tiepolo, head of the Venetian church from 1619 to 1630, stated that the nuns were noblewomen, women "brought up and nourished with the utmost delicacy and respect." Their confinement within the walls of the convent owed nothing to "the spirit of devotion," everything to "the impulse of their parents."[4] Sir Henry Wotton, English ambassador to Venice, had expressed the same view. In a letter of 1608, he wrote that women were being forced into convents against their will by their parents, "who to spare so much marriage money, impose commonly that life upon three daughters at least if they have five, and so in proportion."[5]

By "marriage money," Wotton was referring to the dowry—the woman's portion or share of her family's fortune, which was paid to her on the occasion of her marriage.[6] While the dowry was a woman's legal right, the amount her father was prepared to pay varied according to the condition she was marrying into. An ambitious marriage alliance with potential social or political advantages for the bride's family might be deemed worth the payment of a very large dowry. At the opposite end of the spectrum, there lay the relatively cheap option of the convent. Like other brides, nuns brought a dowry with them, but the sum required by the convent was generally small compared with that demanded in the marriage market. In return, these women were provided with an honorable and secure home until their deaths.

Among the elite of Venetian society, the birth of a baby

girl would always give rise to the same dilemma, *maritar ò monacar:* Would she marry or become a nun? The family's calculations were based on the perceived marriageability of the girl (taking into account such things as her health and physical appearance), on the number of sisters she had and on the funds available for her settlement. The final question was the most pressing, and at a time when the elite marriage market in Venice was characterized by soaring dowry inflation, few noble families could afford to marry off all their daughters. As Wotton suggested, it was the strategy of some noble fathers to parcel out their female offspring into two camps, dispatching certain daughters to the convent while concentrating their dowry expenditure on one or two others so as to secure the most impressive alliances for their families.[7]

The alarming rise in the size of noble-marriage dowries dated at least from the beginning of the fifteenth century, and in 1420 the Venetian Senate imposed its first legal limit, capping the maximum outlay on a dowry at sixteen hundred ducats. Significantly, as the wording of the decree reveals, this measure was partly motivated by concern about forced vocations; because of the rising cost of marriage, fathers were finding themselves constrained "to imprison their daughters in convents, with due weeping and wailing" (the Latin makes it clear that it was the daughters, not the fathers, who were distraught).[8] Testifying to the ineffectiveness of earlier efforts to restrict dowries, in 1505 the Senate passed another law raising the official ceiling to three thousand ducats.[9] Still the legislation failed to achieve its objective. The inflationary trend continued throughout the century, with noble dowries often exceeding twenty thousand ducats. In his letter of 1608, Henry Wotton commented that "no gentleman's daughter requir[ed] less for the bestowing of her than twenty-five or thirty thousand crowns in present money, which some two hundred years since was a good provision in the public treasury."[10] (At this time, a journeyman mason could expect to earn an annual salary of around fifty ducats.)

As Venetian noblemen herded their daughters into the convents, taking little notice of the children's wishes or their spiritual vocations, they excused themselves, in Wotton's words, "with the excessive rate into which marriage portions are mounted here." It was as if the families were unwilling players in a system that had run far beyond their control. But dowry inflation was, in reality, a man-made problem.[11] It occurred as a result of two strategies consciously pursued by the Venetian nobility. The first was the age-old refusal of Venetian patricians to marry outside their caste. The second was marriage limitation, a policy designed to preserve the family fortunes from dispersal among a profusion of heirs. While noble families sought to buttress their wealth and status by securing only the most prestigious alliances for their daughters, they discouraged their sons from marrying at all. Pursuing military, political, professional or commercial careers, it was common for unmarried noblemen to live with their brothers in all-male households. In this way, the elites of early modern Venice practiced birth control.[12] The tactic led to an ever decreasing number of eligible bachelors, and at the same time caused dowries to escalate, as fathers competed with one another to secure the best match for those daughters whose destiny was marriage. In a society where it was unthinkable for noblewomen to marry beneath themselves, convents served to accommodate those who would never marry at all.

The use of the convents as dumping grounds for unmarried noblewomen sat uncomfortably with the objectives of religious reform. This was a concern that preoccupied the authorities of church and state throughout the Catholic lands of Europe. For not only was the practice of forced vocations an abuse in itself, but the presence of involuntary nuns in convents was bound to lead to further cases of corruption and indiscipline. The Council of Trent provided unequivocal condemnation of any person who was in any way complicit in forcing a woman to enter a convent.[13] In order to ensure that candidates for the religious life came of their own free will, they were to be examined by a bishop or his deputy. The candidate for the novitiate was also to be tested on the regulations and requirements of the rule, an examination to be repeated before profession.[14] Besides episcopal approval, professions had to have the blessing of the convent superiors. The council also imposed minimum-age requirements: twelve years for the initial clothing ceremony, when the novice took the religious habit and uttered her first vows, and sixteen years for profession, when the vows were repeated and confirmed. The novice had to have been clothed for at least a year prior to her profession.[15] Reformers emphasized the probationary function of the novitiate. As a further safeguard of the novice's freedom, the council laid down that no dowry was to be paid to the convent until the time of profession.[16]

In the city of Venice, where, as we have seen, the elites depended on the convents to accommodate their unmarried daughters, one might imagine that the directives of the council posed particular difficulties. And yet, local evidence suggests overwhelming deference to the reforms emanating from Trent and a shared concern regarding the abuse of vocations. The attack on forced vocations received wholehearted endorsement in the constitutions and decrees published in 1592 by Bishop Antonio Grimani. In his regulations for the admission of nuns, much of what Grimani instructed was translated directly from the council's rulings.[17] But he also added certain strictures of his own, imposing precise limitations on kinship links within the convent and requiring a two-thirds-majority approval from the convent chapter before a candidate might be admitted to clothing or profession. The strongest indication of Grimani's commitment to eradicating forced vocations was his raising of the minimum age of clothing. Slightly apologetically, he explained his divergence from Trent: Although the holy council had set the minimum age for taking the nun's habit at twelve, this did not prevent provincial authorities from establishing a higher age requirement. And so Grimani laid down his more stringent lower limit of fifteen years, to enable the girl "to make her judgement with greater maturity, and to express her will more freely."[18]

But despite the church's official stance against forced vocations, even the most committed reformers recognized the difficulty of prising the convents from their settled place in the family strategies of the Venetian nobility. Commenting in 1580 on the problem of introducing reforms to the convents of Venice, Alberto Bolognetti, the papal nuncio (literally, "the pope's messenger" in the republic), observed that it was already hard enough for noblemen to persuade their daughters to enter convents; if the reforms were enacted, these same girls would refuse absolutely to take the veil. The striking thing about Bolognetti's argument, dispatched back to his masters in Rome, was his appreciation of the dangers of interfering with the local convents. He understood that any attempt to impose strict discipline on the nuns "would cause the ruin of many families, on account of the excessive dowries which nobles are accustomed to give those daughters who marry."[19]

The plea for a pragmatic approach was articulated most transparently by Patriarch Giovanni Tiepolo, who urged the doge and Senate against too strict an imposition of conventual austerity. Tiepolo proposed that the dilution of traditional monastic obligations—fasting, wearing rough clothes and sleeping on uncomfortable straw mattresses—would ameliorate the situation of involuntary nuns; they would be, "if not consoled, at least less miserable." But while Tiepolo was sympathetic to the plight of women compelled to become nuns against their will, he reiterated the absolute necessity of forced vocations:

> If the two thousand or more noblewomen, who in this City live locked up in convents as if in a public storehouse, had been able or had wanted to dispose of themselves differently, what confusion! What damage! What disorder! What dangers! What scandals, and what terrible consequences would have been witnessed for their families and for the City![20]

Tiepolo clearly believed that without recourse to the "public storehouse" of the convents, families would unleash their willful daughters onto society, plunging the city into chaos and anarchy.

Sacrificing women to Reason of State: This was how the writer Arcangela Tarabotti viewed any such attempt to justify the practice of forced vocations.[21] Her attack draws on the language of political analysis, which in the Renaissance was increasingly directed toward understanding the kind of machinations for secular power that we today still call Machiavellian. The pragmatic compromises of scheming men were intolerable to this nun, herself confined within the walls of Sant'Anna as a result of their tidy social arrangements. In Tarabotti's eyes, no relaxation of the regulations, or bestowal of material favors, could make up for the loss of liberty inflicted on involuntary nuns. Moreover, she also believed that such concessions contributed to the corruption of the convent and were unwelcome to those with a true calling to the religious life. *L'Inferno monacale,* dedicated to "The Most Serene Republic of Venice," challenged the authorities of church and state to dismantle the entire social edifice of the convent as storehouse for women of the elite.

In Tarabotti's impassioned analysis, for an involuntary nun the convent was at once jail, inferno and tomb. Correspondingly, forced vocations amounted to political, spiritual and personal death. Political death, because coercion to take the veil contravened the rights and liberties of the individual. Tarabotti was disgusted at the termination of a woman's freedom to choose her own destiny, a termination that might be effected while the baby was yet in the womb: "With what execrable paternal cruelty do parents consign their daughters to live in a nunnery, even before they are born?"[22] As she argued in another of her polemical treatises, the *Tirannia paterna* (*Paternal Tyranny*), there was no natural reason why girls should be thus deprived of their liberties. Contrasting the humanity of animals with the bestiality of men, she observed that "bears, tigers, vipers, basilisks and every crude, poisonous and untamed beast, feed and tenderly love their offspring, making no distinction between male and female."[23] As for the unequal treatment of girls from the same family, this was just as untenable: "It is impossible to find a law that grants married women greater claims than nuns on the houses of their parents."[24]

Angered by the imprisonment of young women against their will, Tarabotti sanctioned filial disobedience:

Daughters must obey their parents in just and licit matters, not in unreasonable ones; besides which, in operations which respect the internal movement of the will, no creature is held to obey any other than the Creator. And thus the father must not and cannot marry off that daughter who wants to remain a virgin; nor is she obliged to submit to his determination and force. Like-

wise, nor can the father compel his daughter to become
a nun without the cooperation of her free will.[25]

Tarabotti's stance was persuasive, but whether the right of resistance was a practical possibility for women is another matter. Set aside the economic difficulties of refusing the status
quo; as Tarabotti herself vividly demonstrates, the mechanisms
of deception were so well polished that the young woman or
child on the point of entering a convent might be ignorant of
her own will.

Women who became nuns without a true vocation did
not just lose their rights during this life; they jeopardized their
salvation in the next, risking consignment to the everlasting
inferno and spiritual death. Tarabotti believed that forced vocations profaned the house of God, and in this respect her position was shared by many Catholic reformers. Rather than
increasing in virtue, nuns who are placed in convents against
their will "become more sinful and cause offence to their unwillingly accepted Spouse."[26] Vanity and vice are perpetuated
by the older nuns who, embittered by their own experience of
the cloister, fail to provide a model of the true religious life.
When young girls are admitted to the convent, they are instructed by these old women, who

> instead of enjoining them to adopt a rigorous silence,
> assure the girls that they can make as much noise as they
> like. No effort is spared in organizing balls, singing,
> music, masked parties and festive meals. And while they
> neglect to oblige the young nuns to remember to med-
> itate upon the lives of the saints, they diligently celebrate
> the solemn feasts of Saint John and Saint Martin with
> parties and revelry, as if these festivities were unbreak-
> able precepts.[27]

With such corruption and laxity pervading even the highest ranks of the monastic community, Tarabotti perceived the scandals that periodically struck the convents of Venice as inevitable. When it came to pointing the finger of blame at the fathers of unwilling nuns, she did not mince her words. "Just consider this a moment, oh Ministers of Satan, that by forcing your daughters to enter convents, you are participants in all their scandalous deeds."[28]

It is clear that Tarabotti viewed forced vocations as profoundly damaging to the character as well as the soul. This was the third kind of death awaiting the involuntary nun—the convent as emotional tomb. Testifying to the psychological damage suffered by coerced women, she observes that "those who remain shut up in convents against their will, benign, silent and dear things that they are by nature, are angered and offended by the wrong which has been inflicted upon them, and become unworthy and embittered and lose their natural and proper qualities, having been denied the opportunity to act according to their general inclination."[29] Tarabotti's own grief at having been forced to become a nun is perhaps most evident in her accounts of the "funereal ceremonies" of clothing and profession: sacrificing beautiful locks of hair; making the irrevocable vows; sitting in the refectory at the celebratory meal, unable to eat.

Perhaps contrary to the expectations prompted by the title, the *Inferno* is conspicuously not an attack on the religious life per se. Tarabotti protests from the outset that her arguments "are not intended to blaspheme religion, but only to oppose those fathers and other relations who violently gag their daughters."[30] Just as she condemns parents who force their daughters into nunneries, so she denounces those who stand in the way of genuine vocations. Moreover, while she despises the avarice of fathers who subject girls to the "extreme parsimony" of convent life, willing sacrifice is to be applauded. In her most explicit avowal, she declares,

> With head bowed, I kneel down and exalt to the stars the sanctity and merit of those convents and nuns who are properly governed and who, called by heavenly inspiration in accordance with their own will, expose themselves to the sufferings of the monastic life.[31]

The inferno of Tarabotti's title was the hell of the *unwilling* nun.

Yet, while Tarabotti protested against the fate of such involuntary nuns, her sisters seem to have remained largely silent. One does not hear of women being dragged to the convent gate screaming and kicking or of profession ceremonies being stopped short by novices refusing to utter their vows. The reluctance of Venetian women to take the veil was only alluded to indirectly, as when Alberto Bolognetti wrote of the difficulties of imposing disciplinary reforms upon the convents. A comparable comment was made by the abbess of San Biagio e Cataldo in the 1590s, as she accounted for her lenient style of government: She did not consider it appropriate to mete out stiff penances such as flagellation or fasting to her erring charges, given that "the girls are placed here more for safekeeping than as nuns." And yet when each of her nuns was interviewed individually by the patriarch's vicar, and asked expressly about the circumstances of her profession, the answers were uniform: "I made my profession voluntarily and have always been happy."[32]

We cannot take these formulaic responses at face value. The pomp and formality of a patriarchal visitation did not necessarily generate honest, open replies. Moreover, the women would have been aware that it was too late to protest against their vows; to claim that they had made their professions unwillingly would have been tantamount to admitting perjury before God. In a recent study, the historian Jutte Sperling insists that the passage of over 50 percent of Venetian noblewomen into convents must have been the result of coercion.[33] And it is certainly true that those who seek to interpret the flood of female vocations as a spiritual movement will look in vain for evidence from Venice. Likewise, arguments about the appeal of the early modern convent as a haven for female autonomy are hard to sustain in the light of restrictive reforms and, in particular, the imposition of compulsory enclosure—policed and regulated by male authorities. But universal coercion is a strong claim, for which the evidence is sparse.

For Arcangela Tarabotti, the minimum measure of compliance needed to seal a nun's fate was obtained by means of trickery and deceit. As she lamented, "All men are liars in all circumstances, but when it comes to assassinating a miserable girl, their deceptions and falsehoods are greater than ever."[34] False promises of luxury and comfort in the convent and the reassuring pledge of frequent visits from relations became transparent as soon as the first vows had been secured. Fathers received assistance in duping their daughters from older nuns inside the convent, often kinswomen.[35] Thus elderly "aunts" who had themselves been victims of forced vocations avenged their abuse by abusing their young relatives, "weaving the most fabulous yarns undreamt of by even the most famous and gifted of poets" to persuade their nieces to take the veil. Tarabotti claimed that these women would go so far as to adorn the trees in the convent courtyards with sugared almonds and fruits in order to con young girls into believing that the gardens of nunneries yielded sweet things.[36]

Also viewed as conspirators were the mothers of potential

nuns whose own lives had been favored with the privileges of the married state, and who conferred all their affection on those daughters who would become brides.[37] A set of anonymous Venetian verses from the sixteenth century constructs a dialogue between a mother and daughter who are arguing over the proposal that the girl become a nun.[38] The mother concentrates on the spiritual advantages of the religious life, of serving God "outside the travails of the world." But she also invokes negative arguments for the undesirability of marriage: "I know from experience, if you marry you will be sorry for it, so stay out of danger, and listen to my advice." The daughter is unpersuaded and begs her mother not to force her to become a nun. She feels nothing but revulsion for the religious life as she contemplates the prospect of endless services and the continual shouting of the abbess. Furthermore, she is being courted by a handsome young man, whose attentions she would be mad to give up in order to take the veil. In a parting shot, the girl reminds her mother that, whatever she may say against it now, she herself has never been one to eschew the married life:

> Mother, you married
> And when your husband died
> You took another,
> Then a third, and a fourth.
> So don't complain
> If now I take a husband;
> Your advice was good,
> But you didn't follow it yourself.

Like Tarabotti, the poet emphasizes the double standard and hypocrisy of those intent on pushing women into the religious life.

Too bad that we cannot go back to the palaces of late Renaissance Venice to listen in on real conversations and arguments between adolescent girls and their parents. Such conversations, if they happened, may in fact have taken place in the convent parlor, for many women who became nuns had already spent the best part of their childhood within the walls of the convent, being brought up and educated by nuns. While the notorious phenomenon of the child nun had been countered by the decrees of Trent, the admission of boarding girls, or *educande,* from the age of seven ensured that those who were expected to take the veil had seen little of the outside world by the time of their profession.

But beyond the literary record, where do we look to find evidence of the process of deception and coercion? In the case of Venice, trial records point us in the direction of a small number of self-proclaimed "involuntary nuns." These include nuns who had committed sexual transgressions and who testified that they had been forced into the convent against their will.[39] A handful of women who attempted to escape from Venetian convents also claimed to have been victims of forced vocations, insisting that "they put me in the convent by force," or that "I have never been content in the religious life."[40] Locked in her room and held at knifepoint by her father, Suor Crestina Dolfin, who ran away from the convent of Spirito Santo in 1561, provides one of the most clear-cut cases of coercion. Besides physical threats, her father apparently obtained her compliance with flattery and inducements.[41]

In interpreting these tales, we need to be alert to rhetorical ploys. Some women under investigation may have claimed to have been forced into the nunnery in order to mitigate their subsequent misdeeds. Others who had taken religious vows freely and willingly had obviously grown disillusioned with the conventual life. These were circumstances in which nuns might retrospectively fashion themselves as victims of coercion.

A colorful example of just how contradictory the evidence about vocations can be is provided by the case of an escapee nun named Suor Faustina, who fled San Giovanni Lateran in 1555; it was rumored that she was pregnant.[42] Faustina was the illegitimate daughter of Francesco di Polo, who made a lengthy submission to the convent magistrates detailing the circumstances in which his daughter had entered the nunnery. According to Francesco, it was Faustina's aunt, Suor Tadia, a nun in Treviso on the Venetian mainland, who first proposed that she should come to live with her as a boarding girl at her convent of San Theomisto. It was never, Francesco claimed, his intention that Faustina should become a nun. Thus he was rather concerned when, from time to time, he received letters from the girl expressing her intention to take vows. Francesco responded with delaying tactics. Seeking to revive Faustina's taste for the world, he led her to Venice at Carnival time; but with weeping and wailing she begged him every day to return her to the convent. And so, several months later, seeing how fixed Faustina's mind was, Francesco "was forced" to allow his daughter to be clothed as a nun, with a conventual dowry of two hundred ducats (no great sum, incidentally, at least not in comparison with the dowries demanded by convents in the city of Venice).

Faustina lived devoutly at San Theomisto for several years, and went on to take the vows of profession and consecration. But things started to go wrong after the death of her aunt, an event which Faustina darkly attributed to the persecutions and spitefulness of the other nuns. She wrote to her father claiming that she could no longer stand such malign people. Francesco sought to console Faustina, but one day she received a visit from a male cousin and decided to run away with him to the home of a maternal aunt. Being informed of her flight, it fell to Francesco to fetch his daughter and to arrange for her transfer to the Venetian convent of San Giovanni Lateran. Soon afterward, she fell into the company of one of the convent employees, Francesco dalle Crosette. When, some years later, she was found in bed with that man, she and her lover fled. This is where, amid indignant splutterings, the account of Francesco di Polo ends.

Thus Faustina, the girl with the unstoppable childhood vocation, ran away from the conventual life for the second time. Or, as becomes clear later on in the trial, for the third time. For, two years earlier, soon after Faustina's arrival at San Giovanni, several of that convent's neighbors had been disturbed in the middle of the night by a noise on the rooftop. When they opened the hatch onto the roof, they saw the nun, who began to plead with them:"Help me, for the love of God! If you don't let me in, I shall throw myself off the roof. For I have been kept for six months in prison under the stairs of San Zuan [Giovanni] Lateran."[43] The neighbors were sympathetic, and the fugitive nun assured them that not only did she have somewhere to go to, but that she also had a husband. This extraordinary detail, entirely absent from the father's account, is nevertheless substantiated in the testimony of other witnesses. One nun called to give evidence tells of Faustina's sometime betrothal to a man who was subsequently banished from Venetian territory, for what reason we do not know. Francesco dalle Crosette, when interrogated by the convent magistrates, spoke of how Faustina had been "taken away from her husband" by her father. Faustina herself spread the word that she had been forced to become a nun by her father and stepmother.

The accounts of Faustina and her father do not tally. And there is good reason to read all the evidence with a degree of skepticism. On the one hand, Francesco di Polo was clearly protesting too much. His attentiveness to his illegitimate daughter's wishes appears somewhat strained, even before we have heard her side of the story. On the other hand, whatever the circumstances of her vocation, Faustina was now up to her neck in misdemeanors. Her best defense was to claim that she had been forced to take the veil. If we can recover anything from the case of Faustina di Polo, it is that the usual factors of youth, innocence and family pressure contributed to the muddle of the girl's vocation.

Such cases do not bring us much closer to understanding why thousands of Venetian noblewomen of perhaps no more than average religiosity, and with little evidence of divine calling, complied in the process of becoming nuns, and spoke their vows once, twice and three times over, "with their mouths" if not "with their hearts." Fascinating as stories like Faustina's might be, we would perhaps do better to steer clear of the exceptional examples of transgressive nuns; for the proportion of women who ran away from convents was, of course, tiny when set against all those who accepted their lot to live and die within the cloister.

Let us return to the moment at which a nun took her vows. A late eighteenth-century painting by Gabriel Bella of a noblewoman taking the veil at the Venetian convent of San Lorenzo provides an interesting contrast with Tarabotti's accounts of the vow-taking ceremonies. The scene is viewed from the public part of the church, and the focal point of the image is the woman kneeling before the altar while the veil is placed over her head. Behind the gilded grilles of the church, we can make out the faces of nuns watching the proceedings from within the enclosed area. In front, there are scores of musicians—men singing and playing viols—occupying six rows of pews, while the main body of the church is filled with about a hundred laypeople. These are clearly identified by their black robes as noblemen and women, accompanied by their servants. Some of the women are seated at either side of the church, but most of the congregation is milling around or standing in small groups. The picture conveys an atmosphere of cheerful celebration.[44]

Tarabotti makes no mention of such crowds of well-wishers gathered to see a nun on her way. Her description of the festivities and parties with which every convent marked the taking of religious vows reduces these events to a parody of the nun's grief. But the ceremonies of clothing, profession and consecration were often lavish occasions, commonly involving both the convent and the nun's family in considerable financial outlay. Convents were regularly chastised for their excessive expenditure on flour, eggs and almonds, the principal ingredients of the cakes and pastries that were the mainstay of nuns' festivities. And, in a parallel move to the laws regulating marriage dowries, there were repeated efforts from both church and state to restrain the sums of money that Venetian families spent on their daughters in nunneries. According to new laws introduced in the early seventeenth century, the cost of a Venetian nun's dowry was set and standardized at one thousand ducats; alternatively, parents could make a commitment of sixty ducats per annum for their daughter's lifetime. True, the conventual dowry amounted to perhaps only a twentieth of the marriage portions bestowed on a noblewoman. However, whereas a woman's marriage dowry remained her property, to leave to her heirs or take back to her own kin after her husband's death, the conventual dowry could never be reclaimed. A guardian might have hoped to have retained some control over the marriage portions of his female dependents, but he knew that the payments made over to a convent were lost forever. And yet, the records of convent dowries suggest that the payments continued to creep up, with families in the midseventeenth century contracting to pay convents a lump sum of say eight hundred ducats in addition to a sixty- or ninety-ducat annuity.[45]

The dowry was the biggest but not the only cost of becoming a nun in early modern Venice. Most noble nuns brought with them a *cassa,* or chest. It is the same word that is used for the marriage chest (usually called a *cassone* in other parts of Italy), and it refers not just to the box, but also to its contents—clothes, linen, domestic items and accessories. These were the commodities with which the noble nun furnished her cell, enabling her to re-create some of the luxuries and comforts of home life. The new nun was also allocated a sufficient amount of money with which to entertain the rest of the community at her clothing, profession and consecration: fifty or sixty ducats for each of the festivities, as well as coins to give out to all the other nuns in celebration of her arrival. The trend in the provision of such extras remained steadily upward throughout the seventeenth century, and contracts demonstrate that many parents threw in an additional "donation" or gift to the convent to supplement the legally restricted dowry. Nor did the family's financial commitment cease with the nun's admission. It was perfectly common for nuns to continue to rely on further support from their relations during their life inside the convent. The patriarchal visitors compiled lists of those nuns who received regular private incomes deriving from assets that had been given or bequeathed to them. But it is clear that these established revenues reveal only a part of the picture and that financial assistance was more often provided on an ad hoc basis.

The provision of a personal allowance and other material benefits did more than oil the passage of the aristocratic nun into the convent. Such assets were markers of status that enabled the nun to preserve her social and familial identity within the enclosed world of the nunnery. The noble nun did not sever links with her family at the gates of the convent; on the contrary, she fully expected to receive ongoing financial and emotional support from her kindred left outside. The importance of family connections was also evident within the walls of the convents; as we have seen, it was uncommon for a noble girl to enter a nunnery where there were no aunts, cousins or sisters to welcome her.

It is to the family that we must look in seeking to understand why women in Renaissance Venice accepted the convent as their destiny. Women entered the nunnery in response to family pressures. Parents selected daughters for the convent in the same way that they negotiated marriage alliances for their male and female offspring. Just as there were cases of involuntary vocations, so there were also forced marriages, and both would occasionally result in women escaping or petitioning for release from their vows. But, for the most part, nuns—like secular brides—internalized the needs of their families and responded to the call to act in accordance with the family honor.

The force of this call is well illustrated by a letter from the Venetian writer, Giovanni Loredan, sent in the midseventeenth century to his niece, Laura Pasqualigo. Laura, who had apparently agreed to take the veil, was now having doubts. Loredan, a writer most famous for his libertinism and—ironically—a friend of Tarabotti's, urged his niece to have a care for "the reputation of your family and for the quiet of your soul." He went on:

> You are born noble, and of a most worthy family; but seeing as you do not have a dowry equal to your birth you will have either to degrade your condition or to venture into the discomforts of poverty. To stain the

nobility with inferior sorts is to encounter universal contempt. To conjoin with poor fortunes is to share and multiply miseries. Marriages which are unequal in birth and equal in poverty always result in unhappiness. . . . But the good sense of your ladyship condemns my exhortations as superfluous. I know that upon wise deliberation you will wish to console your parents, to bring stability to your lineage, to find security for yourself, to give an example to the young, and to make known to your descendants that prudent minds do not allow themselves to be tyrannized by human considerations but by reason.[46]

Loredan's coercive rhetoric is irksome to the modern reader, but there is every reason to believe that his concern with family reputation would have struck a chord with many women embarking upon the cloistered life.

3. Blood of the Republic

ONE SUMMER'S DAY IN 1521, Doge Antonio Grimani received a visit from an angry woman aged 106. Her name was Anzola Boldù, and she was the abbess of the Franciscan nunnery of Santa Chiara. She headed a delegation of six nuns, all noblewomen, who were accompanied by members of their families; also in attendance was a male representative from the Franciscan order. The nuns came to the doge in order to protest the fact that the governance of Santa Chiara had been taken from them and handed over to a group of women from the convents of Santa Croce and Santa Maria dei Miracoli. This measure was part of a program of reforms initiated by Patriarch Antonio Contarini, which—to use a modern analogy—"bussed" nuns between the model observant convents of the city and those communities known as conventuals, which were considered lax and in need of reform. The ousted nuns claimed that they were being ill-treated under this new regimen. According to Boldù, the observants gave them nothing to eat, and they were starving to death. The situation was insupportable.[1]

In response to Boldù's complaints, the doge acted swiftly, immediately commissioning an inquiry into the affair, to be undertaken by the patriarch and by Cardinal Grimani, the protector of the Franciscan order in Venice. (The cardinal was, as it happened, the doge's son.) But in the meantime, the problem was snowballing. Less than three weeks after Boldù's mission, four more abbesses set out from their convents—Santa

Maria delle Vergini, San Zaccaria, Santa Maria della Celestia, and Santa Marta—destined for the ducal palace. Again, the nuns were accompanied by a host of relatives and supporters. The women threw themselves on their knees before the doge. Then the abbess of Le Vergini spoke on their behalf in Latin, "delivering almost an oration." The next speech was made by Nicolò Michiel, a nobleman with daughters and sisters at San Zaccaria. He railed against the imposition of "nuns of a different order, rule, and habit" upon the noblewomen of San Zaccaria, and—with little concern for accuracy—he characterized the new nuns as "Greeks, bastards, and plebs." Furthermore, he claimed that in the 760 years of the convent's history the nuns of San Zaccaria had invested forty-six thousand ducats in building projects, including the construction of a "most beautiful refectory," all of which had now been taken away from them. The reforming enterprise of the observant nuns was perceived here as nothing less than theft.[2]

Throughout late summer, the protests and petitions kept rolling in. The behavior of the conventual nuns only served to remind the patriarch of the need for reform. He scolded the women who came to the palace for daring to step outside the walls of their convent, and pronounced excommunication upon anyone who helped to further the cause of the conventuals.[3] At the Cistercian convent of La Celestia, the old community tore down a wall of the convent grain store in an attempt to regain control of their food supplies.[4] But while the patriarch continued to lament the unruliness of the conventuals, the state authorities realized that these women had to be appeased. On September seventeenth, following the visit of yet another delegation of relatives to the doge and his counselors, the decision was taken to elect "three honourable gentlemen" to resolve the disputes between conventuals and observants and to see to the fair allocation of resources between them.

This was the origin of the *provveditori sopra monasteri,* the state magistracy that oversaw convents.[5] It was an expensive and radical measure, but it worked. The rampaging nuns were at last quieted.

These events are amply recorded in the diary of Marin Sanuto, the foremost political journalist of his day. Why was Sanuto so interested in the battles of warring nuns? Why, moreover, were a centenarian abbess and her followers able to capture the attention of the Venetian government, and ultimately to persuade it to act in the safeguarding of their interests? Why, in short, were nuns such a hot political issue in late Renaissance Venice?

There is one answer to all these questions—social status. The conventual abbesses who objected to the reforms instituted by the patriarch came from the ancient families of the Venetian nobility, the very families that filled the republic's governing councils and monopolized its offices of state. The protesting nuns had extensive networks of influence outside their convents, a fact made palpable by the presence of relatives who rallied with them to the ducal palace, and further indicated by the patriarch's threat to excommunicate anyone who assisted in the conventuals' cause. The speeches of Nicolò Michiel, with their insulting rhetoric directed against the observant nuns, reveal the extent to which the dispute was articulated in terms of class conflict. Michiel condemned the patriarch's program of reforms as an act of "cruelty used against the nobility."[6]

By and large, the people of sixteenth- and seventeenth-century Europe were not encouraged to believe in social mobility. The social order was presented as being God-given and therefore fixed. Just as kings ruled over subjects, so nobles were superior to commoners, and that innate superiority was often translated directly into political power. Rank was pulled at every level of society. Merchants distinguished themselves from craftsmen by never working with their hands, and only selling goods. The distance between master craftsmen (who were permitted to run their own workshops) and journeymen (who were mere employees) was energetically maintained by the trade guilds. Within the household, the master and mistress were styled rulers of their children, servants and apprentices. But even by the standards of the time, the stratification of Venetian society was particularly rigid. Indeed, the unchanging nature of its social order was taken to be one of the factors behind its enduring political stability. Although other cities in the Italian peninsula were continually afflicted by internal dissension and popular rebellions, Venice was, in the words of the nineteenth-century historian Jacob Burckhardt, "the city of apparent stagnation."[7]

There were three tiers to the Venetian social order: *nobili, cittadini* and *popolani*. The nobility was a defined hereditary caste which, with certain tightly controlled exceptions, had been limited to some two hundred clans and families since 1297. Only in 1648, when the republic was preparing for war against the Turks, was noble status put up for sale, allowing for the ennoblement of forty new families. The nobility was also quite literally the ruling class. All legitimate noblemen over the age of twenty-five sat in the Great Council (*maggior consiglio*), in which sovereignty was vested. Beneath the nobles, the citizens of Venice formed a secondary aristocracy. These included "newcomers" to the city (those who had arrived after 1297!) as well as nouveaux riches. Citizens could never aspire to join the nobility, but they were accorded a certain amount of influence through their monopoly of offices in the doge's chancery, the republic's civil service.[8] Finally, the great mass of Venetians belonged to the plebeian class, encompassing prosperous artisans and shopkeepers as well as the poorest members of society. Excluded from the formal channels of influence, the *popolani* were nevertheless renowned for their acquiescence to the state.[9]

At every level of the caste system, intermarriage—what anthropologists term "endogamy"—was the norm. In the case of the nobility, "marrying out" had serious legal consequences. A law of 1422 excluded from office the sons of noblemen born to "vile" or nonnoble women, and the creation in 1506 of a *Libro d'oro,* or "Golden Book," a register of all noble marriages, served to define and preserve the purity of noble blood. But in practice, the prevention of *mésalliances* depended crucially upon the existence of the nunneries. For thousands of women like Laura Pasqualigo, warned by her uncle Giovanni Loredan that "to stain the nobility with inferior sorts is to encounter universal contempt," the only viable option was to enter the convent. This was why the nobility had such a stake in the convents of Venice and why the highest echelons of government concerned themselves with the plight of the nuns.

The convent's place in the family strategies of the Venetian nobility was suggested by the ceremonies surrounding marriage, both secular and sacred. For many young noblewomen, who had been sent to board in a convent during their childhood and teenage years, married life began on the threshold of the convent. Noble clans met to conclude marriage contracts in the parlors of convents.[10] And on the eve of the wedding, flotillas of gondolas took the bride and her entourage to visit her sisters and other relatives in the local nunneries. While reformers inveighed against this mixing of secular and religious society, and prohibited nuns from touching the hand of the bride, the impetus to involve convent women in the rituals of marriage died hard. The noble girl, about to embark on married life, wished to take leave of her relatives in the convent; the latter provided presents and hospitality to see her on her way.[11] At the same time, many nuns and their relatives saw the ceremonies of clothing, profession and consecration as the occasion for a family celebration. In demographic terms, a nun's celestial marriage was destined to bear no fruit, yet it still had a crucial role to play in the survival of the lineage. When nuns' families gathered, feasted and exchanged gifts at the convent, they were acknowledging the significance of that institution in securing the wealth and health of the noble class.

The class consciousness and exclusivity that characterized the Venetian nobility, and to a lesser extent the citizenry, were mirrored within the walls of the nunnery. Lists of names from ten convents, compiled by Patriarch Vendramin's officials during the period 1609–18, reveal that, on average, just under three quarters of the nuns were noble. The roll call at San Zaccaria, the most renowned and ancient Venetian convent, was impeccably aristocratic: In 1609, of the seventy nuns who were professed or awaiting profession, precisely seventy were born of noble stock. At Santa Caterina, in 1616, the list was almost as pure—just one out of one hundred choir nuns did not register a noble surname—and the proportion of noble nuns did not fall below 94 percent at the convents of Sant'Alvise, Sant'Andrea and Spirito Santo.[12]

Even the more socially heterogeneous houses, in which noble nuns rubbed shoulders with women from the citizen class, retained a strong measure of exclusivity. In 1560, Patriarch Giovanni Trevisan ruled that girls who were either illegitimate or of artisan stock could not be accepted as choir nuns.[13] On the other hand, he issued a general mandate at around the same time censoring "certain houses" for refusing to accept women from the citizenry.[14] Quite apart from the snobbery implicit in Trevisan's regulations, the level of the conventual dowry—fixed from the early seventeenth century at eight hundred to a thousand ducats—put the religious life beyond the reach of the vast majority of women. The only way for a poorer woman to enter one of Venice's enclosed convents was for her to take the simple vows of a *conversa,* marking her for a life of domestic service within the nunnery. Even the dowry of a *conversa*—around three hundred ducats—was not negligible. In any case, the role of *converse* as servants to the choir nuns strengthened rather than undermined the elite character of the convent.[15]

Filled from the ranks of the nobility or, failing that, from the old citizen class of merchants, notaries and secretaries, Venetian convents were microcosms of the city elite.[16] And far from leaving their earthly cares behind them, nuns imported many of the social and political tensions of the lay community into their own enclosed world. In the more aristocratic houses, nuns—supported by private incomes—ate, dressed and behaved as gentlewomen, addressing one another as *Signora* (my lady) in preference to *Suora* (sister), and quarreling over orders of precedence in the choir or dining hall.[17] The practice whereby nuns continued to use their family names, itself an indication of their desire to retain their secular identity, provides evidence of the depth of family associations within the cloisters of Venice. There were, for example, seven Foscarinis, six Querinis, five Gradenigos and five Moresinis at San Zaccaria. At Sant'Andrea de Zirada, the Balbis and the Corners headed the list; Spirito Santo was a stronghold of the Moresini clan; and there were no fewer than fourteen Contarinis at Santa Caterina.[18]

The convents of Renaissance Venice were powered by noble blood. When delegations of noble nuns petitioned the government, as they did in 1521, the force of their high-ranking family connections made their cause hard to ignore. By the late sixteenth century, thanks to the tightening of discipline, it would have been unthinkable for nuns of whatever station to venture outside the convent in order to harangue the authorities of the Venetian state, but written petitions from convents continued to be stamped with the mark of nobility. In 1626, the nuns of San Iseppo complained to the convent magistrates about their Calabrian confessor Veruccio, whose uncouth ways were such that many of the women considered themselves in no fit state to take communion after the priest had heard their confessions. Receiving no reply to their first letter, the nuns wrote again, and again and again, pleading for a replacement confessor to be instated. The third letter (dated April 18) was probably written during Holy Week, for the nuns particularly lamented that they should be deprived of the sacraments in "these holy days." Marshaling their objections against the priest (who only a few years before had served as a hired thug, or *bravo,* and still carried a sword), the nuns appealed to the magistrates to remember their social status: "For we are born of the very blood of this republic, and even those who are not gentlewomen still have their souls, for which Christ came down from the heavens to this earth."[19]

Unlike some of the older and richer convents in Venice, San Iseppo could not boast a pure noble pedigree; according to the records of a visitation carried out four years before those letters, just half the choir nuns came from Venetian noble families.[20] So the nuns hedged their bets, putting forward the joint claims of social superiority and spiritual equality. Double-edged as the issue of nobility might have been at San Iseppo, the nuns' remarks reveal a preoccupation with social class and a faith in its power to sway the authorities. But the convent magistrates hardly needed to be reminded of the noble blood that ran thick in the female religious houses of the city.

Back in 1509, the diarist Girolamo Priuli—self-appointed curmudgeon to the Venetian state—had accused the government of turning a blind eye to the worst transgressions committed at the convents, claiming that those who held power were principally concerned with "looking after their own blood and the honour of their houses."[21] Priuli's analysis of the situation was (characteristically) overhasty. In fact, the inextricability of the convents from the ruling class was the motive for preventing abuses as well as for ignoring them—the impetus alternately for reform and for leniency.[22] Nuns' families launched imperious protests when they considered the state's handling of conventual discipline to be either too strict or too soft. On the one hand, they objected to the enforcement of enclosure wherever it denied them access to their daughters; on the other, they were quick to complain of any external threat to the honor of their womenfolk. Denunciations from relatives (complaining, for example, about the moral quality of convent employees) stressed familial interest and enumerated the daughters, sisters and nieces who lived at the community in question.[23] At the same time, they appealed to the broader interests of the nobility as a whole, urging the convent magistrates to take action on account of "the honour and reputation of the first blood and born of this city."[24]

Steeped in the blood of the ruling class, convents inevitably became involved in the political concerns of the republic. In around 1580, the pope's nuncio, Alberto Bolognetti, complained of the behind-the-scenes interventions of nuns in the deals and counterdeals characteristic of Venetian politics, and especially in the pursuit of offices. According to Bolognetti, "These women, by calling upon their fathers, brothers and other close relatives, and by begging them to favour one man or another, can well help or harm them in their political dealings."[25] The eagerness of nuns to play a role in secular politics may, as the nuncio believed, have been motivated by the hope of obtaining favors and concessions from those in power; it may also have been an end in itself. When

Giovanni Tiepolo, patriarch in the 1620s and himself a member of one of Venice's most illustrious noble houses, wrote of the city's nuns that they were "noblewomen, brought up and nourished with the utmost delicacy and respect," he added, "Had they been of the other sex it would have fallen to them to command and govern the World."[26]

Yet, while laywomen were excluded from most forms of political participation in Venice, nuns were accustomed to the responsibilities of government—if not of the world, then at least of their own communities.[27] Through the institution of the chapter, nuns were collectively responsible for managing the finances of their convent. It was the duty of the chapter to ensure the profitable investment of capital, and in particular of the payments of cash it received from nuns' dowries. To this end, convents invested most commonly in property, trade (by making loans to the guilds under the supervision of the state) or *livelli* (private loans that avoided the prohibitions on usury, since they were released under the guise of fictional property sales). Through their investments, Venetian convents participated actively in the economy, generating wealth and employment.

Although the nuns of Venice were, from the midsixteenth century, strictly enclosed, their economic imaginations necessarily roved far beyond the convent walls. The majority of communities were in possession of extensive "immobile assets," ranging from agricultural land to urban dwellings and shops. The archives of the Venetian convents, contained within the city's State Archive since the convents' suppression under Napoleon, consist above all of documents relating to property: records of the sale or purchase of land, contracts for building work or repairs, rental agreements and endless accounts of litigation. These documents reflect the fact that managing convent lands was a major responsibility for nuns, a challenge which could at times become a worry. The efficient and profitable administration of convent property was dependent in large part upon the business skills of the women in charge.[28]

In the running of their communities, nuns wielded truly exceptional power. In common with their male relatives who sat in the councils of the Venetian state, convent women held office, cast ballots, campaigned in elections, debated and made speeches. The constitutions of a Venetian convent closely paralleled the structures of the Venetian state. Just as the republic was founded on a mixed constitution, consisting of a monarch (doge), aristocracy (Senate) and democracy (Great Council), so the system of conventual government rested on the sharing of authority between the abbess, a group of elders ("the discreet ones" or "mothers of advice") and the chapter, which encompassed all the professed choir nuns. In his regulations of 1592, Antonio Grimani, bishop of Torcello, laid down in detail the precise distribution of power within this three-tiered system of authority:

> We declare that the Abbess is empowered to despatch affairs up to the value of ten ducats, without any other counsel than that which she sees fit to take from the convent treasurer. In matters with a value of ten to fifty ducats, such as small outlays and deals and other similar business, she must consult her advisers. From fifty ducats upwards, she must consult first of all with the advisers, and then propose the matter to be voted on in chapter; and among these important issues, we include the concluding of tenancy agreements; sales and major purchases; changing employees and other matters of similar significance.[29]

Focusing on questions relating to the administration of the convent's economic resources, Grimani's instructions were clearly designed to prevent the interests of any one individual or group from dominating in the convent. The same considerations led to regulations limiting family interests in the chapter. Nuns with personal interests in the matter to be decided upon were to be excluded temporarily from the chapter. And the decisions of the nuns, though meticulously recorded, were on no account to be divulged.[30]

A simple majority of votes in chapter was necessary for decisions to be passed.[31] And nuns were encouraged to exercise their votes judiciously and independently. According to Grimani, although nuns should not vote until two or three years after profession (Priuli reckoned on five), they should attend the chapter and listen to the proceedings in order to learn about the government and business of the convent, "lest, out of inexperience, they be persuaded to cast their votes at the behest of their relations or superiors." Whenever a "very important matter" had to be discussed, Grimani urged that it should not be sprung on the nuns without warning. Rather, they should be notified of the matter in advance, and it should be dealt with in a further meeting, a week later or as appropriate. It was the task of the treasurer or scribe to keep "the book of acts and decrees of the chapter." In this, the date of each meeting would be recorded, along with the names of the superior and of all the nuns present, and the resolutions and voting distributions of any ballots.[32] Through their involvement in the chapter, nuns gained access to what was usually the thoroughly masculine culture of politics. This extraordinary anomaly in the gender order was at its most acute at election time, when women participated in the democratic process, electing and being elected to positions of power within the convent community.

The chapter was responsible for the appointment of nuns to offices at every level of the convent hierarchy. In the apportioning of office, age was prized and, perhaps more significantly, youth was mistrusted. Prelates advised nuns to take special care in the appointment of women to serve as *discrete ascoltatrici* (quite literally "listeners," whose job it was to listen in on nuns' parlor conversations with outsiders), gatekeepers and novice mistresses. Jobs that entailed contact with the outside world—and, in particular, contact with men—required optimal discretion and chastity, such as were considered unlikely to be found in women under forty![33] But it was not simply the preoccupations of male ecclesiastics that ensured that older nuns enjoyed particular status. Within the convent, the privileges afforded to those women who had been in residence the longest were self-perpetuating; as with the venerable statesmen who presided over the republic, senior nuns were unlikely to divest themselves of the power that was traditionally the prerogative of age.[34]

The most prominent jobs were reserved for the most senior members of the community, but almost all professed nuns were allocated a particular responsibility. The appointments procedure was a regular event, since the term of office for all positions (excluding that of abbess) was limited to one or two years, a measure which aimed to prevent nuns from exercising their authority according to personal interest.[35] In reality, it was rare for an office to be contested, so the chapter's role was merely to confirm or veto a decision taken by the abbess and her advisers. The exception was the position of the abbess herself, an office which was apparently always contested, and which, from the late sixteenth century, came up for election on a triennial basis.[36]

The election of the abbess or prioress of a convent was the toughest test of the institution's political probity.[37] The basic requirements for the job were simple: Candidates had to be at least forty years of age and to have been professed at least eight years previously.[38] But to be elected superior of her convent, a nun required the backing of two thirds of the chapter. Extremely sensitive to the possibility of electoral corruption, the ecclesiastical authorities insisted on the nuns voting by secret ballot, under the supervision of a prelate. Voting by proxy was disallowed even for sick nuns. Speaking out against the fraudulent and partial election practices that evidently operated in some nunneries, Bishop Grimani issued the following exhortation:

> Let no one dare to endanger the convent by engaging in . . . illicit and unfitting practices, whether to further herself or to favour another out of friendship, kinship, or particular interest; nor to use fraud or partiality in voting, but to allow everyone to make their decision with freedom and sincere judgement, not obfuscated by evil design, but guided and illuminated by rectitude and the grace of the Holy Spirit.[39]

To avoid external influences, nuns were not allowed to speak to outsiders in the run-up to an election. There was one final precaution against corruption: On no account could the ballot go ahead unless all the nuns with a vote in the chapter had been confessed and received communion.

The instructions written by prelates like Grimani and Priuli set down the ideal of convent government. At every stage, "the particular interest" of individuals and, more important, of families was at least frustrated, at best subdued. But just as the workings of the Venetian state were perennially distorted by the pressures of private influence and corruption, so within the convent theory and practice diverged. The interests of a convent could not be administered mechanically. Decisions had to be made, and there were bound to be external pressures from the relatives and other lay acquaintances of nuns. Nuns' participation in the intrigues and rivalries of the Venetian republic—as described by Bolognetti—was paralleled by lay involvement in the internal politics of the convent. In particular, the election of a new abbess or prioress was liable to become the talk of the town. Two stories of electoral controversy and corruption allow us to sense the reverberations of convent politics throughout the city of Venice.

In early February 1533, the Dominican vicar-general, Fra Serafino, dismissed the prioress of Corpus Domini from her office two months before her term was due to expire so that the ensuing election could take place while he was present in Venice. His actions were tactless, to say the least, and called forth a storm of public indignation. How dare a Florentine friar (second in command of the Dominican order in Italy though he was) thus insult a Venetian noblewoman (the sister of Polo Trevisan, a member of the powerful Council of Ten)? But this was just the beginning of the friar's effrontery. Having got rid of the Trevisan prioress, Fra Serafino then attempted to manipulate the ensuing election by violating the secrecy of the ballot; and when, in spite of his maneuvers, the community elected Veneranda Capello, he refused to confirm her as the new superior. His rather specious argument for debarring the nuns' chosen candidate was that, at forty-seven, Veneranda was too young to hold the office. In two subsequent elections, Capello was excluded and the other candidates involved failed to win sufficient votes for election. Following the intervention of the Council of Ten, Capello took part in yet another election and on February 11 she was legitimately reelected. The heads of the Council of Ten awaited Fra Serafino's confirmation of the new prioress only to find that he had suddenly left Venice and taken himself off to Bologna. But the controversy continued to rage on both sides of the convent walls.

Two parties had developed around the rival candidates, each commanding support throughout the city. Giacoma Torella, of citizen stock, was the favorite of the vicar-general and his local allies. Her noble opponent, Veneranda Capello, was supported by a large party of relatives "who made up the best part of the principal houses of the city"; members of this camp were infuriated by the fact that their kinswoman's election had been continually blocked "as if she were some wretch or madwoman."[40] The papal nuncio, Girolamo Aleandro, blamed the families of the nuns for the ongoing dispute: "The whole problem of arriving at an agreement arises from the discord and resentment and rivalry of their relations, who exist in such great numbers outside."[41] But divisions in the outside world were reflected within the convent. In November 1533, when Veneranda Capello was at last appointed, a clique of nuns around the unsuccessful Torella responded by refusing to obey the new prioress. The papal nuncio excommunicated the rebellious nuns, but even this was insufficient to tame them; the Council of Ten took more effective action, ordering that the convent be raided and that six sisters (two professed nuns, including Torella, and four *converse*) be imprisoned in six different observant nunneries around the city. In the event, the threat did not have to be carried out, for relatives of the rebellious faction came to Corpus Domini and urged the nuns to manifest their obedience and humility both to the prioress and to the secular authorities. From the outbreak of the conflict to its resolution, the interests of the nuns of Corpus Domini proved to be inextricable from those of their families.

As with Corpus Domini more than thirty years earlier, the discord that arose at San Sepolcro in 1567 was initiated by a male superior from the nuns' order. Once again, the crisis resulted from the removal of the community's abbess from her post and several attempts by local friars (in this case, Franciscans) to control the appointment of her successor. On June thirtieth, news reached the convent magistrates that

> in the convent of San Sepolcro, the nuns were in a state of great confusion and uproar, because their superior, the father confessor, a Franciscan, had arrived at the convent last Saturday and had ousted the abbess from office.[42]

This time there was a disciplinary pretext for the interference of the confessor in the affairs of the nunnery, for he held Suor Michaela Beltrame, abbess for the prior two and a half years, responsible for the escape of a young girl named Meneghina, who had been boarding at San Sepolcro. Yet the determination of the friar to force through the election of his own preferred candidate, Suor Daria Navagier, suggests that factors besides the alleged negligence of Suor Michaela drove him to intervene. The magistrates scented trouble.

Statements that have survived from the ensuing investigation indicate the fury that many nuns evinced at the conduct of their confessor. They tell of how he came to the convent, accompanied by the superior of the nearby friary, San Francesco della Vigna, and set about bullying the nuns into submission. First of all, the two friars undertook to interview all the inhabitants of the convent over a period of two days. The events of the third day are recounted skeptically by one of the nuns:

> The confessor came with the superior of San Francesco, and made the gate-keepers open the door, and the pair of them entered, and the confessor rang the bell summoning the nuns into the chapter, and all the nuns came obediently, and then he pronounced that the abbess had been removed from her office, although this was against the will of the majority.[43]

The nun's account goes on to relate how the members of the chapter, reluctant to sanction the actions of the two friars, walked out of the meeting, only to be summoned back by the bell. Many of the nuns refused to return, prompting the confessor to pursue these women in an attempt to force them back. The friars pulled the veils off nuns who failed to comply, a gesture designed to rob the women of their status and dignity.

Eventually, after much more bell ringing, the chapter reassembled, and the father confessor announced that they were to vote openly on whether they favored the old abbess or Suor Daria Navagier. Enraged by this travesty of their electoral system, nuns fled in a riot of flying headgear:

> Many of the nuns pulled their black veils from their heads, and threw them away, and they escaped upstairs, and the fathers wanted to remove their veils, and in this confusion the new abbess was elected by nine nuns who remained in the chapter.[44]

Another witness recalled how several votes were held before the friars got the result they desired from the rump chapter, winning finally by utterly unscrupulous means: "The confessor took the ballots and when he saw the name of the old abbess he withdrew it and put it under his feet . . . and this election was carried by 10 or 12 nuns out of the 60 who are in this convent."[45] The nun who reported this comically inept attempt at ballot rigging was keenly aware of the failure of Navagier to secure an electoral mandate.

Of course, Navagier had her supporters. One was Suor Franceschina Moresini, who insisted on the legitimacy of the election with a similar precision as to the division of votes. "And then suor Daria was made abbess, canonically," she claimed, "for we were 50 in total and of the 50 nuns nine did not vote (some were ill; suor Michaela and the gate-keeper were excluded), and suor Daria obtained 23 votes, and thus she was elected canonically."[46] But even if Suor Franceschina's figures are reliable, Suor Daria could only have been elected by a simple majority, not by the two-thirds majority that was generally required.

In common with the disputed election that had occurred at Corpus Domini, family rivalries fired the controversy at San Sepolcro. As the investigation progressed, it emerged that the old abbess, Suor Michaela, had been feuding with the Navagier family for some time. The object of their contention was the proposal of the Navagiers to construct a balcony in the church—such private investments were the equivalent of corporate sponsorship during the Renaissance, and most ecclesiastical buildings were heavily marked with monuments, altars, tombs and other showpieces of munificence. But the Navagier scheme was problematic because the balcony under discussion was deemed to compromise the nuns' enclosure. Suor Aurelia Pizzoni gave this account:

> And when suor Michaela was first made abbess, the dispute with the Navagier family regarding the balcony which they wanted to build in church was still running, and suor Michaela put an end to the matter, ensuring that the balcony was not built, because it would be possible to see into the convent from it; and this was the cause of great displeasure to suor Daria.[47]

The convent was split between the two abbesses. There were those who claimed that Suor Michaela had deliberately allowed the escape of Meneghina; others protested her innocence, blaming the interference of the friars for the crisis in the convent. In the words of one witness, the seventy-eight-year-old Suor Cecilia Lion:

> I have been in this convent for 58 years, and we have always lived in peace, and poor suor Michaela is a saint, and I believe that she will achieve miracles at her death, and she has lived with great patience, and I do not know how she survives, and the cause of every ill is the father confessor who came here, and I believe that the devil is the cause of all this.[48]

Suor Eugenia Vianuola was also in no doubt as to whom to blame for the instability in the nunnery: "The friars are the principal cause of our discord, for it is they who put all the discords among us."[49] Furthermore, the friars, who had been at the convent for more than seventeen days, were eating the nuns out of house and home, for their allies in the nunnery provided them with "capons, doves, cakes, cream, malmsey, sweet wine." Meanwhile, all the nuns had to eat were a few beans and some rough oil—the food that the friars had spurned.[50]

While Michaela's supporters complained at the interference of the friars, the Navagier party objected to the involvement of the convent magistrates—the embodiment of the state—on the grounds that outside authorities, and in particular laymen, should keep out of an internal affair. One nun, Suor Arcanzola Contarini, protested that the magistrates "arrived some days ago to carry out their investigation, creating a disturbance among us, and laymen have never before interfered in this convent, for God said 'Touch not mine anointed.' "[51] Judging from the welcome afforded to Piero Navagier and Suor Arcanzola's own relatives, Hieronimo and Vicenzo Contarini, this principle was not always upheld.

A panoply of different interest groups was involved in the affairs of nunneries. Apart from the perennial interventions of nuns' families, power-hungry friars, papal nuncios and state magistrates also pursued their differences into the territory of the convent. As we have seen, reforming prelates like Antonio Grimani and Lorenzo Priuli would later insist on the integrity of the chapter in an attempt to isolate convents from the disruptive interventions of outside parties. Ultimately, however, it was the nuns, from within the walls of the convent, who controlled the level of external influence upon their affairs. It was they who opened up channels to the outside world. And it was they who fought off interference when they so wished, invoking the constitutions of their internal government in defense of their autonomy.

The myth of Venice, the city of stable government in which a perfectly formed constitution prevented opportunities for self-interest and dissension, provides an obvious analogy for the kind of mechanical government that sixteenth-century prelates sought to impose on the city's nunneries. The myth—classically articulated by the Venetian historian and reformer, Gasparo Contarini, in the 1520s—flourished from the early sixteenth century until around 1650. From the later seventeenth century it was opposed by an antimyth, forged principally by French critics, which presented Venice as a center of corruption, intrigue and tyranny.[52] Apologists for the Venetian republic stressed the importance of its constitutional mechanisms—the rotation of offices and the secret ballot—in rendering government impervious to corruption. Later critics scorned the notion of Venetian political integrity. They pointed out that it was in the *broglio,* an area of Piazza San Marco that became a synonym for corruption, that the real business was done. Here, nobles bought and sold votes and plotted to further their careers at the expense of others. Their selfishness and irresponsibility were concealed beneath the cloak of the secret ballot.[53]

The political system shared by the Venetian state and its convents is emblematic of the centrality of nuns within civic culture. Secret ballots, records of divisions, the rotation of offices, gerontocracy, the exclusion of interested parties and shared authority all reflected the traditions of the republic in the convent.[54] But the reality of convent politics, riddled with partialities and special interests imported from the lay world, gave still clearer witness to the links that bound noble nuns to the ruling class. In the parlors of convents, nuns and their relatives dealt and schemed, pursuing their private concerns and forming factions. Even the *broglio,* that unofficial yet crucial aspect of the Venetian political scene, found an echo within the enclosed world of the nunnery.

4. Sacred and Profane

O n February 2, 1612, two prostitutes made their way to the Franciscan convent church of Santa Maria Maggiore on the far western side of Venice. For both women, the church was only a few minutes' walk from home. One, Laura Todeschin, lived just south of the convent on the banks of the lagoon; the other, Signora Grana, closer still on Calle Sporca, literally "Filth Street," a narrow and—we may hazard—once stinking alley that still exists today, across the canal from the convent. The two women did not attend the church together, and yet their respective appearances on that particular day were not entirely coincidental. Both were drawn to make their devotions because it was the Feast of Candlemas. Celebrating the Purification of the Virgin after the birth of Christ, this was one of four major festivals devoted to Mary and—as we shall see—a prominent event in the Venetian ceremonial calendar. In addition, Laura Todeschin had a personal reason for going to church that day, and for stopping to hear mass twice over— once at the altar dedicated to Christ and again at the altar of the Blessed Sacrament. She had received a proposal of marriage from the gentleman who kept her, a certain Loredan, and she sought divine guidance as to whether or not she should accept his offer. As the two prostitutes knelt at the altars of Santa Maria Maggiore, unburdening their consciences and seeking spiritual sustenance, one hundred or more nuns went about their day's business behind the imposing brick walls of the convent. They, too, would be making their devotions to the Madonna that day, screened off from public view. It was a strange convergence of nuns and prostitutes, united for a moment in their combined adoration of the Virgin Mary, on a feast day replete with associations of female purity and fertility.[1]

Strange to us perhaps, but not so to the people of late Renaissance Venice, who would have understood at a glance the intimate relationship between sacred and profane that was being played out in Santa Maria Maggiore. For although nuns and prostitutes stood at opposite ends of the spectrum of human sinfulness, a silent treaty bound these two groups of women in the common cause of the city's salvation. According to Catholic theologians, the vice trade was a necessary evil that functioned like a latrine to preserve the cleanliness of the community by removing the filth. Prostitutes, therefore, although themselves sinners, helped to maintain the virtue of the city as a whole.[2] Nunneries, in contrast, were perceived as a positive spiritual resource, repositories of piety and chastity that counterbalanced the worldliness of the community at large. In embracing celibacy, which was held by Catholics to be the state most pleasing to God, and praying regularly throughout the day and night, nuns pursued a course of life impractical for members of the laity. Their closeness to God made them especially effective intercessors on behalf of secular society; their purity atoned for the sins of the city.

It was to this notion of the convent as a shared spiritual resource that the two prostitutes turned, with a piety that was doubtless sincere. For them, the convent church dedicated to Mary, the ultimate model of female chastity, was the ideal site for their prayers of penitence, the Marian festival of Candlemas the ideal moment. By attending the church of Santa Maria Maggiore on that day, they hoped to tap into the virginal assets of the nunnery, and so set their own spiritual accounts aright.

Towering over the fishing neighborhood on the western periphery of Venice, the massive Franciscan edifice of Santa Maria Maggiore was a commanding religious center for the people who lived in its shadow—not just prostitutes, of course, but men, women and children of all ages and professions. It was one of several churches where local people might go to pray or hear mass: The Angelo Raffaele, San Niccolò dei Tolentini, San Niccolò dei Mendicoli, and dei Carmini were all close by. Questioned about her churchgoing habits, Signora Grana stated that she was accustomed to hear mass at dei Carmini, at Santa Maria Maggiore, and "in other places, according to circumstance."[3] The nunneries of Venice formed part of a complex network of religious institutions—a web of links and associations within which ordinary people spun their spiritual lives.

Throughout the city, there were literally hundreds of churches, each of which had its own particular associations and functions. The official ecclesiastical center and the seat of the patriarch was not San Marco but San Pietro, on the far eastern edge of Venice, as far from the geographical center as could be. Then there were the parishes, seventy of them in the city of Venice. Units of civil as well as ecclesiastical administration, their churches were meeting places as well as sites of prayer.[4] The oratories of confraternities offered another devotional focus for the Venetian laity, at least for men. These brotherhoods met regularly to hear masses for the souls of departed members; they also administered charity to living members and their families and participated in citywide processions, clad in their distinctive liveries. Apart from the *scuole grandi*—the six great confraternities of San Rocco, the Carità, San Giovanni Evangelista, the Misericordia, San Marco, and San Teodoro were each legally entitled to admit five hundred to six hundred members—there were between one hundred and three hundred lesser confraternities, known as the *scuole piccole*.[5] Finally, the city of Venice accommodated over sixty religious houses of friars, monks and nuns; to each of these institutions a public church was attached. The thirty or so male houses included Franciscan grey friars and Dominican black friars, Benedictine monks and Augustinian canons, Carmelites, Gerolomites, Servites and Capuchins. Each community had its lay following, which might in part be sustained by neighborhood or family links, but which was often further stimulated by a particular cult or style of worship. Situated on opposite sides of the city, and rivaling one another for grandeur as only the Franciscans and the Dominicans knew how, the vast medieval churches of the Frari and San Giovanni e Paolo operated almost as devotional villages or malls, parading an array of chapels and altars, and providing multiple opportunities for lay patronage.

The role of nuns within the community of the faithful was inevitably played out at a greater remove. Male communities included ordained members who could administer the sacraments, not only to their own members but also to the laity. In their role as preachers and confessors, monks and friars communicated directly with laypeople in a way that was impossible for nuns. Convent churches were staffed by male clergy, brought in from outside to service the spiritual needs of the laity. The sheer number of priests employed by individual nunneries—commonly between ten and twenty—is testimony to the extent of that demand.[6] Laypeople might attend mass in a convent church; they might even be married or baptized there; they were frequently buried there.[7] Local legends and traditions, or the presence of a significant relic or shrine, served to nurture a following at particular convents. While San Zaccaria and San Lorenzo owned the most impressive sets of saints' remains, the less prestigious convents usually had something worth displaying. Santa Marta possessed the hand of its titular saint; the nuns of Santa Chiara kept one of the nails from Christ's cross; the church of Santa Giustina incorporated the stone where the eponymous martyr had knelt.[8] San Bernardo, on the island of Murano, acquired new credit toward the end of the sixteenth century when a miraculous image of the Virgin Mary situated above the church door became "a source of great consolation to all the people of the island." The marble sculpture first spoke to a poor laywoman, Donna Laura, in 1581, and provided her and her children with bread. Such was the miracle's popularity that in 1584 the nuns gained permission for a lay confraternity of men and women to be established at San Bernardo, "to make intercessions to Our glorious Mother Advocate."[9]

For some, the convent church was a place of regular worship; for others, it assumed importance sporadically, at times of spiritual crisis. During the devastating plague of 1630–31, which killed one third of the city's population, the employees of the Venetian Arsenal, the republic's shipyard, sought to appease God by making a substantial benefaction to the local convent of Sant'Anna. Until recently it was possible to read the inscription on the crumbling walls of the chapel to the right of the main altar in the convent church:

THIS CHAPEL AND ALTAR
WERE BUILT AS AN OFFERING
BY THE WORKERS
OF THE ARSENAL
IN THE TIME OF THE PLAGUE
OUT OF THEIR OWN MEANS
IN THE YEAR MDCXXXI.
CARPENTERS, CAULKERS,
OAR-MAKERS AND SAWYERS.[10]

Prompted by that same calamitous epidemic, the Arsenal workers commissioned the painting that hung in the chapel. The work of Gian Battista Lorenzetti, it depicted Christ with the Blessed Virgin, and Saints Rocco, Anna, Sebastiano and Lorenzo Giustinian (a set of saints chosen for their local significance and for their reputed powers of protection against the plague).[11] There is something incongruous about these rough manual laborers, more noted for drinking than for piety, clubbing together to build and adorn a chapel at Sant'Anna. The working men can have felt little affinity with the noblewomen of the convent. And while Sant'Anna—situated just south of the Arsenal—may have appealed to their sense of neighborhood, we might have expected the men to have conferred their benefaction upon the church at the heart of their community, Beata Madonna dell'Arsenale. But their choice of the convent church was a considered one. By investing in the church of Sant'Anna, a place made doubly sacred by the invisible presence of its virgin nuns, the men of the Arsenal—like the prostitutes of Santa Maria Maggiore—strove to mitigate the profaneness of their way of life.[12]

These displays of lay devotion, focused upon convents, are echoed in the wills of numerous Venetians who left bequests to the city's nunneries, sought to be buried in convent churches or paid for redemptive masses to be said in them. An illiterate wine merchant, Zuane di Mascaroni, made amends for his sins in 1601 by leaving the communities of Le Convertite and Santa Croce di Venezia twelve barrels of wine each, "for his soul, and in remission of his sins, declaring that the wine given to these convents should be of good quality." By remembering the nuns in his will, Zuane was able to enter one last deed of merit into his spiritual account book. His actions and motives were conditioned by the Catholic theology of salvation: Although divine grace was a precondition of being saved, men and women must also strive to please their Lord through their individual and collective efforts. We do not know Zuane's motives for favoring the convents of Le Convertite and Santa Croce; perhaps, he had family connections with those communities, or perhaps the nuns had been his clients.[13] But whether or not Zuane was personally connected to the convents he chose to benefit, his inclusion of nuns in his testament was entirely unexceptional for a lay Venetian.

At one end of the scale, there were disinterested and almost formulaic benefactions to the most pious Franciscan convents—Santa Croce, Santa Maria Maggiore, the Miracoli, San Sepolcro and Santa Chiara di Murano. The amount bequeathed to each nunnery might vary from a small annuity of 2 ducats a year to a hefty lump-sum payment of two hundred fifty ducats. Either way, the testator's objective was much the same: to affirm his or her piety in the face of divine judgment.[14] At the other extreme, we find laypeople using their wills to express far more personal links to particular religious institutions. Lucretia Corner, a noblewoman, made her will in 1601 and bequeathed the sum of 20 ducats to Santa Croce. She also left a personal annuity of 20 ducats to her sister, Suor Prudentia, a nun at the same convent. And although she chose to be buried in the church of San Sebastiano, in the tomb of her late husband, and left money to pay for a redemptive mass to be said twice a week in that church, Lucretia requested that her body be dressed in the habit of the nuns of Santa Croce and that it be accompanied at her burial by women from the convent. She also named the nuns as the executors of her will. Lucretia therefore split her patronage between two religious institutions in Venice, one of which linked her to her sister, the other to her deceased husband.[15]

The question of where to lay one's body to rest could be a complex one, activating a range of sometimes contradictory affinities. In 1602, the nobleman Sebastian Capello left instructions for his burial some way from his home parish of Santa Sofia (Cannaregio), in the convent church of San Cosma e Damiano on the Giudecca. His daughter Suor Contarina was a nun in that convent, and the abbess had promised him a vault in the chapel of the Most Holy Sacrament—a prime site indeed, where the Capellos would rub shoulders (so to speak) with the Veniers, another noble clan buried there. At the same time, Capello requested that the bodies of his first wife, Contarina, and his daughter Moresina, currently resting in the nearby convent church of Santa Croce della Giudecca, be brought to join him at San Cosma e Damiano; this despite the fact that another daughter, Suor Gratia, was a nun at Santa Croce. Capello's apparent switch of allegiances was not straightforward, for in the same will he left personal annuities to both his daughters and also favored both convents with small legacies. But such evenhandedness came to an end with the decision to establish the family vault at San Cosma e Damiano. What was the motive behind this decision? Did Suor Gratia feel hurt or slighted by the removal of her mother's and sister's bodies to the convent down the road? Among the upper ranks of Venetian society, where, typically, every generation produced a crop of nuns, monks and priests, such split loyalties and dilemmas must have been common.[16]

Linked by gender, family and social status to the massive population of nuns in the city, noblewomen were frequent among the testators who remembered the convents of Venice in their wills. Perhaps contemplating how their lives might have been if they themselves had been sent to the convent, they often left personal bequests and annuities to sisters, cousins and aunts who were nuns. The favors, however, were not always one-way. Some laywomen asked nuns individually or corporately to serve as their executors; others, such as Lucretia Corner, sought to be buried in nun's garb.[17] The English travel writer Thomas Coryat, who visited the city in 1609, mocked the "fond and impious opinion" of Venetian men who believed that "there is such vertue in the Friers cowle that it will procure them remission of the third part of their sinnes."[18] The same salvation strategy was adopted by Venetian women, who hoped that in assuming the habit of a female religious order, they could cast off the vanities of the world and envelop themselves in the cloak of virginity. It was as if, for an outlay of around five ducats, the married woman could repurchase her chastity.[19]

The commodification of devotion, of which the Protestant Coryat so heartily disapproved, was most clearly expressed in the Catholic practice of paying for redemptive masses. Some testators were boundless in their enthusiasm for establishing masses for their own and their relatives' souls in convents, monasteries and parish churches across the city. Personal connections enabled nunneries to catch a large share of the trade in masses. This was partly a sentimental issue: Franceschina Littegato had several friends at the convent of San Iseppo, so it was natural that she should include that convent among the four churches where she wished masses to be said immediately after her death. But there were also practical considerations in selecting a convent where a friend or relative could ensure that the testator's wishes were respected. Sebastian Capello requested masses to be said at San Cosma e Damiano three times a week in perpetuity, entrusting his daughter Suor Contarina with seeing that the masses were administered as he instructed. With their detailed financial provisions, wills draw attention to the fact that salvation had its price. In 1592, the prioress of Santa Giustina wrote to the patriarch lamenting the convent's obligation to administer four masses a year for the soul of a nobleman, Alvise Priuli, in return for his meager bequest of two ducats a year.[20] Her hardheadedness was understandable for, as the Counter-Reformation pushed nuns behind closed doors, redemptive masses became an increasingly important source of revenue for convents.

From prostitutes and shipbuilders to merchants and nobles, the value of the nunneries within the spiritual economy of the city was understood and manipulated at every level of society. The nuns were well aware of their intercessory power, which formed an integral part of their strategies for survival.[21] In a letter of supplication dated October 7, 1620, the nuns of Santa Chiara di Murano sought an exemption from one of the regulations underpinning enclosure. They reminded the convent magistrates of their status as servants of God, assuring them that "day and night, we are continuously praying to our Lord for the conservation and greatness of this holy and blessed Republic, which is guarded and felicitously preserved by His divine majesty."[22] Such claims were the common currency of negotiations between convents and the authorities of church and state before and after the reforms of Trent. But the impetus to invest in the religious life was, as we have seen, deeply rooted in lay society.

The Venetian state itself took a lead in granting economic support to nunneries, conscious that such acts of charity boosted the republic's spiritual credit as well as the nuns' coffers. (It is worth remembering, though, that the alms bestowed upon the nunneries by the government were trifling in comparison with the sums paid by those same institutions in the form of taxes.)[23] Convents were among those hospitals and other pious foundations that received annual wheat handouts from the government.[24] The state was also on occasion prepared to throw a line to a convent in financial distress "as a sign of the piety and benignity of the government."[25] Investing in nuns could have a blatant propaganda value as when, in 1627, the Senate undertook to pay the conventual dowry of a girl named as the daughter of Acuash Agà. A convert from Islam, "particularly inspired by the Lord God," the girl was apparently determined to become a nun, against the wishes of her father. The Senate offered its support eagerly: "It is a fitting tribute to the piety of the *Signoria* and to the honor of God, who has so greatly favored this Creature with his graces, to give her the means of effecting such a praiseworthy and holy vocation."[26] At other times, governmental munificence was bestowed with ostentatious ceremony. In 1597, the Dogaressa Morosina Morosini, wife of the newly elected Doge Marin Grimani, gained a dispensation from the pope to visit all the city's nunneries. A letter from the patriarch to the nuns of Venice, briefing them on the forthcoming visit, explained that she intended "to learn of your domestic needs, and to see your condition with her own eyes, in order that she and her most Serene Consort might protect you ever more ardently."[27]

Three convents had special roles to play in the ritual transactions that bound the Venetian state, embodied by the doge, to the nuns of the city—San Zaccaria, Santa Giustina, and Santa Maria delle Vergini. San Zaccaria had always had a close relationship with the doges. The oldest convent in Venice, and also one of the richest, the convent's first patron was Doge Giustiniano Partecipizio (in office 827–29). Legend has it that Abbess Agostina Morosini gave to Doge Pietro Tradonico (Partecipizio's successor) the first of the trademark ducal horned caps.[28] In recognition of this ancient bond, doges since Tradonico had visited the nuns every Easter. The doge's annual procession to Santa Giustina in Castello was, in comparison, a more modern tradition. This convent, founded in the midfifteenth century and not renowned for its material wealth, ac-

quired special recognition from the doge as a result of the
Venetian naval victory over the Turks at Lepanto in 1571, for
the date of the battle, October seventh, coincided with the
feast of its patron saint. The virgin and martyr Giustina had always been a favorite with the Venetians; following Lepanto, her
feast became one of the major events in the civic calendar.
From 1572, the day was celebrated with a ceremonial procession to the church of Santa Giustina; the doge and noblemen,
adorned with the full regalia of office, and accompanied by
ambassadors and foreign dignitaries, processed from Piazza San
Marco to the convent. After solemn mass had been celebrated
by one of the canons of San Marco, attention focused on the
nuns as the doge presented them with specially minted coins
known as *giustine*.[29]

But nowhere was the holy alliance of Venetian nuns with
the city-state more graphically demonstrated than in the "marriage" of the doge of Venice to the abbess of Santa Maria delle
Vergini. This extraordinary custom had its origins in the thirteenth century and formed an essential part of the abbess's investiture ceremony. Known simply as Le Vergini, the nuns
owed their foundation in 1224 to the munificence of Doge
Pietro Ziani, and the role of the doge in confirming the election of the abbess underlined his rights of patronage. Placing
the precious ring of Saint Mark upon her finger, the doge
"married" the newly elected abbess "in recognition of his ancient preeminence."[30]

The metaphorical marriage between the doge and the
abbess imitated another, better-known ritual in the doge's ceremonial repertoire. This event, known as the *Sensa*, took place
on Ascension Day (the fortieth day after Easter), which was
the anniversary of the reconciliation between the Holy Roman Emperor Frederick Barbarossa and Pope Alexander III,
achieved on Venetian soil and as a result of Venetian naval in-

tervention in 1177. According to legend, Alexander demonstrated his gratitude to the Venetians by giving a gold ring to Doge Sebastiano Ziani and granting him the right to "marry" the sea, in recognition of the republic's dominion. Within a century, the marriage to the sea had become an annual celebration. After a service at San Marco, the doge was rowed out to the Lido in his ceremonial galley where, in front of a crowd of thousands, he threw a wedding ring into the Adriatic and spoke the words, "We espouse thee, O sea, as a sign of true and perpetual dominion."[31]

While the *Sensa* took place out in the lagoon, and the investiture ceremony occurred in the indoor space of an urban convent, the similarity between these two rites would have been clear to Venetians. By the sixteenth century, the chronicle of Le Vergini—a sumptuously illuminated manuscript history—explicitly linked the origins of the ceremonies, claiming (erroneously) that the convent had been founded in the wake of the 1177 accord between pope and emperor, and that it was Doge Sebastiano Ziani (rather than the later Pietro) who had "married" the first abbess.[32] But although the parallels between the two nuptials were striking, the metaphor of marriage functioned differently in each. If the *Sensa* was fundamentally a ritual of subordination, in which Venice played husband to a publicly subjected wife, the marriage of the doge to the abbess of Le Vergini took place on more equal terms.[33] To begin with, the nuns, unlike the sea, were in a position to answer back: Central to the proceedings of the ceremony was a Latin oration given by one of the most learned women of the convent in honor of the new abbess.[34] Then there was the wedding banquet, a grand opportunity for the convent to offer hospitality to the dignitaries and other members of the local nobility.[35] Far from being understood as rituals of subjection, the investiture ceremonies were viewed by the nuns as glorious moments in the history of the convent, and they were lovingly recounted and illustrated in the convent chronicle.

The transactions between abbess and doge at Le Vergini indicated the reciprocity of the relationship between Venice and its nunneries. Just as the doge gave the abbess temporal authority, with which to govern her community, so the abbess invested the ducal authority with sanctity.[36] That sanctity was the guarantee of the continuing prosperity and power of the city, a city which drew heavily upon its special associations with the Madonna and which was itself frequently cast as a virgin. In the words of Thomas Coryat:

> It is a matter very worthy the consideration, to thinke how this noble citie hath like a pure Virgin and incontaminated mayde . . . kept her virginity vntouched these thousand two hundred and twelue yeares . . . though Emperours, Kings, Princes and mighty Potentates, being allured with her glorious beauty haue attempted to deflowre her, euery one receiuing the repulse: a thing most wonderfull and strange.[37]

In common with many other Italian states, including Florence and Siena, Venice claimed the protection of the Virgin Mary, but its relationship with her was engrained in particularly developed traditions of history and iconography, which were in turn fed by the idea of the city as an inviolable island. To begin with, the city of Venice was supposedly founded in 421 on the Feast of the Annunciation, March twenty-fifth, and the Venetians took the anniversary of that date as the start of the new year. Images of the Virgin and the Angel Gabriel adorned the façade of the church of San Marco, the walls of the Ducal Palace, and even the Rialto Bridge. The Feast of the

Annunciation, along with that of Candlemas and the Assumption of the Virgin (August fifteenth), were among the principal occasions for ceremony and celebration in the civic calendar. In addition, the doge paid special tribute to Mary by attending mass at San Marco on all of her feast days. The presence of the Madonna extended well beyond the political center. By the middle of the fifteenth century, there were, according to one count, more than twenty "great temples" and three hundred altars dedicated to the Virgin's name.[38]

Besides its churches and altars, Venice was home to a large population of living and breathing virgins in the form of consecrated nuns. Even though they were deliberately situated on the peripheries, away from the bustling political and commercial centers of San Marco and the Rialto, the nunneries were inextricably enmeshed in the social and economic fabric of the city. They were also vital to the republic's spiritual economy. But although the nuns of Venice were conceived of as a spiritual asset, they could all too easily become a liability. And at the beginning of the sixteenth century, as Venice itself stood on the brink of severe spiritual recession, it is little wonder that the authorities of church and state began to concern themselves avidly with the reform of the city's convents. A virgin city, and a city of virgins, Venice strove to make the nunneries impenetrable.

5. The Boundaries of Reform

$\mathscr{A}$CROSS EUROPE, convents were under assault. Their properties were being seized, their buildings looted, their inhabitants subjected to insult and abuse. In the Baltic town of Stralsund, a mob pelted a community of nuns with mud and stones during a church service, jeering at them as "heavenly harlots." At Medingen, in north Germany, a group of men led by the Duke of Brunswick forced their way into a convent and bashed a hole into the nun's choir, where the inmates were taking refuge; they also silenced the building by divesting the bell of its rope and clapper. On the Swiss-German border, at Katherinenthal, iconoclasts tore the habits from the nuns and stuffed the clothing into sacks, which they publicly burned. In England, it was rumored that state officials sent to inspect convents for signs of corruption attempted to seduce the women they found there. Dutch Calvinists were reputed to have paraded nuns naked through their army camps.[1]

The spur for this surge of violence directed against nuns was, of course, the Protestant Reformation, which rent the fabric of Christendom in the early sixteenth century. As religious differences tore families, communities and kingdoms apart, convents found themselves at the center of the propaganda wars. Catholic polemicists—nuns included—consolidated the rumors of cruelty and abuse, eager to make martyrs of their sisters and demons of their enemies. They also played a part in fashioning the tales of heroic resistance that have come down to us. Refusing to listen to the heretical sermons of

Protestant reformers, Ursula Bock, the Dominican prioress of Saint Margaret's in Strasbourg, set up dummies in place of nuns in the choir behind the grille. The nuns of Lüne, in north Germany, set fire to old felt slippers to drive out the Protestant preacher with smoke.[2]

If the nuns had been prepared to listen to the reformers, they would probably have been treated to the equally colorful outpourings of the Protestant propaganda machine. They would have been told that the monastic life they had been leading was an unnatural state, and one that was highly conducive to sexual corruption. In the Protestant imagination, priests were inevitably whoremongers, monks masturbated in the privacy of their cells, nuns slipped into sexual error. In these representations, religious women were often shown as victims rather than culprits; there were exposés of child nuns forced to take vows by their parents and of communities of women terrorized and exploited by their male religious supervisors. In response to the tales of women resisting the closure of their convents, Protestant pamphleteers publicized the heroics of reformist nuns who escaped, most famously Katherine von Bora (the future wife of Luther) and her disillusioned sisters, who fled the convent at Nimbschen in a cart full of herring barrels.[3]

The Reformation campaign against convents was not so much the cause as the effect of deep-rooted anxieties concerning the social and sexual status of nuns. Women who became nuns could wield power and influence both within and beyond their communities. They owed their privileges not just to their elite social origins, but also to their unique position within the pre-Reformation gender system. In this system, virginity was prized above marriage, and nuns—as brides of Christ—escaped the subordination imposed by men upon their lay wives. The Protestant assault on the convents was therefore a central element in a broader campaign to establish a new and more rigidly patriarchal social order, founded on marriage and the family.[4] In the reformers' utopia, there would be no convents, no brothels and no adultery. Instead, men and women would work together in benign, if unequal, partnerships, serving God, rearing children and contributing to the domestic economy. Protestants claimed the authority of Scripture for their values, for nowhere, they argued, did God command men and women to withdraw to cloisters, but rather "to marry, work hard, love our children and serve our neighbors." Even the image of the Virgin Mary was refashioned to fit in with this workaday vision: In Protestant iconography, her virginity was played down, and she was portrayed as a dedicated wife and mother who washed pots and milked cows.[5]

At the onset of the Reformation, it was the celibate ideal that looked to be the Achilles' heel of the Catholic Church. So easy to scorn, celibacy was far harder to defend because of its shallow foundations in Scripture. But above all, it was hard to maintain. Celibacy was difficult, and that was the point. The Catholic Church could never hope to rid its ranks of all taint of sexual corruption. By upholding such a fragile ideal, it could look forward to centuries of embarrassment and ridicule. For a brief period in the early sixteenth century, the issue sparked off controversy within the Catholic Church itself. There were those who questioned their church's commitment to a celibate priesthood. Others proposed the abolition of the religious orders on the grounds that they were corrupt beyond redemption.[6] But, in 1563, the Council of Trent dug its heels in. It settled on a hardline policy, establishing the superiority of celibacy as a point of faith, and pronouncing anathema on all who dared to assert that the married state was more worthy than virginity.[7] For better or worse, celibacy was here to stay.

At the twenty-fifth and final session of the council, when the assembled prelates were weary and impatient to leave, attention turned to the reform of monks, friars and nuns.[8] The tone was set by the preamble of the "Decree on regulars and nuns":

> The holy council is aware how much grace and benefit arises in the church from monasteries which are devoutly founded and rightly administered. It considers it necessary for ancient and regular discipline to be restored where it has collapsed, and to be pursued with greater resolve where it has been preserved. That this may come about more quickly and easily the council has decided to enact . . . that all regulars, both male and female, should order and arrange their lives according to the rule they profess; and that above all they should faithfully observe the fundamental requirements of their profession, such as the vows of obedience, poverty and chastity, together with any other special precepts intrinsic to their rule or order and to the preservation of the common life, diet and clothing. . . . For if the very bases and foundations of all religious discipline are not carefully preserved, the whole building will necessarily topple.[9]

Familiar exhortations to adhere to the rule and the vows were followed by detailed guidelines on the admission and profession of new nuns, including a raft of new measures designed to prevent forced vocations. There were also significant directives concerning the temporal and spiritual government of religious houses. Most notably, bishops were to be given an increased role in the administration of nuns—the ruling that would empower the Priulis and Vendramins of the future.

Among this package of regulations and resolutions, canon

five of the final decree looked inconspicuous enough, but its implications for women in convents were to prove enormous:

> After religious profession no nun may go out of her convent on any pretext, even for a short time, except for a legitimate reason approved by the bishop, notwithstanding any concessions and privileges. And no one of any kind or condition or sex or age may enter the convent without the permission of the bishop or superior given in writing, under pain of excommunication automatically incurred.[10]

This was the church's solution to the problem of maintaining its ideal of celibacy—compulsory enclosure for all nuns.

It was not a new idea, and it was sexist in the extreme. One of the earliest proponents of enclosure, Bishop Caesarius of Arles (470–542), warned of the dangers of permitting a woman "chaste and consecrated to God" to associate with outsiders, even relatives, "lest she hear what is not proper, or say what is not fitting, or see what could be injurious to chastity."[11] That warning encapsulates the rationale of enclosure, which emerged almost exclusively as a requirement for nuns, not monks.[12] The female religious life was held to be especially problematic because (it was widely believed) women's lusts were insatiable. Without husbands to satisfy or govern their desires, women could not hope to be chaste. In a widespread Latin saying, which went one further than the Venetian *maritar ò monacar*, the problem of the female appetites was thus summed up: *Aut maritus, aut murus* (if not a husband to govern her, then a girl needed a wall to contain her).[13]

The Council of Trent presented its parting shot on enclosure as a straightforward reenactment of the 1298 bull (known as *Periculoso*) of Pope Boniface VIII.[14] It called for the maintenance of enclosure or its reintroduction "wherever it had been violated." But the appeal to medieval precedent, and the invocation of a golden age when enclosure had supposedly been the norm, was largely rhetorical. While churchmen had propagated the virtues of female enclosure throughout the Middle Ages, its implementation had only been sporadic at best. Certain reformed female houses and orders had incorporated enclosure into their rule, among them the Poor Clares (whose constitution dates from 1259), the Briggitines (1346), and the first Carmelite sisters (1453).[15] Pope Boniface had decreed that all nunneries should submit to enclosure, yet strict observance remained the exception rather than the norm. Now all nunneries, no matter what was laid down in the rules and constitutions of their orders, were going to be forced into submission.

For in its glib appropriation of the 1298 bull, the Council of Trent completely failed to address the diverse customs of existing nunneries. Where did canon five leave the numerous convents where enclosure had never existed? In such cases it was illogical to talk of enclosure having been violated.[16] What of the mendicant or begging orders, which had always enjoyed the right to come and go from their convents and who depended on contact with the world to obtain their livelihood?[17] Then there was the unclear area of third-order nuns, who lived outside formal communities, and of *converse,* the convent servants who were accustomed to coming and going on a daily basis. Were they included in the new regulations laid down for professed nuns?[18] The technical ambiguities of this blunt pronouncement were debated by cardinals and others in the wake of the council. With the bull *Circa Pastoralis* of May 29, 1566, Pope Pius V hoped to end discussions about the interpretation of canon five. It was asserted that all professed nuns, by virtue of their profession, were bound to strict enclosure whatever the nature of their rule or their customary rights. Pius's bull, while more precise than the conciliar ruling, was certainly no more sensitive to the realities and varieties of convent life.[19]

In Venice, the decrees that issued from the Council of Trent were taken as strong support for disciplinary measures that the republic had already put in place. So familiar was the principle of enclosure that in 1593 Patriarch Lorenzo Priuli could tell the nuns of San Biagio e Cataldo that "the enclosure of nuns was born together with nunneries themselves. Where there is no enclosure, there is no nunnery."[20] Again, this appeal to a mythical past was disingenuous, an overestimation both of the success of the policy of enclosure and of its universality. As recently as 1581, a Venetian lawyer, Francesco Zabarella, had argued that the nuns of his city could never be liable to excommunication for breach of enclosure, for, he stated, here the majority of convents were "open."[21] This was a mistake, but a revealing one. As for the enclosure of nuns being born with the nunneries themselves, that claim disguised the fact that legislation to prevent outsiders entering convents, and nuns leaving them, had begun to find its way onto the Venetian statute books only from the beginning of the sixteenth century.

From 1521, the principal agents of the Venetian government with responsibility for the nunneries were the convent magistrates. These three nobles had a variety of roles that developed over time, with ever increasing emphasis on the enforcement of enclosure. In the first place, it was their duty to promulgate the rules. A decree of 1551 emanating from the Council of Ten, one of the most powerful bodies of state, made it the responsibility of the magistrates "to inform all the venerable Abbesses and Prioresses of our orders regarding visitors to nunneries, giving them notice of the degrees of kin that are allowed to visit each nun, according to the form of our laws." It also fell to the magistracy to bring to justice any outsiders who broke those rules, as the same decree stipulated:

> These three nobles will have the authority to punish wrongdoers with the penalties laid down in the laws, and when all three are in agreement, they must sentence the wrongdoers, without further counsel.[22]

In pursuit of this judicial remit, the convent magistrates regularly investigated cases unearthed by their officials or brought to their attention by denunciations (letters of accusation that played an essential part in the policing of Renaissance Venice).

In other aspects of their business, the convent magistrates, assisted by their spies, scribes and other officials, were expected to cooperate closely with the ecclesiastical authorities. From 1562, the magistrates were legally bound to carry out a series of twice-yearly inspections into the nunneries of Venice and the islands, a task which they shared with the patriarch's vicar (or, in the case of the lagoon convents, a delegate of the bishop of Torcello). The inspections were focused on points of access to the convents; in particular, the magistrates were obliged to see that the doors leading from the confessor's quarters to the enclosed part of the nunnery were walled up. If these inspections brought to light "the need for further provision," the magistrates were to report back to the Heads of the Ten, who would in turn propose new legislative measures to the council.[23] Again, in 1569, the magistrates and the patriarch were instructed to inspect the convents with a view to imposing enclosure:

> They must go to each of the said convents, and inspect all the doors and other places where one might enter

and leave the convent; and where they discover more
than two doors, one accessible from the land and one
from the water, they must immediately wall them up
and block them so that they may no longer be
used . . . and they must instruct the Abbesses and Prioresses to take all necessary care to have good keys
made, and that they must keep those doors which are to
remain in use well guarded.[24]

Thus the Venetian authorities—whose efforts to impose discipline on the convents evidently predated Trent—embraced
and internalized the directives of the reforming council.

At its most basic level, enclosure signified the total separation of nuns from the lay world. In the words of Patriarch
Priuli:

You must observe the area of enclosure absolutely, never
stepping even a single pace beyond it, either in the
church or in the parlour; nor may you receive anyone
within it, of whatever kind, condition, or age, without
our express licence in writing.[25]

Such injunctions were backed up with bricks and mortar. Priuli instructed that nunneries should be "encircled by walls so
high" that it would be impossible either to scale them, or to see
over them from places nearby.[26] High walls had a symbolic as
well as a practical force, reminding both insiders and outsiders
of nuns' removal from the contaminating influence of society.
A physical breach of enclosure warranted excommunication,
and even the most glancing contact with the laity could
threaten the immaculacy of a convent. Patriarch Vendramin instructed the nuns of San Rocco & Santa Margarita to block up
the holes ventilating their latrine, for fear that they might catch

a glimpse of the street below through them.[27] Bishop Antonio Grimani of Torcello ordered that all windows looking onto the street or other public areas "exposed to the eyes of passers-by," as well as those visible from the private houses of laypeople, must be bricked up.[28] In the orders issued to Sant'Andrea di Zirada following the 1596 visitation, the community was reminded that their "campanile . . . must be permanently locked up"; thirty years previously, the convent magistrates had investigated the charge that some of the nuns had climbed to the top of the bell tower and flaunted themselves before the neighborhood.[29]

Some access to a nunnery was, of course, necessary, but it was to be kept to a bare minimum. Echoing the Council of Ten decree of 1569, Bishop Grimani ordered that convents were to have just two doors, one opening onto land and the other onto water, for unloading essential goods. The water entrance was to be used only when absolutely unavoidable, and all deliveries were to take place under the supervision of two of the oldest and most trusted nuns. Grimani went on to give precise instructions as to the strength and quality of the doors. They must be made "of good strong double planks, without any fissure or hole through which one can see inside; their thresholds made of stone, and fitting well, so that there is no gap."[30] The main land door would have the additional feature of an iron grate backed by black cloth, to screen the doorkeeper from view and enable her to respond to callers without opening the door. However, it was hoped that the convent doors would normally be quite redundant since, wherever possible, the *ruota* (wheel) could be used. This ingenious feature of convent architecture enabled food and other essentials to be passed through a hatch without revealing anyone or anything on the other side of the wall. On the construction of these devices, Grimani specified that they should be finely adapted so that, whether standing still or moving, they allow no opening, nor occasion even the slightest fissure, through which it might be possible to see the nuns inside.[31]

Such machinery sought to fulfill the practical requirements of convent life while preserving the precarious ideal of enclosure.

Only within tightly defined contexts was communication with lay folk sanctioned. For such purposes convents had long incorporated at least one parlor, a public space adjacent to the enclosed area and separated from it by a wall in which was set a grated window. It was here that nuns met close relations, and convent officials did business with the outside world. Many reformers considered the parlor a perturbingly vulnerable spot in the convent's defenses, and the concern of Priuli is evident in his publication in 1591 of *Orders & admonitions* [. . .] *concerning visitors to convents and the maintenance of enclosure.* The rigor with which these orders are formulated to cover all eventualities and to minimize every risk shows Priuli at his most paranoid. Where he was forced to make concessions to "necessity," he tried to overcome his helplessness by insisting on his personal license being requested at every stage.

The *Orders* begin by specifying the male relations permitted to visit nuns: fathers, brothers and immediate uncles. Such visitors could not go directly to the parlor but were first required to make their presence known at the wheel. Usually, conversations between nuns and male visitors had to be listened to by a specially appointed nun. But where family business demanded privacy, Priuli conceded that the *ascoltatrice* (listener), as she was known, could stand out of earshot. It was also the task of the listener to control the length of interviews, and to keep a list of names of all the men who were allowed to visit the nuns, as well as a logbook of those who had paid visits.[32] Men who fell outside the immediate family would need to obtain a license from the patriarch himself. Female visitors were viewed with slightly less suspicion, and even those without family ties could arrange to talk with nuns without applying for a patriarchal license. The approval of the nun in charge of the wheel still had to be gained, however, and she was to admit only women who were "honorable and honest, known by you and of good reputation."[33]

Use of the parlor was, of course, limited to times when nuns were not engaged in services, eating or other communal activities. Nor was visiting allowed on days when communion was celebrated. Reports of parlors being used by nuns and lay folk for feasts and merrymaking were a familiar concern. Indeed, in the early sixteenth century, the parlors of the more aristocratic Venetian convents were renowned as centers of high sociability. In 1509, for example, a group of young patricians was charged with dancing the night away at La Celestia.[34] When Patriarch Trevisan visited San Maffio di Mazzorbo in 1564, the nuns were keen to assert that "they no longer eat in the parlors."[35] But partying seems to have continued in the parlors of many convents.[36]

Bishop Grimani of Torcello was forced to concede that there might be instances when nuns' families had to take a meal in the parlor before heading back to Venice or the mainland from remote lagoon islands.[37] In such cases, there was to be no singing or dancing, and visitors were to provide their own food so as not to burden the community. Grimani also accepted that relations of nuns might be stranded overnight if weather conditions prevented them from traveling home by boat, and admitted that this was a "legitimate cause" for them to stay in the *forestaria* (guest house). The guest house was also used by the confessor, by those employed to manage the nuns' business interests and by others working for the convent when necessary. Predictably, Grimani provided a long list of regulations regarding its construction and purpose to ensure that it in no way jeopardized the nuns' enclosure. The building could not have any windows overlooking the nunnery, however small; the persons permitted to stay there were to be closely controlled; as with the parlor, it should not become a venue for partying; and a wheel should connect guest house and convent to enable food to be passed through, thus preventing any more direct contact between nuns and their guests.[38]

In a very small number of cases, lay presence within the enclosure itself was permitted. It was reluctantly accepted even by the most zealous of reformers that sick nuns should be allowed to see doctors. As men whose very profession brought them into close bodily contact with their patients, it is no surprise that they were viewed with a high level of suspicion, prompting yet more rules. Doctors employed by nunneries were to be of good name and approved life, and over forty years old. They were to be licensed by the bishop and had to swear an oath of obedience to his orders. Their visits were discouraged and they were only supposed to enter the convent "when urgent necessity requires it, and not for every light occasion." If the patient was capable of coming to the grate instead, then this was preferable; if the patient was too sick to move, other nuns might discuss her case in the parlor with the doctor and seek advice that they could then implement themselves. However, if there was genuinely no alternative to the doctor's presence at the bedside, then the bell should be rung to warn the nuns so that they might retreat into their cells. Veiled from top to toe in black, two old and trustworthy members of the community should accompany the doctor to the sickbed.[39]

Just as doctors were occasionally called upon to see to the physical needs of nuns, so the internal fabric of the monastery sometimes demanded the attention of skilled laymen. It was acknowledged that carpenters and builders might be required within the enclosure; their intermittent presence at the convent was another of those unavoidable compromises that could be regulated but not eliminated. Episcopal or patriarchal license was in all cases to be obtained, and Bishop Grimani even provided an oath to be taken by workmen.[40] Yet contemporary trials give ample evidence of casual employees failing to apply for the necessary permission before embarking on what they saw as perfectly innocuous tasks.

During the years 1611–12, the magistrates dealt with four cases of builders or other workmen entering female convents without the appropriate license from the magistrates. All claimed total ignorance as to how they had transgressed the law. Maestro Battista freely admitted to having worked at Sant' Anna, introducing a dividing wall to make two cells out of one room and—on a previous occasion—repairing the convent roof. Apparently unaware of the need for a license from the office of the magistrates, he confidently asserted: "I have a licence which the Abbess showed to me."[41] In April 1611, Zuane da Rivoltela was summoned before the magistracy on a similar charge of entering a convent without the requisite license. Showing some knowledge of the regulations concerning enclosure, he stressed that he had been employed to work only on the exterior of the convent and that the nuns employed a certain Maestro Giacomo for any jobs within the enclosed area. However, Zuane had been required to enter the convent in order to take out wood and other building materials, and for this purpose the abbess had, he believed, obtained a license on his behalf. Chided for acting solely on the word of the abbess without knowing who had authorized the license she presented to him, Zuane excused himself, saying, "I only entered the convent twice, believing that the papers were in order, for I do not know how to read or write."[42]

Zuane Radichio, a stonemason, was tried by the magistracy in May 1612.[43] He had been employed to construct a staircase leading to the organ and to carry out work on the high altar of the convent church of San Girolamo. These tasks had entailed conversations with several nuns, including the abbess, but witnesses attested that these meetings had been held openly and were of a purely professional nature. Zuane was able to present the magistrates with a license from the patriarch; they reiterated the obligation to apply for permission from the magistracy itself.

In none of the three cases examined above were any aspersions cast upon the moral conduct of the workmen. All believed they were being legitimately employed to carry out standard jobs. As Zuane da Rivoltela remarked, "I knew nothing except what the abbess told me, else I would not have entered for ten ducats."[44] But the innocence of one builder, another Battista, in a case of April 1612, carries a particular irony. For Battista was employed by the convent of Ogni Santi to close up one of the parlors with a wall ten to twelve feet long, in accordance with the patriarch's orders for tighter enclosure.[45] Thus enclosure was undermined as a result of one community's efforts to implement the separation from the world that the reformers had called for. In the words of the builder, "I was just doing my job."

Self-contained though an enclosed nunnery might at first appear, the cloistered life remained dependent on the outside world, and that uncomfortable fact was evident in the paraphernalia of devices put in place by the authorities with the aim of limiting contact between nuns and the rest of society. Physical barriers were to be backed up by unceasing vigilance—hence the many functions reserved for "old and discreet nuns" in supervising doors, keys and the comings and goings of outsiders. In turn, the efforts of the inmates were to be supported by patriarchs and magistrates armed with licenses, oaths and punishments. Those authorities spread their nets ever wider in the pursuit of even the most minor transgressions.

Even in the early decades of the campaign to enforce enclosure, the reformers displayed a preoccupation with the areas immediately outside the enclosed convent. In 1554, the magistrates initiated proceedings against a group of Venetian men who were in the habit of crossing the lagoon to Malamocco to hang out in the little street that ran alongside the convent. Witnesses reported that the men spoke familiarly with the nuns, and it was fair to conclude that the honor of the community was in jeopardy.[46] Equally suspicious was the group of musicians charged with playing a *matinada* (the dawn equivalent of a serenade) in a boat outside La Celestia in 1569.[47]

Increasingly, the areas surrounding convents were turned into exclusion zones; placards dating from the seventeenth century may still be seen near the former convents of San Zaccaria and Spirito Santo, prohibiting "all games, tumults, noises, speaking obscene words, committing improper acts, fouling the ground, leaving the masts of boats, refuse, or anything else lying around," and threatening "grave penalties" for offenders.[48] The notices, which were put up by the *essecutori contra la bestemmia* (the magistrates responsible for countering blasphemy in the city), encouraged the local people to keep at a respectful distance from the convents, a principle reiterated again and again by the convent magistracy.

By the early seventeenth century it seems that any laypeople caught loitering outside a convent, regardless of their intent, might be deemed worthy of investigation. Take the case of Zuane de Romiso, a young man from the Trentino, the hilly region to the north of Venice. In November 1621, Zuane was sentenced by the convent magistrates to two months' imprisonment "for having unknowingly entered a garden of a nuns' convent outside this city in order to eat fruit."[49] The convent in question was San Bernardo, on the island of Murano, and in his defense Zuane explained how he had entered the nunnery garden quite by accident. He had, he claimed, been out in a boat off the northern banks of the island with two friends, also Trentini, when one of them, Piero dalla Rasega, had mentioned a nearby orchard in which there were figs and pomegranates. Piero led them to the place, and Zuane (who had, he said, arrived from the country just a fortnight before) followed, with no idea where they were. Once among the fruit trees, the men set about sating their appetites, although (as Zuane commented ruefully) the fruit was of poor quality, "and I ate only three figs and mulberries which were not even good, nor were there pomegranates or anything else, and I did this because I was extremely hungry." Zuane insisted that he never would have dreamed of entering the garden had he known that it belonged to a convent. The case points to the patchiness with which the planned enclosure had been carried through a century after the establishment of the convent magistracy—had San Bernardo been properly sealed up, its orchards would not have been so open to accidental trespassing. But it also suggests the extraordinary vigilance of the magistrates intent on pursuing even the most trivial crimes.

That vigilance appears particularly extreme in relation to certain kinds of infringement. In April 1611, two Jews who had arranged to meet a business colleague who was going with them "to survey certain carpets and rugs of a wool merchant" took the *traghetto* (ferry) to Santa Croce. Awaiting the arrival of their friend's gondola, they sought shade and sat down "on the public canal bank by the door of the nuns of Corpus Domini." Shortly afterward the convent door opened and a carpenter deposited his tools outside; then he returned into the enclo-sure, leaving the door open behind him. Two nuns—possibly *converse*—appeared at the door and asked the men loitering there if they were Venetian. No sooner had the Jews answered than an agent of the convent magistracy popped up and ar-rested them.[50]

In June of the same year, Battista, a fruiterer's boy, was in very serious trouble for having passed by the convent of Sant' Anna in a boat, at night, while singing drunken obscenities. The subject of his song was a woman called Lucia, and there is little reason to suppose his words were directed at the nuns. However, his interrogator assured him:

> You will be severely punished by the Justice for having uttered these obscene words, that are thoroughly inap-propriate to any public place, let alone to be spoken in the vicinity of a sacred place of tender virgins conse-crated to Our Lord.

Battista was sentenced to six months' imprisonment.[51]

Meanwhile, between 1610 and 1612, the convent magis-trates heard five cases against prostitutes who had attended services at nunnery churches. Signora Novella had allegedly "made a great deal of noise" in the convent church of Sant' Andrea de Zirada. She had arrived there ostentatiously, at-tended by a gaggle of admiring gentlemen, and during the course of the service she had picked a fight with a gentle-woman. Furthermore, it was reported that she had begun to frequent the convent parlor.[52] The desirability of keeping such a woman well away from the nunnery was clear. But others of the prostitutes were less obviously worthy of prosecution.

Laura, who, as we have seen, slipped into mass at Santa Maria Maggiore on the feast of the Madonna delle Candele, did not behave indecorously.[53] And although Crestina, caught entering the church of Santa Giustina in March 1612, was conspicuously bedecked with personal ornaments, her deportment there does not appear to have attracted criticism.[54]

What motivated the churchmen and magistrates prosecuting these cases? Were prostitutes kept away from convents because contact with them was viewed as the thin end of the wedge—a route to the active corruption of religious women? Or was their mere presence in churches—even when they were there for pious reasons, and were in any case totally invisible to the nuns—perceived as polluting? The fear of sexual contamination is most explicit in the proceedings against a musician called Pasqualin, tried in 1611 for "showing his member in the churches of nuns." Pasqualin had done the rounds of the Venetian nunneries, waiting in their churches or parlors until a nun appeared at the grate, at which point he would reveal "his obscene parts." His actions earned him a sentence of ten years on the galleys.[55] But while the concern of the magistrates in this case is readily comprehensible, the corrupting influence of the laity was strongly perceived even when there was no direct risk to the nuns. The women who lived inside the convents were often indifferent to or even ignorant of the laypeople who were brought for trial.

Jews, drunks, prostitutes and flashers—perhaps the concurrence of stories about this assemblage of subversives should alert us to a wider set of concerns on the part of the Venetian state. One historian writing about Venice's blasphemy magistracy (set up in 1537, just sixteen years after the convent magistracy) has observed that this period saw a series of conspicuous efforts by the Venetian government to impose moral reforms on its people.[56] Measures aimed at preserving the quiet and decorum of the city were taken against blasphemy, drunkenness and nocturnal revelry. There was new legislation against sodomy and other forms of perceived sexual deviancy. And there were new policies of containment for evils that were there to stay, or that were even perceived as necessary. Thus from 1516, the Jews of Venice were hemmed in by high walls around the ghetto and hampered by the close regulation of their movements outside. Throughout the period, prostitutes were the subject of laws that confined them to particular parts of the city and required them to wear the distinctive yellow neckband denoting their status.[57] Just as these impure elements of Venetian society were cordoned off into particular zones, so nuns were shut up in supposedly incorruptible isolation.

The strict enclosure of convents and the energetic pursuit of those who, by their very presence, smudged the boundaries between the world of sin and these islands of sinlessness (a distinction that had to be vehemently asserted, since the facts did not always bear it out) may be seen as a form of "moral cleansing."[58] Enclosure fitted into a program of purification directed at the whole of Venetian society, a program that (as we have seen) reflected the republic's insecurity in an age of war and crisis. The Venetian state's willingness to embrace the Council of Trent's calls for enclosure flowed from concerns that went beyond a desire to impose discipline on its communities of religious women. Indeed, many of the trials conducted by the magistrates had little at all to do with nuns. Yet it was those who lived within the convent walls who were most affected by this policy of isolation.

6. Sustaining Networks

Oh how wearing it is to find oneself always sitting at the same table with the same food! How tormenting to retire every night to the same bed, always to breathe the same air, always to conduct the same conversations and to see the same faces![1]

CLAUSTROPHOBIA! This was Arcangela Tarabotti's reaction to the cloistered life. Professed nuns wore the ring that symbolized their marriage with Christ, but of more immediate practical significance was their commitment to the community in which they were bound to live until separation by death. The membership of a nunnery was slow to change and commonly consisted of between fifty and a hundred women. These ranged from teenagers to the very old, and varied in social status as well as hierarchical rank. That such communities were prone to internal tensions is scarcely surprising. Exhortations to concord and reconciliation were ignored, and the communal ideal was continually undermined by cliques, feuds, slander and general bitchiness. In their insistence on "the common life," the outside authorities governing religious women tried to deprive them of any form of relief. Individuality was denied and intimacy disallowed, creating an environment characterized by the sameness of which Suor Arcangela complained.

If freedom from earthly relationships and subjection to the institution had always been the ideals of monastic life, how much more oppressive were these tenets when combined with the mandate for total enclosure which, following Trent, now applied to every nunnery? Windows were walled up, doors were sealed, gardens were put out of bounds, and the light was shut out with blinds and curtains. But efforts to keep nuns apart from the laity did not imply only physical separation. Religious women were to be protected from the contamination of worldly emotions. The ties of love and affection that competed with devotion to the religious life were to be severed wherever possible; reminders of the secular realm were to be kept at bay. Within the institutional ideal envisaged by reformers like Priuli and Grimani, there was no room for personal relationships of any kind. Grimani's musings on the vow of chastity ended up by condemning affection itself:

> Thus the occasion and the root whence experience has taught us all disorders arise is that particular and extraordinary love, which is carried from one sister to another, or from a nun to a secular person of either sex.[2]

The absolute insistence on enclosure and the zealous attention paid to implementing it sought to place nuns in a vacuum, sealed off from human relations. In compensation, nuns were cast as Christ's brides, a role that provided a suitable outlet for their unspent emotions. Lacking a true sense of vocation, however, many women in convents bridled against their lot and craved above all the sustenance of family and friends.

When interviewed by the convent magistrates in 1620, the confessor to the nuns of Santa Marta commented, "I have always persuaded the nuns to relinquish their particular friendships both inside and outside the convent: because *amicitia huius mundi est inimica Deo* [the friendship of this world is inimical to God]."[3] This principle, fundamental to the doctrine of the common life, was nevertheless one of the hardest to enforce, and it is particularly difficult to conceive of how external authorities hoped to be able to control the fondness of nuns for one another. The rationale behind their continued attempts was threefold. First, on purely religious grounds, the reformers could not allow earthly friendships to distract from nuns' devotion to their celestial spouse and to the spiritual rigors of the rule. Second, as a result of disciplinary and moral concerns, they feared that such relations might lead to lustful practices within the convent. Third, they believed that "particular affections" threatened the institutional stability of the community, opening up possibilities for corruption and mismanagement and often souring the atmosphere.[4] The reformers were right. Particular intimacies and cliques did indeed disturb the peace of convents; records of such incidents both highlight the overheated quality of emotional relationships within convent walls, and point to the attempts of some nuns to escape the constraints of their institutional existence by forging alternative identities.

At the convent of San Iseppo—a socially heterogeneous community of around eighty nuns—the problems focused on a particular clique.[5] A patriarchal visitation of 1595 refers to "three nuns [who] greatly trouble the convent": Suor Marietta Dolfin, Suor Dorothea Sforza and Suor Mansueta Pase. In addition, Marietta Dolfin was close to a *conversa* named Lorenza—so close, in fact, that the two women (the former from a venerable noble lineage, the other inevitably of inferior social standing) shared a bed. It was, however, the more general disobedience of this group that caused concern. Not only did these nuns rarely frequent the choir, but they also marked themselves apart by their decadence of dress: "The three nuns named above are the vainest of them all." Suor Marietta Dolfin had been found "with ornaments and high-heeled clogs, and wears silk stockings with gilt lace."

Following the visitation at San Iseppo, the patriarch summoned the four main culprits and informed them

> that by virtue of holy obedience they must no longer
> consort together nor speak to one another, unless they
> do so in the common areas, in the presence of other
> nuns, and for necessary purposes, under pain of depriva-
> tion from the parlours for one year and other discre-
> tionary penalties.

But it was clear that the breakdown of the community had gone beyond the antics of the nuns specifically named. The observations of the patriarchal visitors reveal that groupings founded on age and kinship—the two factors that most commonly gave rise to disunion—rivaled the convent's institutional identity. The youth contingent was boosted at San Iseppo by the presence of seventeen boarding girls, and it was reported that "the young do not pay due respect to the Superior and to their elders"; further, that "some of these young nuns and others remain together in their own cells until six hours after dusk with the pretense of working, and they cause uproars and irregularities." Whereas young nuns looked to each other's company for more boisterous entertainments, in deference to the habits of the lay world they would rejoin their families at mealtimes.

Similar tales echo through the records of other convents. During the rounds of Priuli's visitations, his vicars reported that at Santa Giustina there were "twelve nuns opposed to the prioress," while at Santa Lucia "there are friends who consort together far more closely than is necessary."[6] Suor Paula Lippamano headed a clique at San Sepolcro, and her "disciples," it was said, "never eat in the refectory in the evening," preferring to dine together in a separate group.[7] The same old abuses recurred in the visitation reports of Patriarch Vendramin. In 1609, at Sant'Andrea de Zirada—a convent with a history of division—it was reported that there were four nuns who refused to eat with the rest of the community, preferring to take meals in their cells.[8] In the same year, this offense was also registered at San Zaccaria:

> His Lordship is greatly displeased by the abuse of those who use the pretext of their particular responsibilities in order to eat outside the Refectory, especially in the evening, using the same excuse for hours on end during the night, when they are obviously chatting and muttering.[9]

Generational divides were widespread, and the older nuns were forever complaining about the behavior of their younger sisters. At Sant'Alvise in 1595, the patriarchal visitors noted (patronizingly) that "many of the young nuns are overexuberant, and they go at pleasure to speak at the convent gate and to natter with little women."[10] A similar concern with the insobriety of youth emanates from Santa Croce in 1611: "The young nuns . . . are too headstrong, and show little obedience to the abbess."[11] The remarks of the older nuns at Santa Maria dei Miracoli suggest that their community had become self-consciously polarized along the lines of age. They complained "that the young nuns don't want to speak with the old nuns, but stick together in their personal oratories" (by "oratories," they referred to the private areas intended for prayer forming part of each nun's cell).[12]

While there was a tendency for nuns of similar ages to club together within the convent, the toughest bonds, as has been discussed, were those of kinship. Families developed conventions concerning the choice of nunneries for their female dependents, and young girls were often eased into convent life by the comforting thought that their sisters, cousins and aunts would be there to look after them.[13] Although the deceit of certain "aunts" who tricked young girls into taking the veil earned the condemnation of Tarabotti, on the whole, familial closeness was enduring.[14] At Ogni Santi in 1594, nuns from the Barbarigo clan formed an exclusive group:

> Above the large parlour, there is a big room furnished with beds where Suor Valeria Barbarigo sleeps along with certain of her nieces and other dependants. . . . And here are to be found cupboards containing various things, that is commodities for cooking and a barrel of wine.[15]

Gathered around a barrel of wine, the Barbarigos set up an alternative community within the walls of the nunnery.

The special relationships that united particular groups of nuns disunited convents. Personal friendships provided an escape from the tedium of institutional life and opportunities for socializing as well as outlets for cramped emotions.[16] But they also contributed to the tensions characterizing the cloistered existence: cliquishness, rivalry and disobedience. A more effective antidote to claustrophobia was, therefore, the web of relationships fostered on the edge of enclosure, which reunited nuns with the wider world. Social exchange between nuns and outsiders was, of course, hampered by those external authorities who sought to impose total enclosure on nunneries. But the bulky weight of evidence for legislation and disciplinary proceedings against unlicensed visitors to convents testifies to the ongoing failure, as well as to the persistence, of these efforts.

As with every other aspect of conventual life, nuns' relations with their families came under strict regulation in the rush of legislation precipitated by the reforms of the Council of Trent. Visits from family members were subject to the limitations of time and purpose laid down in the rules governing use of the parlor, and male relatives were only allowed to visit if they came within the required "degrees of kinship."[17] Such restrictions might be considered to have served the interests of those selfish relatives portrayed by Tarabotti, who, after tricking their female dependents into "the ultimate and irrevocable sentence of eternal imprisonment," had no intention of keeping up convivial contact with their victims. Thus she writes of how, in the days running up to nuns' professions, "fathers, brothers and other relatives pretend to love them with all their hearts, paying frequent visits and bestowing generous gifts upon them"; then as soon as the deed is done, "they cease their visits."[18] Tarabotti's pessimistic assessment is far from borne out by the evidence. On the contrary, the relatives of many nuns were assiduous frequenters of the convent parlors. And yet it is true to say that their visits were not always motivated by disinterested love alone.

Although sworn to poverty, nuns had access to certain material goods, supposedly held in common, which enabled them to exercise personal largesse when occasion offered itself. Their tendency to *dar fuor robba* (give stuff away) was a frequent concern of the ecclesiastical authorities in Venice, not only because it was incompatible with nuns' renunciation of property, but also because it could jeopardize the economic stability of the nunneries involved. Such practices of giving died hard, for they were cherished by nuns as a means of maintaining relations with the world outside. Nuns could assert their usefulness to their families by offering them some small measure of material support. At the same time, the family that had provided a nun's dowry might feel justly repaid in accepting food or hospitality from the convent cupboards. Given that some convents were powerful economic institutions, nuns could on occasion use their influence to bring more substantial benefits to their families. In 1595, at Santa Croce della Giudecca, nuns belonging to a branch of the Mollino clan were doing just that:

> The management of the temporal affairs of the convent has effectively been placed in the hands of certain nuns belonging to the Mollino family, since for many years they have monopolized the offices of bookkeepers. Their administration has been found unsatisfactory, on the grounds that certain houses belonging to the nunnery have been let to the relations of these Mollino nuns at a cheap rent without the consent of the chapter; it is unknown exactly how much they pay.[19]

Priuli had earlier ruled that "no more than two blood sisters may vote in the chapter."[20] Yet the Mollino nuns, operating in flagrant defiance of the chapter, had circumvented such rules.

The relations between nuns and their families reflected their mutual interests, and it was unusual for a nun to have built up so much resentment against her relatives that she wished to break off contact with them.[21] Generally, favors were reciprocal, though the onus fell on the nuns to ensure that they maintained a sufficiently hospitable establishment to attract visits from their families. The unequal degree of compulsion in demonstrations of generosity between nuns and their families is perhaps implicit in these remarks made after the 1596 visitation of San Zaccaria:

> The nuns keep for themselves those gifts which they receive from their homes, without showing them to the Abbess. . . . Likewise, when they send presents to their

relations, they do not inform the Abbess . . . and this accounts for half the food which the convent is squandering, because the nuns are continually making biscuits, cakes, doughnuts and pastries in great quantities. And to this end, at certain times of the year, several *quarteroli* of flour are doled out to the nuns, with the result that they consume five hundred *stara* of grain a year, two hundred *stara* more than they should reasonably expect to use.[22]

Such frenzies of cake making, which strained the resources of the convent, were commonly reported in the records of contemporary visitations.

The willingness of nuns to court affection and attention from their families is further indicated by their response to marriages occurring among their sisters and other female relatives. Whereas Tarabotti describes such events as the ultimate humiliation for the nun, who inevitably compared the feasting and extravagance of the marital rites with her own shabby and marginalized existence, some nuns were eager to be involved in the family festivities. In the first wave of patriarchal legislation concerned with the imposition of enclosure, a special law was passed condemning the practice whereby brides would visit convents in all their splendor on their wedding days.[23] Patriarch Trevisan alluded to the same custom in his instruction to the nuns of Corpus Domini: "Neither relations nor brides may be admitted to the gate of the convent, either to see the nuns, or to touch their hands."[24] But nuns remained keen to gather at the windows of the parlor to view the brides.

In 1617, members of a wedding party who had visited the nuns of San Maffio di Murano were called before the convent magistrates. On this occasion, the wedding guests were not themselves charged, but they were interrogated as possible

witnesses to the presence of Nicolò Cressi, a compulsive fre-
quenter of nuns' parlors, who was apparently present at San
Maffio on the very day that he had been released from prison
for previous offenses. Even so, the readiness with which the
wedding guests told of their visit to the convent allows us to
see just how innocent, how "normal" their own behavior must
have seemed to them. The best man described how he went to
San Maffio di Murano, "along with some other friends, to give
a hand to the bride and the other women who had gone to
visit the nuns there." Another of the groom's friends testified
that the visit took place late at night, after dinner, and yet another revealed that the progress included a visit to San Sepolcro in Castello as well as to the Murano convent.[25] Flotillas of
gondolas taking brides to visit their relations in the convents
were—as we can see from Giacomo Franco's illustration in his
Habiti delle donne, published in 1610—an established part of
Venetian wedding rituals.

One of Tarabotti's most poignant images is of the nun
staying up day and night before her sister's wedding in order to
sew the bride a gift, which the recipient, overwhelmed by the
lavishness of her own "most illustrious marriage" derides.[26]
Some nuns were unstoppable in their desire to fete their sisters
on their wedding days.[27] In a report from San Servolo of 1610,
the patriarchal visitors suggested that gifts were sent to brides
in anticipation of reciprocal munificence but urged nuns to ignore such potential benefits:

> It is an abuse severely to be condemned that nuns are
> accustomed to make excessive gifts to brides, on the
> pretext that the latter give presents to the nuns. There-
> fore, the most illustrious Patriarch orders that nuns
> should on no account make such gifts, disregarding any
> future remuneration they might hope for.[28]

But the reciprocal expectations of the nuns were not always so "tit for tat" as a simple exchange of presents. Although nuns relied on their families most obviously for material support, they were perhaps even more concerned to maintain some social and affective rapport with their relatives in the outside world. Contacts of this sort gave nuns an emotional life beyond the cloistered community, afforded them a certain status among their fellow nuns and offered precious opportunities for a change of company and some recreational variety.

That nuns' relatives often responded to the needs of their cloistered womenfolk is evident from the efforts of both ecclesiastical and temporal authorities to assert control over family gatherings at Venetian convents. Indeed, the uncompromising line of the convent magistrates who endeavored to stamp out even the most harmless of transgressions leads one to wonder whether Tarabotti was misplacing her attacks when she blamed the families of nuns for neglecting those who were imprisoned by conventual chains. It is hard to conceive as threatening the visit of the Pisani brothers to La Celestia in 1626 to "wish good day" to their sister, Suor Benetta, yet they found themselves hauled before the magistrates for their actions.[29] Invoking the absolute ban on monks and friars visiting nuns, the magistrates were again unbending in their attitude toward a certain Fra Cornelio, who went to the parlor of San Girolamo to speak with his sister. When Cornelio was interviewed and asked why he had been summoned, he replied, "I cannot imagine, unless it is because I went to see my sister, a nun at San Girolamo . . . following the death of my mother." He had failed to obtain a license "not knowing that the prohibition extended to a brother." But whatever pressing family business might arise in future, he was told, he must apply for special dispensation to visit his sister.[30]

Following a rather charming incident of honest family

fun, which nevertheless failed to charm the convent magistrates, Piero da Mosto was called to trial in 1618. In his own summary of events, he explained how he had been visited over the Easter holidays by two girls from the country who were hoping to enjoy the seasonal festivities that Venice had to offer. It was on the last of the feast days that Piero's sister, a widow, suggested that they take the girls out in a boat to have supper. Plans for their nighttime picnic at first developed fortuitously: "In the course of our trip we met a fishing boat, and I bought 10 or 12 mackerels, and some other fish; and on discussing where we could go to get the fish cooked, my sister said, 'Let's pay a visit to our aunt at Sant'Anna.'" Since Piero's sister had not seen this aunt for three or four years, he endorsed her proposal, evidently perceiving the visit as a good way to kill two birds with one stone: "And so I sent a servant onto land with a bailing scoop full of fish to pay our respects to Suor Cherubina of the da Mosto house, our aunt; and to ask her to cook the fish for us." Suor Cherubina, delighted by the visit of her sister, sent word that she must disembark. When the latter protested that she could not leave the boat, since she was wearing rough shoes and had no hat, a compromise was devised whereby the visitors took the boat round to the canal running alongside the convent cellars. "Thither we went, and our aunt and two of my cousins, Suor Nicolosa of Ca'Foscarini, and Suor Costantina of Ca'Zorzi, came round to us and we chatted with them." The occasion now constituted quite a family gathering, and the party amused itself for a quarter of an hour until sighted by an agent of the magistrates patrolling the area. Although no verdict for the case survives, we may assume that the gathering was broken up before the fish were cooked, and that Piero received at the very least a stiff warning against revels of this kind.[31]

Insofar as they were successful, the efforts of external authorities to isolate nuns from their families denied the women an important means of relief from the hemmed-in existence of the convent. In fact, the measures that attempted to stifle the "natural" affections of familial relations met with a fair amount of resistance from nuns and lay folk alike. One family determined to assert its rights to retain affectionate contact with particular nuns crops up several times in the records of the magistrates, for the merchant Oratio Coreggio and his wife Paulina seem to have been more than usually attentive to the young female dependents whom they had placed in the convent of San Maffio di Murano. The first we hear of the family is in 1609, when Oratio organized a meal in the parlor of San Maffio after the clothing ceremony of one of his nieces.[32] Although he was charged with bringing an unnecessarily large flock of well-wishers to the convent and remaining in the parlor until late at night, he perceived his own actions as utterly reputable. Oratio explained first of all how he had raised his niece and borne the costs of her admission as a nun. "With my own means I placed a daughter of my sister in the convent: I paid for a cell to be bought for her, I supplied the conventual dowry, and I brought her up from the age of six." He then went on to describe the modest festivities he had undertaken to lay on:

> On the feast of San Martino, the day that the girl was clothed, we went to the convent. The party consisted of my mother, aged 78, my wife, my sisters, 6 of my other unmarried nieces and female relatives, and 6 of my married nieces; also my mother-in-law, my sisters-in-law and cousins. And because we had not eaten anything, we desired a room to retire to, and we were granted use of the parlour, next to the waterside, where we gave to

these our closest kinswomen some biscuits and other
things, in recognition of the nun's spiritual marriage.

Coreggio viewed the hospitality he had provided for his relatives not only as a practical necessity, but as an appropriate
manner in which to mark the occasion, "in recognition of the
nun's spiritual marriage."[33] This opinion was not shared by the
magistrates, who fined Oratio twenty ducats.

When we next hear of the family, it is Paulina who is
deemed overzealous in her attentions to her wards at San Maffio. By 1617, it would seem that four of her charges were at the
convent, and in February of that year it was reported that she
had offered these girls refreshments in the parlor: "She brought
them some marzipan, 2 *bozze* [that is, 5–6 litres!] of white wine,
and some biscuits of one sort or another." Brought before the
magistracy, Paulina claimed total ignorance as to the illegality of
her actions. She argued that it was "the custom manifestly exercised by all fathers, mothers and brothers to go quite openly
during Carnival to spend time with their daughters and sisters
in convents." Furthermore, she demonstrated an awareness that
these young girls were owed a certain compensation for having
been placed in the nunnery by their family. Moved by "natural
reason and love of these four young girls, destined by me at a
tender age to the service of God, and finding it necessary to incline them to this worthy proposition with loving visits,"
Paulina hoped to ease the lot of her wards. And so, "In order to
amuse the girls, and to console these tender little creatures, I
brought them some sweetmeats, and some cream."[34]

We do not know if the magistrates ever came to a verdict
on this case. (A denunciation of April 1617, urging the magistracy to sentence Paulina, suggests that they may have been
undecided about how to resolve the matter.) But in 1621, an

appeal was made to the magistrates by Elena Barbaro, on behalf of two nuns, Suor Crestina and Suor Paulina Coreggio, that their aunt, "Paulina Coreggio, widow," might be permitted to visit them at San Maffio, "since these two young nuns have no closer blood relative in this world." In the first instance, license was granted for Paulina to visit the nuns on a single set occasion; then the permission was extended indefinitely. It would seem that the magistrates could no longer resist the determination of this woman to do her duty by her nieces.[35]

Nuns and their families frequently demonstrated the will to keep in touch with one another. Family events, such as weddings, or the nuns' own ceremonies on feast days or at vow taking, provided opportunities for kin to gather at convents. On a more everyday basis, relations would visit the parlor to speak with nuns, and food and drink would often be consumed, despite laws condemning such practices.[36] The affection that some laypeople retained for their relations in nunneries is well illustrated by their posthumous instructions. Bequests to nuns could be quite considerable, and it was also common to entrust particular relatives with the responsibility of looking after nuns in the family. For example, Iacomo Bragadin, in his will of 1605, instructed his wife

> to pay to my beloved sister suor Lodovica Bragadin in the convent of Sant'Andrea . . . forty ducats a year and to provide her with everything she needs; and I entreat my wife to take her and keep her as her own dear sister, and to act as I would have done, and this I ask her to do up to the year when she dies.[37]

But the efforts of families to maintain contact with nuns were now countered by the policies of church and state, which aspired to cut religious women off from the rest of society. Sometimes those who were brought before the courts for visiting nuns could scarcely believe the inflexibility of the regulations. In a spirited defense of her own conduct, Paulina Coreggio argued that

> such a law, although just and holy, has never been used against mothers, whose incaution is not derived from scandalous intent; but rather, on account of love for their children, they have acted by most excusable and involuntary motives.[38]

This indignant assertion of a mother's rights in the face of the state suggests the extent to which the "reform" of the nunneries jarred with existing social customs and expectations. Ultimately, no amount of legislation could break the ties of love and affection that bound nuns to the outside world.

7. The Conversation of Women

IN A CHAPTER of his conduct book for Christian women, entitled *How the Nun Must Flee from the Parlours,* Agostino Valier, bishop of Verona and an ardent exponent of the Counter-Reformation, urged nuns not to listen to news from the miserable world outside, insisting that they could derive nothing from conversation with laywomen:

> Do not delight in the conversation of laywomen, for they are accustomed to praise the things that they love; since they love the affairs of the world, they will speak of worldly matters; since they are fascinated by earthly concerns, they will provide news of such things; likewise, they desire transitory things, and with transitory things they will fill your ears.[1]

The bishop's instructions will be familiar enough by now, for they chime with the orders regularly issued by the patriarchal authorities in Venice. They contrast vividly with the scenes that are dramatized in a series of comic dialogues, published in 1675, entitled *Il nuovo parlatorio delle monache* (*The New Parlour of Nuns*). The sixth of these takes place between a nun named Suor Tarsia and a certain Donna Menica, one of her family's servants. The opening lines suggest above all the nun's voracious appetite for news:

> Oh Donna Menica, what good things have you brought me? How are you all? What's going on at home? When

is my sister coming? Has my brother-in-law overcome
his dishonour yet?

Menica responds censoriously, chastising Tarsia for confusing
her with all her questions. Beseeching her to calm down, she
warns the nun that she is the bearer of bad news, a revelation
which sets Tarsia off again:

> What bad news can this be? Has my brother-in-law lost
> a great sum at cards? Has he been burgled? Or have the
> animals died? Do not let me languish upon these uncer-
> tainties, but tell all!

And after more ticking off from Menica, we learn that the
nun's sister, Signora Isabella, is cuckolding her husband. Need-
less to say, Tarsia insists on hearing all the juicy details.[2]

Reformers like Valier were all too well aware of how much
nuns valued their relations with laypeople, and of how important it was for them to obtain regular bulletins of what was going on in the outside world. The information networks that
served the convent were predominantly, though not exclusively, female. Nuns surrounded themselves with *petegole* (gossips) or *donnette* (little women) who acted as purveyors of news
and gave a perspective on life beyond the convent walls. The
Venetian authorities fought a running battle against "the conversation and conduct of those women and girls, who frequent
the convents, under the pretext of providing services."[3] In at-
tempting to isolate religious women, they claimed that they
were shielding them from the taint of secular society. And yet
the boundaries between secular and sacred were not so clearly
drawn. Even within the convent community, the presence of
certain kinds of women, whose experiences, preoccupations
and, indeed, conversations were often distinctly this-worldly,

threatened to contaminate the holy institutions that harbored them. These ambiguous cases fell into three principal categories: laywomen, boarding girls and widows.

While the traditional practice of offering hospitality to laywomen as paying guests was on the wane in this period, convents continued to provide a refuge for women who were in special need or trouble.[4] In particular, victims of marital violence, having initiated proceedings for separation in the patriarchal court, commonly retreated to one of the nunneries for the duration of the ecclesiastical investigation.[5] A decree of February 1622 registers the Council of Ten's ambivalence about this appropriation of the convent as a refuge. The preamble noted that married women were sometimes received into convents in cases of extreme urgency, and it paid tribute to the nuns' role in rescuing these unfortunates from scandal and seeking to reconcile them with their husbands and families. However, it went on to resolve that, in future, such women would only be admitted to the convents with the permission of the Council of Ten, which could only be granted with a three-quarters majority. Although the Venetian state evidently wished to retain the convents' function as safe houses for otherwise unprotected women, it also saw the potential dangers of mixing lay and religious women and sought to regulate arrangements ever more closely.

The temporary admission of married women to the convent was viewed as a special event; by contrast, the acceptance of boarding girls was standard practice, and they were supposed to observe the full rigors of enclosure. Patriarch Priuli stressed that if a girl stepped outside the convent, she was on no account to be allowed back in unless she intended to become a nun.[6] But even while they stayed securely within the sacred walls, these girls represented a worldly element in the religious community. Following the visitation of Santa Marta in 1594, it was reported that

> the boarding-girls are a great disturbance to the convent and cause more harm than good, because the majority of them pay only 40 ducats a year. . . . Moreover, some of them are kept by the novice-mistresses in their own cells where they sleep, and they go around the dormitory as they please, wandering about in a disorderly fashion. And they play cards all night long, scandalously.[7]

The presence in the nunnery of lay girls, aged between seven and twenty-five, was not always conducive to discipline. They had taken no vows, and many of them were destined for earthly marriages.[8] It is significant that the ecclesiastical authorities were particularly concerned about keeping the boarders apart from nuns once the former's betrothals had taken place. The following instruction was sent to San Servolo in 1610:

> When boarding-girls are betrothed as brides, they should be sent back to their homes. It is not permissible that they remain in the convent, dressed as married women, nor that their husbands scandalously come to visit them at the grated window. . . . And if the parents do not send for their daughter once she is betrothed, the Abbess must put her in a gondola and send her back to the house of her relations, under whatever grave punishments shall seem fit to His Most Illustrious Lordship.[9]

Close friendships inevitably developed between nuns and boarding girls, who passed the best part of their childhood and adolescence within the walls of the convent. And despite the regulations, such relationships often persisted once the lay-women had gone back to the world.[10] But although the au-thorities tried to control the practice of accepting boarding girls within the nunneries, they did not even attempt to pre-vent it. The economic importance of the girls for providing a steady income was well understood.[11] Once again, practical considerations allowed a convention that ran contrary to the principle of enclosure to persist, giving nuns scope for devel-oping relationships with women who would one day be living in the tainted, secular world.

Widows—the third category of convent inhabitant whose status challenged the enclosed ideal—became increasingly un-common in the nunneries of late Renaissance Venice. As sex-ually experienced women, who had lived in the world, these represented the opposite end of the spectrum from those chaste young boarding girls who were destined for marriage. Their case was discussed in detail in Benedetto Buommattei's *Order for the Consecration of Virgins,* a liturgical work published in Venice in 1622. Given that the core of the consecration cer-emony consisted of the virgin marrying Christ, Buommattei argued that it was inappropriate for a woman who had already taken an earthly husband. Instead, widows (or other nonvir-ginal nuns) were eligible for a ceremony of "conversion," or "continence" with the emphasis being placed on sexual absti-nence, rather than immaculacy. The service followed the same pattern as the ceremony of consecration, with the words "vir-gins" and "virginity" replaced by "holy nuns" and "chastity."[12]

Buommattei's comments might be taken to imply that widows were not uncomon among religious communities of the early seventeenth century. And yet their absence from the extensive and meticulous regulations produced by the Venet-ian prelacy is noticeable: Widows are not mentioned in the lists of nuns which sometimes form part of the patriarchal visitation reports. In fact, research for this book has uncovered only one definite reference to a nun of widow status, and this case is very early.[13] (By contrast, sixteen of the forty-eight nuns listed in a fifteenth-century necrology, or death register, from the convent of Corpus Domini were widows.)[14] Two factors may have caused the sharp decline in this phenomenon. First, the socioeconomic conditions that promoted the religious life as an alternative to marriage among young noblewomen discouraged it as a step for widows. Having already made the initial outlay of a marital dowry, the widow's family would be likely to oppose the payment of a nonrefundable conventual dowry, or even an annuity, as a poor investment. Second, most patrician widows enjoyed viable and more attractive alternatives. Whereas, in previous ages, the convent might have appealed as a comfortable place of retirement, in the climate of the Counter-Reformation it offered little to any but the most devout widow. And so, in Venice, the widowed nun—whose existence sat uneasily within the ideology of enclosure—became virtually extinct.

Other headaches for the authorities were not going to go away so easily. Married women, boarding girls and widows were potentially controllable problems; far more intractable threats were presented by the servants of convents. After all, convents could not subsist without servants. Across their imposing walls, innumerable economic transactions took place. Goods and services had to be paid for, products marketed and sold, farms managed, rents exacted, capital invested. Under enclosure it was, of course, impossible for professed nuns to wander out of their community in order to do business with shopkeepers or negotiate with tenants. Consequently, enclosed women relied on the assistance of two categories of servants or employees to look after the interests of the convent in the outside world. First, there were the *converse,* the internal servants of the convent; second, there were external employees, ranging from male business managers, charged with overseeing the convent's investments, to local women who carried out shopping and other chores for the nuns.

Although *converse* were, on the whole, bound by enclosure, in every convent there were a number of unenclosed *converse* who were licensed to venture out in order to carry out business on behalf of their community. In constructing the new measures regarding the enclosure of nunneries, Pope Pius V had made this concession grudgingly, on condition that henceforth *converse* would not be allowed to be professed, but could take only simple vows.[15] The compromise was in part motivated by the traditional dependence of mendicant or begging communities on alms given by the laity. The principle was adopted by the Venetian prelates, who licensed certain unprofessed *converse,* aged forty or over, to go into the city or onto the mainland "to seek alms or for other services."[16] Referring specifically to Pope Pius's bull *Circa Pastoralis* of 1566, Patriarch Priuli instructed the nuns of Sant'Andrea di Zirada in 1596 that for important business they should "elect four of the said *converse,* who are aged over forty years, and who on other counts are among the most discreet women in the convent."[17] Priuli's visitations testify to the conscientious enforcement of this rule. The patriarchal vicar regularly took note of the names of the four *converse* who were licensed to serve the nuns' interests in the outside world.

Yet despite the attentive monitoring of *converse,* this type of nun consistently appears in the visitation records as a source of disruption and disorder. The patriarchal visitors were evidently skeptical about the benefits of *converse* engaging in traditional mendicant activities. Following their visitation of Sant'Alvise in 1595, they observed disapprovingly that "the said *converse* go through Venice begging bread from certain houses, but without necessity, and with loss of time and little profit."[18] More worrying was the freedom of the unenclosed *converse* to travel around the *terraferma*. For example, at San Sepolcro in 1595 the patriarchal visitors noted that

> every year they send out two *converse* to seek alms in Portogruaro [in Friuli], two to the Padovan towards Este, and sometimes to the Trevisan to a property of the convent called Rovese in order to collect rents.[19]

This degree of freedom of movement made *converse* a troublesome quantity, even if they remained technically within the rules. Unsurprisingly, they were inclined to abuse their liberty. At Corpus Domini in 1595, it was reported that "the unenclosed *converse* go into the countryside, and wherever they please, with great scandal."[20] Some of the most detailed descriptions of scandalous behavior were noted by the patriarchal visitors of Santa Maria Maggiore.

> The *converse* enjoy too much liberty, going out on highdays and holidays. . . . They sometimes go to make their devotions to the Christ of Poveggia and to the Madonna of Chioggia, in pursuit of amusement; and the most presumptuous of these are Suor Micchiela, Suor Giustina, Suor Lodovica and Suor Chiara. These 4 nuns often go out together, and this is bad. And sometimes they go out of the convent to eat in the homes of their families; they are accustomed to go to the mainland to seek alms, that is to Udine, or to Porto, which activities usually result in disorder. There are too many *converse*, and for this reason, it is necessary to refrain from admitting any others for some time.[21]

For this anomalous category of unenclosed nun, life appeared to be one long holiday.

By allowing unenclosed women to coexist with professed nuns within the walls of the convent, the Counter-Reformation authorities admitted a compromise that was at once necessary and undermining. *Converse* who crossed the convent walls smudged the boundaries of enclosure. The problem was not simply that these unprotected women subjected themselves to the dangers and temptations of the world, but that they brought something of that corrupt world back into the cloister with them.

Meanwhile, the principal threat to the purity and innocence of enclosed nuns remained, of course, outsiders. Even contacts with the lay world that were founded in piety could be treated as pernicious. When, for example, a weaver who supplied services to Santa Maria Maggiore was asked by the magistrates, in 1565, why he gave up working time in order to attend to the nuns, he replied, "Sometimes that which I do is motivated by charity and by the devotion that I have for this place, blessed to the honour of God." In return for his labors, his reward was modest—"a pan of cream, a piece of bread in broth, and some water."[22] Yet as the Counter-Reformation obsession with enclosure developed, even the most innocuous infringements of the regulations were subject to rigorous investigation.

At its most malevolent, contact with the lay servants might undermine the chastity of Christ's brides. Recall the case of Suor Faustina, who ran away from San Giovanni Lateran in 1555. Her alleged lover and accomplice in escape, Francesco dalle Crosette, was employed by the convent to fulfill a variety of tasks, wherever the need arose. These included carrying water and building materials, as well as helping nuns to make bread inside the enclosure. In the course of his depositions to the convent magistrates, he freely admitted the frequency of his visits: "I went there ten times a day, whenever they required my help." [23] Francesco referred to himself as "a son of the convent," and it is easy to imagine how he grew intimate with Faustina. Suor Zuana di Thomasi testified that

> sometimes he came to the nunnery to carry out some service, because he had an aunt, Mother Seraphina, who was the prioress of the convent. And thus he took up a friendship with the said suor Faustina . . . and he often spoke with her and he spent a deal of time in the parlour, and he told us other nuns that she sent him to do various services for her. [24]

The growing friendship between nun and male employee was founded on a relationship of service.

At the convent of Spirito Santo, a sickly nun named Suor Crestina employed Pasqua—formerly a domestic servant of her own family—to take away her dirty clothes. Pasqua explained:

> I only went there when she sent for me. She used to give me her sheets to wash, because she said that it made the nuns feel sick to wash them since she had an infected wound in her leg. She always said to me that I would wash her sheets, and she would pay me. [25]

Not only did Crestina have a personal servant, but the servant also justified their arrangement by reference to a lapse in fellow feeling within the sisterhood. So much for the common life!

The employment of laywomen to carry out services for the convent and its inmates was strongly associated with nuns' propensity for gift giving. The material benefits to which convent servants could look forward were twofold: They were the gainers not only of paid employment, but also of endless perks in the form of food and drink to take away. As we have seen, nuns were notorious for their production and distribution of edible goodies. Not infrequently, the illicit largesse of its inhabitants was pinpointed as the reason why a particular convent was undergoing major financial problems. Patriarch Priuli's report from Santa Maria delle Vergini in 1596, with strong echoes of his remarks about San Zaccaria the same year, was quite explicit:

> They consume six hundred or more *stara* of wheat per annum, although there are only 68 nuns. . . . And they consume a great deal of flour in making biscuits, pastries, and other things, whenever they make bread. . . . They have debts of three thousand ducats, despite the fact that their revenues are fat.[26]

At the end of this visitation, Priuli turned his attention specifically to the financial problems that had arisen at the convent as a result of the nuns' excessive baking. He ordered that in future, bread should be made outside the convent; workmen should be paid in money, not in kind; and strict limits should be imposed on "charity." The patriarch hoped by this ruling to bring about a saving of 200 *stara* (approximately 16,660 liters) of flour per annum.[27]

Nuns' relatives were not the only beneficiaries of their largesse; they also regularly gave food to friends, neighbors and employees. Gift giving was, moreover, an essential part of courting the attention of male admirers. So compelled were nuns to engage in baking cakes and biscuits for others that they happily sacrificed some of their own rations to this end. We learn from a visitation to Santa Chiara "that the nuns demand to be given raw eggs at table, and they do not eat them, but save them in order to make doughnuts and cakes to give away."[28] The rationale behind this apparent altruism may well have been self-empowerment. Research into the spending habits of Venetian noblewomen has shown how they were able to assert themselves by buying extravagant clothes, making testamentary bequests and giving presents.[29] In small but significant ways, nuns—like their lay sisters—also exercised power through expenditure.

The place of gift giving in nuns' relations with the laity is well illustrated in the convent magistrates' investigation of various disciplinary lapses that took place at the convent of Sant' Andrea de Zirada between 1567 and 1568.[30] The siphoning off of the convent's resources here went hand in hand with disobedience, division and the formation of illicit and damaging relationships on the periphery of the enclosure. Of those laypeople who frequented the convent there were, to begin with, the regular employees of the community. Zorzi, the boatman, gave this description of his role: "I carry out all those services which the nuns ask me to do: I go out to collect rents when they send me . . . I do shopping for the convent, and also for the chaplain." Then there was Hieronimo, a porter, who explained that he had done fewer jobs for the convent since the employment of Zorzi, but was still required for carrying certain goods: "I am also employed to bring grain, flour, wood and anything else which is needed to the convent, according to the orders which I receive."[31] Seemingly less legitimate were those women employed on a more casual basis, often to perform particular services for individual nuns. Of one Zuana—known as *la gagiarda* (the strong one)—it was reported that

> she keeps eight or ten chickens belonging to Madonna
> Suor Gabriela at her house, and in return for feeding the
> chickens, Madonna Suor Gabriela . . . supplies her with
> bread and wine, and with every other thing.[32]

This Zuana was one of a group of women, described disparagingly by witnesses as "gossips," who lived "on the shoulders of the convent." Taking food from the nuns, these women constituted a very real threat both to the dignity and the prosperity of the convent.

Yet more damaging to Sant'Andrea was the presence of a certain Felicità, the mistress of the confessor. Not only did Felicità live at the confessor's home at the convent's expense, but her eight children were also provided for, and her daughter Tesaura was employed at the hospital for widows that was attached to the nunnery. The testimonies of the hospital inmates reveal the resentment they felt toward Felicità and other servants who lived off the community's resources, whom they perceived as the cause of their own material deprivation. "We are dying of hunger on account of bad government," was the complaint of one widow.[33]

The convent's debauched and spendthrift confessor, who encouraged Felicità and her family in their parasitic extravagance, was clearly a liability. But the problem was vastly exacerbated by the welcome afforded to Felicità, strong Zuana, and various other hangers-on by certain of the nuns themselves. Consistently identified by witnesses as Suor Anna Giustiniana, Suor Gabriela Salamon, Suor Elena Capello, Suor Beatrice Moro and the *conversa* Suor Anfrosina, these nuns formed an autonomous enclave within the community of Sant'Andrea:

> Those who hang out by the door . . . are always to be
> found there; they never go with the other nuns to the

choir, nor to the refectory, nor do they pay obedience to Madonna the Prioress.[34]

Significantly, these disobedient nuns chose to situate themselves at the very edge of enclosure, where contact with the world was at its freest.[35] From this position, they were able to send laypeople out on errands or with messages. Zorzi reported how he was once employed by Suor Beatrice to deliver flour (hidden among dirty washing being taken from the nunnery) to a sister of hers:

> Suor Beatrice Moro made me bring my boat and put me in the boat and made me carry away three baskets of dirty washing, and underneath this washing in each basket there was a bag of flour . . . and we unloaded them at Santa Caterina at the house of one of the sisters of Madonna Suor Beatrice.[36]

Such demonstrations of largesse perhaps point to a wish on the part of nuns to overcome their denial of personal property. Beatrice's gift of flour to her sister is a comparatively minor instance; the greatest losses were of those goods that leaked out to neighboring laywomen, either as presents or in payment for their services. Helena, a witness from the widows' hospital, testified that "we saw baskets and bags being taken away by women, by gossips and the country people who bring chickens, and they took bread, bran, flour and other stuff."[37]

Besides fulfilling occasional services for the nuns, these gossips had another important commodity to offer those who lived within the enclosure of Sant'Andrea—news. The ecclesiastical authorities were, as we have seen, keenly aware of the undesirability of allowing communities of nuns to bring news in from outside, or to broadcast their own. On the one hand, where nunneries had experienced disciplinary lapses, it was considered safer to suppress the information rather than to expose communities to public scandal. Hence Patriarch Trevisan ruled "that the misdeeds and occurrences of nuns and convents should no longer be passed on to seculars, whether by spoken or written word."[38] On the other hand, it was imperative that nuns should not be subjected to the taint of worldly gossip—a risk that, as we can tell from Bishop Grimani's censorious remarks, was strongly associated with the employment of laywomen:

> Since the presence of many little women in the service of the convent, who are always to be found chatting at the convent gates and windows, lends only damage and little reputation to the convent, we would like to see them removed, or at least reduced in number.[39]

At Sant'Andrea, gossipmongering had become a full-time pursuit for those nuns who spent their days sitting at the gates of the convent. Their prime informant was the troublesome Felicità, whose reports were enriched by leaked intelligences from the confessional. As Maria, a widow from the hospital, related,

> She is always there, and indeed she was there yesterday, and she carries words backwards and forwards, for she stays a good three hours in the little cell chatting with those nuns I've named, and she takes gossip hither and thither, and I've observed that she reports the secrets of the confession and passes them on to everyone; and she has caused a scandal because she relayed to the nuns the confessions which she had heard.[40]

Reading this case one gets the impression of a group of uncommitted and probably vocationless nuns, building up a dependence on the titillating entertainments of Felicità. Not only did she bring them news of the world, and the confessional secrets of their fellow sisters, but she also flirted with them. Zorzi testified that

> I see Felicità going inside the door, sitting down on the benches in the company of those reverend nuns Madonna Suor Gabriela and the others. And as soon as they are there, I see them holding hands, and Felicità puts her hand on the breast of Suor Gabriela and they kiss one another all over.[41]

In return for material support, Felicità and the other women could trade worldly commodities in the form of words or acts.[42] The transaction is clearly articulated by the aforementioned Donna Maria: "They carry away food, and they bring gossip back and forth."[43]

The network of lay contacts that grew around the convent of Sant'Andrea was largely neighborhood based. In July 1568, after two years of investigation by the convent magistrates, eight women and three men were prohibited from going to the convent, speaking with the nuns or approaching the parlor "for any reason whatsoever," under pain of being banned from the wider area in which the nunnery was located, from the bridge of La Croce to the convent itself. The document that records this verdict also notes the name and provenance of each of the offenders:

> Strong Zuana, who lives on the *fondamenta* of Sant'Andrea in a narrow alley, and her daughter;
> Pasqua, from the Friuli, who lives at Santa Chiara
> Lame Lugretia, who lives at San Polo
> Franceschina, a widow, who lives at the wooden bridge, at the end of the campo

> Anzola, dress-maker, at Santa Chiara
> Maddalena; lives at Santa Chiara
> Donado, porter; lives by the Frari
> Donna Andreinna Filacanevo; lives by the church
> Alvise, the son of Donna Felicità . . .
> and Zan Francesco, tailor; at the wooden bridge, at the
>   end of the campo.[44]

From this record we learn where ten out of eleven employees lived. Only Alvise, the son of Felicità (who had been banned from the convent a year earlier), is given no address. Of the remaining ten offenders, eight lived very close to the convent where they worked: The locations of their homes are described either in relation to Sant'Andrea (the *fondamenta,* church or *campo*) or to the neighboring convent of Santa Chiara. Just two of the offenders lived farther afield, by the Frari and at San Polo, both in the center of the city. Although networks of employees sprawled beyond the immediate vicinity of the convent, it is clear that an enclosed nunnery provided a source of work, income and sociability for its neighbors, women in particular.[45]

Networks of women of slightly dubious honor had a remarkable tendency to build up on the peripheries of nunneries. Such were the "great fooleries" and "uproars" occasioned in 1617 by a prostitute, Donna Bella, and her daughter Meneghina outside the convent of Santa Caterina that the priest was unable to hear the confessions of the nuns.[46] At San Servolo in 1621, it was reported that

> it is necessary to keep guard all day long, because there are little women of every kind, who come to the convent, and who are its ruin: whores, bawds and witches.[47]

"Whores, bawds and witches" may have been a hysterical exaggeration. But the frequency with which nuns and prostitutes would strike up a rapport was certainly a major concern of the magistrates. A denunciation of 1612 against the "perverse and immodest Donna Malipiera Malipiero," for her familiarity with the nuns of Spirito Santo, began with a general condemnation of "the temerity of those . . . women who disdain every law, order, and protest." The crime of this particular woman was her enjoyment of a degree of intimacy with the nuns that was wholly unacceptable, even disregarding her own status as a prostitute:

> On the vigil of St Thomas the Apostle, this wicked woman, who was dressed in the clothes of a prostitute or a courting girl, came into the church of Spirito Santo and, what is worse, entered the parlour, and she stayed there talking for a long time with Suor Lucietta Foscarini, with whom she exchanged many kisses, together with a number of other nuns who came into the parlour.[48]

Another prostitute, Anzola, was denounced in 1626 for her visits to the parlor of San Servolo: "She was speaking to nuns from the Bonome family in the said convent, and creating a grand to-do, laughing loudly as whores will."[49] That nuns should have welcomed prostitutes into their midst demonstrates their willingness to entertain even the depths of worldliness in order to keep open their lines of communication with the world outside. But it is also interesting that prostitutes should have found convents an attractive environment in which to spend their leisure time.

It is one of the paradoxes of convent life that it was at once more private and more public than were the lives of elite women outside the cloister. On the one hand, the nunnery offered a much more confined model of female existence than did the noble household. On the other, the city's convents and their exclusively female membership enjoyed a public presence that lay noblewomen did not. Although they were constricted by the limits of enclosure, nuns had access to two different spheres in forging links of friendship, sociability and patronage. They could nurture contacts of a semipersonal nature in the immediate environs of their convents, but they could also operate corporately and exploit their civic status.[50] This duality is reflected in nuns' relationships with the prostitutes who were in many ways their mirror images. Crucial to the civic economy of sin, prostitutes were also socially amphibious, sometimes inhabiting the neighborly circles in which laywomen found their sustenance, at other times exploiting the less personal world of drifting, citywide associations. The transgressive conversation of nuns with prostitutes points to their curious affinities with each other and with men. But the most striking opportunity for nuns to manipulate a role for themselves in the male sphere of civic sociability came annually during the festive period leading up to Lent.

8. Carnival in the Cloister

ONCE A YEAR, on the morning of *Giovedi Grasso,* the last Thursday before the beginning of Lent, an extraordinary event would take place in Piazza San Marco. In front of a dignified assemblage comprising the doge, assorted noblemen and sundry foreign ambassadors, and in the presence of a crowd of jeering onlookers, a bull and twelve pigs were formally sentenced to death. Having been chased relentlessly around the Piazzetta—the section of the square that opens onto the waterfront, which was the site of public executions—the animals were rounded up and slaughtered, and their meat was shared out (traditionally among the nobles). Like so many of the peculiar rituals that marked the Venetian calendar, this one dated back to the thirteenth century and contributed to the myth of the republic's indomitability. According to legend, the animals formed part of an annual tribute paid to the Venetians by an ecclesiastical potentate (the patriarch of Aquileia) whose jurisdictional claims had once been fiercely contested by the republic. The public slaughter of the animals served as a reminder of the defeat of the patriarch and his men.[1]

Despite the political message, the bloody spectacle of animals being butchered in the central ceremonial space of the city fitted Venice's serene image somewhat poorly. Small wonder, then, that in the early sixteenth century, at a time when intense efforts were being made to impose greater discipline and order on society, the authorities should have taken measures to clean up such a messy and undignified custom. But a decree of

1525, which attempted to render the ritual more decent by doing away with the pigs and sanctioning the slaughter of one bull alone, was ignored for some time. The popular demand for pigs lived on.[2]

These scenes of gore and brutality tell us a great deal about the experience of Carnival in Renaissance Venice, which was a far cry from the sanitized festivities re-created for today's tourists.[3] Lasting from Christmas to the beginning of Lent, during the coldest, dampest and most miserable months of the Venetian year, Carnival was by no means a time of unmitigated gaiety. True, there were fireworks, doughnuts, human pyramids and other harmless entertainments. But beneath the revelries there ran a current of cruelty and disorder; this was a time for vicious jokes, abusive courtships and drunken violence. The authorities were all too aware of this ugly and subversive side of Carnival. While the state sought to win the popularity of its subjects by sponsoring certain events, and strove to impose order and purpose on customs that, although undesirably rowdy, could not be eradicated, the annual buildup of criminal prosecutions during this period bore witness to its persistently destabilizing effects.

Key to the lawlessness and disorder that characterized Carnival was anonymity. Venetians of all social classes walked the streets *in maschera,* a term which still refers to both the costumes and the masks donned by revelers. In a city famous for its sumptuary legislation—legislation that aspired to consolidate social hierarchies through the strict regulation of clothing—the adoption of alternative costumes was not simply a matter of fancy dress. As for masks, these not only hid the faces of the pickpocket or the con man, adding to the criminal potential of Carnival, but they also enabled individuals to slip between social stations or even genders, turning the whole world upside down.

All this, one might think, could have little effect on the cloistered women of the Venetian convents. And yet, time and again, the authorities of church and state were moved to condemn "the abuses and excesses which occur in the churches and parlours of nuns especially at times of Carnival with refreshments, eating and drinking, playing, singing and dancing, or people entering convents wearing masks to the dishonour of God and of our Religion."[4] Wholly incompatible with the dignity expected of nuns and with the principle of enclosure, such practices nevertheless proved enduring, further evidence of the extent to which religious communities were integrated into the social life of the wider community, and into the city's year-round festive calendar.[5] And it is no coincidence that a high proportion of the transgressions brought before the magistrates occurred in the weeks leading up to Lent.[6] At Carnival or at other times of civic merrymaking—as we have already seen on a smaller scale with family festivities—revelers were happy to include nunneries in their boisterous progresses, and nuns were keen to reciprocate with hospitality and entertainment.

Nuns who craved variety in their recreation, and an escape from the unchanging routine of religious life, may have looked upon Carnival as a good excuse to exploit to the full the small amount of seasonal license afforded them. In theory, at least, nuns were allowed to engage in convent theater at this time as long as the subject was pious and the participants retained their religious garb.[7] Priuli prefaced a particularly severe condemnation of nuns who contravened these principles with the avowal that "although we do not intend to ban nuns from participating in honest and virtuous recreations at certain times of the year, we are obliged to prevent those activities which are totally contrary to the religious life, and which greatly offend the Lord God, and the commands of the Holy Church."[8]

Clearly, it was difficult to control the theatrical efforts of nuns performing among themselves. Visitation reports suggest that certain communities took advantage of their cloistered existence to break some of the rules in privacy. For example, at the Miracoli it was recorded

> that sometimes the nuns sing profane songs, and they play the guitar and the lute, and they dress up as men in order to put on plays. . . . It is ordered that they should not wear secular clothes when they perform plays.[9]

Here again we see the paradox of enclosure, which in cutting nuns off from the world could actually increase their freedom to behave as they wished.

We remain frustratingly ignorant of what plays Venetian nuns put on. But we may hazard a guess that their dramatic offerings were not so very different from those of their Tuscan sisters who (according to one study) enacted scenes from the secular world "almost to the exclusion of the world the women actually knew."[10] At an imaginative level, therefore, drama afforded these nuns a means of escaping from the confined life of the convent. But, in Venice at least, convent theater also functioned to reconnect nuns with the world outside in a more literal and immediate way. For, from the repeated orders to keep outsiders from attending convent productions, and from the cases brought before the convent magistrates, we can be sure that Venetian nuns frequently procured a public audience for their performances.[11] The patriarchal visitors reported back from San Sepolcro in 1595 that

> much to our displeasure, we have heard that the parlours of your convent remain open until one hour after sun-

set, and that disorders occur particularly in the little parlour, since people lock themselves in so as to talk with
nuns at prohibited hours, carrying sheets and other
props backwards and forwards all day long, in order that
they may put on tragedies and other plays, which occurrences cause great confusion within the nunnery and
great scandal without.[12]

Following the 1609 visitation to San Girolamo, Vendramin
spelled out that nuns were only allowed to perform "without letting anyone—not even women—into the parlour to
watch."[13] These theatrical events, doubtless rendered all the
more palatable by the provision of cakes and wine, were yet
another means of attracting lay folk to the nunnery.

The prospect of watching the nuns of San Servolo in dramatic productions furnished a fine pretext for a group of
pleasure-seeking local friars to extend their visits into the
night. As one witness reported:

I know for a certain fact, for I observed it myself, that on
two occasions Don Tranquillo stayed out all night until
the early hours with Don Concordio of Venice and
Don Cornelio of Mantua, who was a visitor at that
time; and it was thought that they had gone to supper at
San Servolo, and that they stayed there to watch the
plays.[14]

That convent theater was viewed by nuns as one of several
means of enticing outsiders into the convent is suggested by
the fact that the friars also "played cards and dice . . . with the
nuns at Carnival."[15] Compare the disapproving remarks of
Suor Francesca Zen at San Lorenzo in 1622 regarding the antics of her fellow nuns:

At Carnival, they put on plays; this year, they put on two comedies which were worthy and one printed work which was wicked, and I seized the copies of this play and burnt them. After Christmas, they begin to play at cards, and they play day and night, and sometimes lose as much as ten ducats each, and two or three of the *converse* also play.[16]

Amateur dramatics at Carnival time were just the tip of an iceberg, part of nuns' year-round efforts to attract the attention of the wider world.

Dramatic representations could, and often did, involve putting on costumes for the stage, and nuns appear to have delighted in the chance to don secular garb belonging to either sex. But even without theater, Carnival was a time for dressing up and for flirting with alternative identities. In 1614, at a time when San Zaccaria had fallen prey to the most scandalous disciplinary lapses, and two nuns had brought their male lovers to live within the confines of enclosure, the abbess reported of the men in question that "these youths went about the convent at night, dressed up as nuns."[17] Questioned about this, Suor Laura Querini, who was accused of having brought the men to the convent, denied that they had done any such thing. But she freely admitted that "the nuns are accustomed to dress up, both as men and women, and to go about the convent at night."[18] Suor Zaccaria, a *conversa,* testified to her own involvement in such nocturnal revelries: "It's true that I led Suor Gregoria, my friend the *conversa,* dressed up as a man, to the cell of the above-named Suor Laura, joking to her that this was a man."[19] The practice of cross-dressing surfaces again in a case at La Celestia commencing in 1617, this time relating to events that had occurred in the *carnevaletto* (little carnival) preceding Advent. On this occasion, Nicolò Cressi (whom we met in a previous chap-

BORDERS

BORDERS
BOOKS AND MUSIC
1801 K STREET NW
(BETWEEN 18TH AND L STREET
WASHINGTON DC 20006

STORE: 0050   REG: 02/33 TRAN#: 4935
SALE   03/14/2003 EMP: 00085

EUROPE IN HIGH MIDDLE AGES
        7064727   CL T   27.95
VIRGINS OF VENICE
        7064735   CL T   24.95

              Subtotal   52.90
              DC 5.75%   3.04
2 Items   Total   55.94
              VISA   55.94
ACCT # /S XXXXXXXXXXXX2033
                AUTH: 568745
NAME: PAGE/JOHN R

CUSTOMER COPY

03/14/2003 02:46PM

THANK YOU FOR SHOPPING AT BORDERS
PLEASE ASK ABOUT OUR SPECIAL EVENTS
        (202) 466-4999

Visit our website @ www.Borders.com!

ter skulking around the parlor of San Maffio di Mazzorbo) told how he was asked by his friend, a priest named Gerolemo Grandi, to lend him a suit of men's clothing so that the priest could dress up his favored nun, the *conversa* Suor Lucia. According to Cressi, the quid pro quo of this arrangement was that Gerolemo "promised to let me see her dressed up as a man."[20]

Dressing up and cross-dressing served to give relief and entertainment to the nuns themselves, while simultaneously attracting those who got a voyeuristic thrill from the idea of cloistered women subverting their godly image and their sexual identities.[21] The designs of the priest Gerolemo had transparently erotic implications, and Suor Laura's antics covered for real sexual misdemeanors. But the aspirations of nuns who engaged in dressing-up games were not necessarily sexual. Suor Elena Badoer, from the nunnery at Malamocco, was denounced by her own abbess in 1626 for having organized what appears to have been a thoroughly convivial gathering of women:

> This Carnival, on three or four days, especially on the feast of Sant'Apolonia, she dressed up in secular clothes as a gentlewoman, with a veil over her face, and she went to dance in the parlours in the presence of her gossips and of a man who was playing the violin.[22]

Continual warnings against the sin of vanity can only have heightened the frisson of dressing up.

The conviviality of scenes like the last one points again to the semipublic nature of the convent, something that is also registered in the orders issued to nuns prohibiting the hospitality they were allowed to offer to carousers:

> It is with great displeasure that His Most Illustrious Lordship has heard of an undue corruption; namely, that

there are nuns who make savoury and fried snacks, and give wine, biscuits and other things to revellers who turn up at the convent.[23]

Such orders betray a recognition that the resources of the convents were often viewed as public assets, their spaces as venues for public entertainments. Musicians staged serenades—or their dawn equivalents—beneath the veiled windows; masked men entered the parlor for refreshments and dancing; revelers stopped by, expecting to be fed by the nuns.[24] In a variety of ways, Venetians viewed nunneries as open houses, and nuns were able to exploit this attitude in their efforts to maintain contact with the outside world.

Religious houses were subjected to regulations far stricter than those that applied in private households. But like other comparable institutions—think of schools, where writing on desks has always seemed entirely acceptable—nunneries could allow their inmates to suspend their sense of personal responsibility for what went on in them. Women who might have conformed to the highest standards of respectability had they been destined for marriage and domesticity could behave far more unpredictably when they were consigned, often unwillingly, to the convent. Outsiders who frequented the nunneries of Venice would have registered the absence of controlling husbands and fathers; the convent magistrates, who might eventually catch up with them and bring them to trial, were a distant prospect. So on both sides there was a renunciation of accountability. And that mutual renunciation could only be bolstered by the practice of wearing masks and concealing personal identity. Elena Badoer's crime of dressing up and making merry in the parlor followed from the incitements of the Carnival period, but it was also a consequence of the queasy instability of the conventual life.

9. Crimes of Sacrilege

N ONE OF HIS MOST provocative dialogues, the six-teenth-century Venetian satirist Pietro Aretino explored the three destinies allotted to the female sex—those of nun, wife and whore. The dialogue involves two prostitutes, one of whom, Nanna, has direct experience of all three states of womanhood, having first embarked upon the religious life before running away to take a husband, and eventually suc-cumbing to the oldest profession. Recalling her brief experi-ence of the cloister, Nanna tells how she found herself being bundled off to the nunnery church where, surrounded by rel-atives, she would take the veil. While her account does not sug-gest that she spoke out openly against the life that had been chosen for her, it is clear enough that her heart was not in it; she already enjoyed the admiration of several men, one of whom could be heard sobbing throughout the clothing cere-mony. As she passed from the church to the convent, the door slammed behind her, shutting out the world; she had not even been allowed to say farewell to her relations. Nanna recalls:

> I believed I was entering a tomb alive, and I thought I
> saw the corpses of women who had perished from fast-
> ing and flagellation; and I no longer wept for my family,
> but for myself.[1]

A moment later and the darkness was dispelled. Nanna re-ceived a warm welcome from the nuns, who—contrary to her fears—were radiant with affection and vivacity. And in the refectory she discovered that there was no dearth of male company either: A group comprising priests, friars and even laymen was visiting the convent. Nanna judged them to be the best and finest and most cheerful men she had ever seen.

As the account progresses, we witness the confounding of all of Nanna's expectations of convent life. Far from being a place of austerity and self-denial, the nunnery turned out to cater to every earthly pleasure. To begin with, Nanna partook of a sumptuous feast—with food such as the pope himself had never tasted. But the true highlight of the occasion was reserved until after the meal, when a servant brought on a basket of dildos (made of Murano glass) to be distributed among the convent's women. Then, once the hilarity had died down, the nuns took Nanna on a tour of the buildings to admire the parlors covered in paintings of erotic scenes. And she later discovered that even the layout of the rooms had been arranged so as to maximize the voyeuristic possibilities. Left alone in her cell, Nanna found herself spying through a chink in the wall, transfixed by the extraordinary displays of group sex taking place in the abbess's quarters. Nanna's own desires were finally attended to by a lusty young friar, and as she contemplated her pleasure, "She praised the hour and the moment in which she had become a nun, considering the life of the sisters to be a true paradise."[2]

It will come as no surprise that Nanna's recollections do not provide an accurate picture of life in an Italian nunnery, even for the period before the reforms instituted by the Council of Trent. But, cutting through the thick layers of satire and pornographic fantasy, Aretino's tale is revealing of contemporary perceptions: the reluctant nun, compelled to enter the convent on account of family pressures; the attempt to bury her desires within the tomb of the convent; the practical impossibility of reducing women to chastity. For Aretino's readers, the slippery progress of Nanna from transgressive nun to adulterous wife to ruined prostitute would have come as no surprise. Contradictory though it may seem, in both popular and elite consciousness, nuns and whores were closely aligned.

In a series of tirades against the immorality of Venetian society, the diarist Girolamo Priuli repeatedly likened the nunneries to brothels. He struck his first blow in 1501, when he dubbed the city's nuns "public prostitutes," and described their convents, paradoxically, as "honest whore-houses."[3] Some years later, in the wake of the crushing Venetian defeat at Agnadello, his attacks gathered pace. His lengthy entry for June 6, 1509, stated that there were "more than 15 convents of similar kind, which bore the reputation of public bordellos and public whore-houses" and that "noble girls, born of the foremost nobility and parentage of the city" had been transformed into "public whores."[4] Later the same month, Priuli was again bewailing the "public bordellos," which were nunneries in name alone. The situation warranted extreme measures, and the indignant diarist proclaimed that "there was no other remedy than to burn down the said convents together with the nuns for the sake of the Venetian State."[5]

Priuli was not the first nor the last to invoke the metaphor of the brothel to describe the nunneries of Venice.[6] In 1497, the Franciscan Timoteo da Lucca, preaching in San Marco, had lamented the fact that "whenever a foreign gentleman comes to this city, they show him the nunneries, scarcely nunneries at all in fact but brothels and public bordellos."[7] Gasparo Contarini later made use of the same imagery, writing in his *De officio episcopi* of 1516 that "many convents of virgins, dedicated to God, stand in for bordellos."[8] Echoes of Girolamo Priuli's diary entries could be heard in a supplication from the nuns of San Maffio di Mazzorbo to the convent magistrates, dated July 1564. Harking back to 1509, the nuns warned:

> Your illustrious Lords know how in the year 1509 divine justice sharply struck this Republic on account of the horrors which were continually committed by the conventual nunneries of this City, and that these nunneries were reduced to the state of public brothels.[9]

Such charges continued to be directed against nunneries and their occupants, as in 1620, when a denunciation remarked of San Servolo "that it appeared not to be a place of religious women but rather of true whores,"[10] or when, also in 1620, following a quarrel, a priest sent his housekeeper along to tell the abbess of San Vido di Burano, "You are a public whore."[11]

At one level, "whore" was merely a commonplace insult. It was also a standard metaphor for everything immoral and corrupt. But there were more meaningful associations between the brothel and the nunnery. First, brothels and prostitutes were public (as was emphasized repeatedly in the language of insult). As we have seen, convents shared something of that public status; despite the Counter-Reformation stress on enclosure, they continued to provide open house to all and sundry. Moreover, disregarding the legal proscriptions, prostitutes themselves had a propensity to hang around nunneries. Second, nuns, like prostitutes, were unkept women, and as such were viewed as being vulnerable to sexual temptation. Prostitutes, of course, had already fallen; but, as is clear from the verbal attacks on Venetian convents, it was well within the bounds of the contemporary imagination to envisage nuns dropping to their level. Finally, there existed institutions in Counter-Reformation Venice that blurred the distinction between the chaste nun and the sexually corrupted woman. The Convertite was a nunnery not for virgins, but for fallen women. The Soccorso (so called because it succored women who had lost their honor) and the Zitelle (which protected girls whose honour was imperiled) were both quasimonastic institutions.[12] For these reasons, whenever confidence in the chastity of Christ's brides wavered, the polarization of nun and whore readily collapsed.

The association between the convent and the brothel was not simply the product of Renaissance misogyny (though there was plenty of that about). The analogy suggests a distaste directed beyond the nuns (the metaphorical whores) at the men who were their putative customers. Both parties were acknowledged in the contemporary rhetoric. Girolamo Priuli singled out "young Venetian noblemen and foreign youths" as the two kinds of men who were attracted to the nunneries, and he averred that they were willing to pay in order to court the affections of cloistered women: "Enamoured of these same young and beautiful nuns, they would part with their money in order to have their pleasure."[13] A denunciation of 1613 against a group of young noblemen who made a habit of frequenting Santa Caterina di Mazzorbo complained of their nocturnal visits in the following terms: "They go into the parlour next to the church, and to the doors of the convent, where they remain for a long time exchanging dishonest words with the said nuns, as if they were in a public bordello."[14] The concern to track down and punish such men was paramount in the development of legislation regarding the convents.

In Renaissance Venice, to have sexual relations with a nun was a crime that came under the jurisdiction of the secular authorities. In 1551, the convent magistrates were made responsible for trying the perpetrators of this crime.[15] Their proceedings focused on the male transgressors who dared to engage in such liaisons, rather than on their lovers from the nunneries. Exempt from temporal jurisdiction, nuns were subject instead to disciplinary proceedings by the patriarch. Alas, the records of the trials of nuns kept in the patriarchal archives were destroyed in the nineteenth century. In only a handful of cases, where transcripts of these trials have survived, can we dovetail the investigations of nuns with investigations of their lovers. The survival of one set of documents and the disappearance of the other means that the evidence we have is heavily skewed. But that fact only serves to draw attention to the contempt in which the city held those men who threatened the chastity of its convents.

Monachini was the somewhat quaint term used to describe men who courted nuns (*monache*). The severity of the secular law in relation to *monachini* derived in part from the categorization of their crime as one of sacrilege. According to the definition offered by the eighteenth-century Venetian legal historian Marco Ferro, in its most general sense sacrilege meant "any profanation of things which are sacred or dedicated to God."[16] Of the various instances Ferro goes on to cite, sexual intercourse with a bride of Christ is presented as a particularly serious profanation, punishable with the death penalty. As with other acts of sacrilege, blame was directed at the subject not the object of the deed. (If a man urinated in the holy water, it was the man, not the holy water, who was held to account!)

In his pioneering study of sexuality in Venice during the fourteenth and fifteenth centuries, the historian Guido Ruggiero argues that fornication with a nun was understood as a "sex crime against God." He highlights four types of sexual transgressions deemed to injure God directly. These were:

1) sex with a priest; 2) sex with a nun; 3) sex "in an ecclesiastical setting" (for example, under the church organ!); and 4) sex with a Jew. According to Ruggiero, the offense paid to God by men who had sexual intercourse with nuns was conceived in particularly graphic terms: "Fornication with nuns, the 'brides of Christ,' literally put Christ in the same position as any other cuckolded husband."[17] In a trial of 1395 against Antonio Vianaro, charged with entering the convent of Santa Croce della Giudecca several times in order to have sexual relations with Suor Ursia Tressa in her cell, the offender was accused of "not considering how much injury he caused the Highest Creator by violating the bride of Jesus Christ" and of "committing wicked incest, fornication, adultery and sacrilege, not keeping God before his eyes."[18]

Sex crimes against God were, of course, different from other sexual transgressions and demanded a different form of legal response. The disciplinary policies aimed at fornicators, adulterers and even rapists were intended to be functional and pragmatic. A man who had deflowered a young girl could make good his crime by agreeing to marry her (since he had severely jeopardized her chances on the marriage market). In responding to cases of adultery, the law's priority was with reconstituting the family unit and protecting property, rather than with the eradication of moral vice. But where the offended party was divine rather than mortal, and the injury spiritual rather than material, the purpose of the law could no longer be said to be about redress and restitution in any practical sense. Instead, the law was shaped to protect the honor of God; in return Venice might hope to receive God's protection.[19]

During the course of the sixteenth century, the motives of the legislators would shift, slightly but significantly. On June

29, 1509, in the wake of the Agnadello crisis, the Senate passed the severest legislation to date "against those wicked and sacrilegious men who violate the convents of nuns dedicated to the service and worship of God." Perpetual banishment from Venice and from the surrounding district was to be the fate of the worst transgressors, who were defined as "all those who have their way with nuns, inside or outside the convent, and similarly those who take nuns out of their convents, even if they excuse themselves on account of not having had sex with them."[20] Thus the same punishment was prescribed for those who had sexual intercourse with nuns and those who led nuns out of their convent, regardless of whether they had sexual relations with them (and so regardless of whether they had cuckolded the deity). Unlawful entry to the convent was also heavily punished with a ten-year ban. Those who facilitated a nun's escape, "boatmen and others," were liable to six months' imprisonment. The crime of sacrilege was given a less distinct status than might be expected, and was cast as just one (albeit the worst) of a range of transgressions that violated the convent's sacred integrity.

Three further laws followed, all emanating from the Council of Ten. The first came in 1514 and harked back to the old emphasis on preserving the divine honor. The preamble to this new law spoke of how, from earliest times, the Venetian government had made provision for every crime except "the nefarious vice and sin of sacrilege, that is the contamination of sacred virgins dedicated to God." The fathers of the republic had omitted to legislate against this for they had not believed it possible that "an act so abominable as violating the wives of Christ Our Lord God could ever occur to the mind of a Christian man." Over the years, in response to the growth of the crime, various measures had been introduced, yet the punishments still remained insufficient to meet the enormities committed by "such evil delinquents and rebels against divine will." The preamble ended by promising a very tough line on these most wicked of men:

> Whence, in order to gratify the highest creator and to rid our land of this horrendous vice—the most atrocious occurrence, a form of treason against God—it is wholly necessary to subject it to the same censure with which other crimes of treason are judged and punished, and at the same time to proceed to the removal of those aforementioned causes which result in such offence to the Divine Majesty.[21]

No holds are barred in this condemnation. Yet the provisions that follow are anticlimactic in two respects. First, contrary to the expectations raised by the preamble, the penalties never quite reach "that tremendous censure which is appropriate to the enormity of the crime." Indeed, several of the punishments arguably represent a decline in severity from the 1509 legislation.[22] Second, and more significant, is the failure to single out the crime of sacrilege for unique treatment after a preamble that played so heavily on the uniqueness of that crime. In the middle of a long list of provisions for the greater security of convents, penalties are prescribed for any man "convicted of carnal union with nuns, whether or not they had taken final vows, inside or outside the convent, or of having entered a convent during the day or night." According to the scale of punishments, having sexual intercourse with one of Christ's brides was now no worse a crime than simply entering a convent without due cause.

By 1566, when the Council of Ten instituted the next major development in the legislation regarding *monachini,* extravagant rhetoric was evidently deemed less of a necessity. The

preamble to the new laws began with a brief exclamation—
"How odious the sacrilegious have always been to Our
Lord"—and went on to lament the growth in transgressions. A
change in the perception of sacrilege is perhaps suggested by
the reference to the "violators of our convents": Back in 1514,
it was the "wives of Christ" who were said to be violated,
rather than the convents, and in 1509, it was "convents of sacred nuns dedicated to the service and worship of God." The
sense of personal injury to God and his brides was waning, and
the greater damage was now perceived as being to the institution. According to the new legislation, however, the highest
penalties were reserved for any man "convicted of having had
carnal commerce with a nun." This warranted ten years' banishment, which could only be initiated after payment of
a weighty thousand-ducat fine. If the convicted man was unable to pay this fine, he would have to spend three years in
prison prior to beginning his exile. These punishments were to
be exactly halved for any man "found inside a convent of
nuns . . . even if he is not convicted of carnal commerce."[23]

In 1605, the Council of Ten produced its toughest legislation to date against *monachini,* prescribing the death penalty
for the first time. Yet the crime was no longer conceived in carnal terms. Rather than placing the emphasis on the sexual violation of Christ's brides, engagement in sexual relations had
apparently become an irrelevance. The wording was as follows:

> And if anyone in the future, whoever he may be,
> excepting those who are admitted by the laws, is found
> inside any convent, or is accused of having been inside,
> by day or night, even if he is not convicted of carnal
> commerce, once he is arrested and the truth has been
> ascertained, let his head be cut off so that it is separated
> from the body, and so that death ensues.[24]

Unlawful entry into a convent, whatever one's business, was now punishable by death.

The evolution of laws against *monachini* in this period did not follow a thoroughly coherent pattern, nor did those laws break decisively with the rhetoric that had been employed in the fourteenth and fifteenth centuries. The crime was always conceived in religious terms; the legislators always vaunted their pious objectives. But it is possible to identify certain underlying developments, even if they were introduced at an uneven pace. The fear of offending God, so prominent in the earlier period, would ultimately be replaced by a concern with "the scandals and dangers of the world." Worldly contamination, not sexual violation, was now presented as the most detestable element of the crimes against convents. Furthermore, it was more often the institution of the nunnery rather than the individual nun that was deemed to have been contaminated. It may not be an overstatement to say that, in the minds of the secular legislators, enclosure per se had supplanted chastity as the ultimate ideal for female monastic life.

Any analysis of the legislation deals, of course, with the theory rather than the practice of measures against sacrilege. A look at the trials themselves undertaken by the convent magistrates from the middle of the sixteenth century alerts us to certain discrepancies between legal provision and actual enforcement; for example, the persistent failure to employ the death penalty, despite its introduction in 1605.[25] This may sometimes be accounted for by the fact that the accused had fled from Venice and could not be found. In such cases, the only course of action available to the magistrates was to banish the culprits from Venetian territories, leaving the threat of death hanging over them if they should dare to break their exile. But it is also true to say that leniency was sometimes exercised on account of political motives, in particular the desire to suppress a scandal that might adversely affect members of the nobility or other prominent figures.[26]

Although there was flexibility regarding sentencing, in the matters of defining crime and establishing a hierarchy of transgressions, the trials generally followed the legislation closely. The concern to protect the sacred space of the convent is evident from the early trials of the convent magistrates (1550s–70s) and greatly escalates from the beginning of the seventeenth century.[27] There was an abundance of trials against petty transgressors of enclosure, but comparatively few directed at men committing explicitly sexual offenses.

Consider the thoroughly unsensational cases tried by the convent magistrates during the years 1625–26, a two-year period that happens to provide us with a particularly dense crop of trials.[28] Of a total of forty-seven trials, twenty-seven were brought against laymen accused of illicit conduct with nuns. Twelve of these arose from simple breaches of the laws regulating visits to the parlor: most commonly, either because the men were not within the permissible bounds of kinship or because their visits took place outside the allowed hours. To these may be added five more cases of men eating in the parlor, and one further case of a group of men who took a meal in the company of two nuns in the convent cellar. Perhaps the most serious of these cases was one in which a man and his wife had apparently taken up temporary residence at Santa Caterina, in Mazzorbo; they were seen "eating with some nuns during prohibited hours, and there was a bed set up in the parlor."[29] Among the remaining cases, three concerned men who were accused of verbal abuse or other "insolences," and another involved three noblemen "who were making a lot of noise in the large parlour with some of the nuns."[30] Two further cases may be distinguished by their concern with what the men were wearing in the presence of nuns: One was accused of sporting a revealing shirt; the other

. The convent of Sant'Alvise in Cannaregio.

2. Surviving arch from the demolished convent of Santa Maria delle Vergini (Le Vergini), now part of a wall of the Arsenal. The Virgin and Child are flanked by Saint Mark (patron saint of Venice) and Saint Augustine (founder of the order to which the nuns belonged). The plaque, dated May 2, 1557, declares, "Hope and love keep us in this pleasant prison."

3 & 4. Title pages of published decrees regulating the behavior of visitors and prostitutes in the ambit of convents. A wealth of legislation concerning the nunneries was issued during the Counter-Reformation. As with all Venetian laws, these were well advertised in highly recognizable pamphlets bearing the lion of Saint Mark.

5. *The Clothing Ceremony of a Nun at San Lorenzo,* in a painting by Gabriel Bella (1789). Nobles mill around in the foreground, musicians play from the pews and nuns look out from behind the grilles that separate the public from the enclosed half of the church.

6. Roundel on an outside wall of the convent church of the Miracoli, showing the idealized figure of a Franciscan nun.

7. *Portrait of Caterina Cornaro* (1454–1510), a famous Venetian noblewoman who married the ruler of Cyprus in 1468. Her lavish clothes and elaborate coiffure give an idea of the kind of fashions that nuns sometimes sought to emulate.

8. Embroidered altar frontal from the convent church of Sant'Anna, meticulously reproducing Tintoretto's *Crucifixion* in the Scuola Grande di San Rocco. The frontal was the work of two of the artist's daughters, Ottavia and Perina, who were nuns at Sant'Anna in the early seventeenth century.

9. Gentile Bellini, *Procession in Piazza San Marco* (1496). In a characteristic display of civic devotion, members of the Confraternity of San Giovanni Evangelista parade their prized relic, a piece of the True Cross. The doge and ruling nobles of the city join with prelates, priests and friars in the exclusively male procession.

10. The doge of Venice "marries" the first abbess of Le Vergini in the presence of the Holy Roman Emperor Frederick Barbarossa and Pope Alexander III, in an illustration from the convent chronicle. According to the chronicle, the abbess in question was the emperor's daughter Julia. However, the scene is in fact mythical, blurring the foundation of the convent in 1224 with diplomatic events that had taken place half a century earlier, in 1177.

11. Doge Leonardo Loredan "marries" Clara Donao, abbess of Le Vergini, in 1513. This is the last image in the convent chronicle, which depicts every investiture from the foundation through to the early sixteenth century.

12. Easter procession of the doge and *Signoria* to San Zaccaria. The doge and *dogaressa* are seen under a canopy in the foreground; before them a servant carries the trademark ducal horned cap, supposedly a gift of the convent's first abbess. Somewhat fancifully, nuns are shown peering from the outer windows of the convent; in reality all the windows would probably have been closed with *trombe* (restrictive shutters) like those seen on just two of them. Beneath the *trombe*, a man urinates against the wall, in flagrant defiance of the sacred enclosure.

13. One of the two great cloisters at San Zaccaria, the oldest convent in the city of Venice, now the headquarters of the *carabinieri* (the police branch of the Italian army).

14. In this seventeenth-century painting from the convent church of San Zaccaria, nuns are seen standing at the grate during the annual visit of the doge.

A QVESTO MODO VANO LE NOVIZZE
IN GONDOLA
Per visitar le loro parenti ne'monasterij accompagnate da gran n.º di Gondole

5. Venetian brides and their wedding parties visiting their relatives in onvents, from a seventeenth-century costume book, *Habiti delle donne*.

16. The convent parlor at San Lorenzo, in an early eighteenth-century engraving.

17. Guardi's painting of a convent parlor, in which the nuns gather at the grates in order to watch a puppet show.

was described as being "lasciviously dressed."[31] Only two cases give any indication of "particular relationships" between nuns and laymen. In 1625, an official of the magistrates reported having seen a man who had climbed up the wall of San Sepolcro, and was "hanging on to an iron railing very high up talking to one of the nuns." This brief report may lend itself to romantic interpretation, but the evidence is insufficient to be sure.[32] We are left, therefore, with just one trial where an established intimacy is definitely perceived. The case relates again to San Sepolcro, and the charge is against Ser Nicolo Barbarigo, of whom it was reported, "This gentleman maintains a continuous and dishonest relationship with Suor Cintia Bembo on the pretext of being her relation, though in fact he is no such thing, and he comes every day to see her."[33]

These twenty-seven cases reveal that a culture of illicit visiting had grown up around the convents of Venice. But there is little to suggest that this culture had a prominent sexual dimension. Many of the relationships revealed in the trials were familial (although the "degrees of kinship" were insufficiently close in the eyes of the law); most followed the patterns of sociability explored in previous chapters. Thanks to evidence like this, some historians have argued that a stiffening of the legislation against *monachini* in this period went hand in hand with a decline in their activities. The heyday of sexual crime in the nunneries was over:

> After 1500, sexuality . . . became episodic and marginal, and was substituted almost everywhere by forms of conviviality . . . (parties, theatrical events, meetings in the parlour).[34]

But this judgment, lamenting the decline of sexuality, smacks of anachronism. Rather than dismissing the "conviviality" that

bulks so large in the records of Venetian convents from the sixteenth century onward, we should look more closely at the
role played by apparently nonsexual relationships between
nuns and men. There is certainly something suspicious about
the persistence with which certain men made their illegal visits, often late at night, and the regularity with which they reof-
fended.[35] Those cases that go into detail suggest three types of
underlying motivation for these visits.

The first area of appeal is revealed in the conduct of those
men who showed a penchant for talking (or acting) dirty in
and around the convent: behaving in a manner wholly inappropriate to the company of virgin nuns, possibly with the intention of shocking or titillating them, though not requiring
their direct involvement. The male employees who worked for
San Daniel were prime culprits. In 1609, a petition was sent by
some of the nuns to the magistrates complaining that the two
men brought "their whores" into their parlor and that the
convent scribes had joined their company, "engaging continuously in profane and dishonest conversations." One witness
had this to say about the conduct of one of the men:

> While he was in the parlour, chatting to the scribes, he
> spoke of profane matters, holding forth dishonestly
> about women, saying of the whores that this lady was
> more beautiful than that one or the other.[36]

The Neapolitan men who lived opposite San Giovanni
Lateran also found it thrilling to behave badly in front of nuns:
In 1620, it was reported "that day and night they make a grand
to-do, flashing their members at the nuns whenever they come
to the window."[37] And we have already encountered Pasqualin
the musician, who loitered in the churches and parlors of
Venetian convents and "showed his shameful parts" whenever

he spotted a nun at the grate.[38] Although details do not always survive, the considerable number of men who were accused of the generic crimes of "causing a scene" or "making a din" in nunneries and conventual churches doubtless found their misconduct all the more delightful when spectated by Christ's brides.

The second motive of men who frequented nunneries was the expectation of material rewards. We have already seen how irrepressible were nuns' urges to provide hospitality and hand out food. In 1619, following an incident at San Marco e Sant' Andrea, a denunciation was brought against the twenty-two-year-old Battista, who had been observed "within the convent enclosure, reclining before a laid table, and a nun was bringing him food to the table."[39] It is easy to see why a hungry young man might find a visit to a convent appealing in these circumstances. At Le Vergini, the nuns bestowed their maternal munificence upon the convent organist:

> The organist, Maestro Paulo, goes there too often, and behaves with too great a familiarity in the parlours; whenever he goes to Castello, he stops off at Le Vergini, and they feed him; and, once he has eaten his meal, they give him more food to take away.[40]

Vicenzo Trevisan, chancellor of Torcello, enjoyed a particularly long-standing relationship with the local nuns at Sant' Antonio, and was brought before the magistrates several times as a result.[41] His father had been a servant to the community, and the nuns claimed to have known him since he was a boy. In 1621, the magistrates learned of his close friendship with Suor Clementia, an intimacy which apparently thrived on the exchange of delicacies. While we are assured that he sent gifts as well as received them, it is hard to believe that these matched the plethora of food-filled baskets emanating from Suor Clementia—"now cakes, now biscuits," "some meat, some fish," and so on.[42]

Some men came to rely on nuns to cook and carry out other domestic chores for them. From a trial of 1619, we learn that Alessandro Branazzini, a lawyer employed on an ad hoc basis at San Sepolcro, enjoyed a close relationship with a certain Suor Cornelia. Their intimacy dated back to a period when he had been ill and had supposedly depended upon food being sent to him from the nuns. (He sent them fish in return.) Once he had recovered, he evidently continued to value the nuns' food parcels. A boatman reported that when Alessandro was going to Loreto on pilgrimage, he made his party stop their boat outside the convent in order to pick up some cakes and biscuits.[43] During the course of his trial, a number of sexual allegations were made against Branazzini, but none of them could be proved. The more general picture painted by the witnesses is of a lower-key relationship with the nuns. One man related how Alessandro had once proposed to him, "Come along and see the beautiful nuns, we'll have a laugh and they'll give us biscuits."[44]

The third area of attraction offered by the nunnery was that men could enjoy a low-level, noncommittal form of sexual engagement with nuns: flirtation, petting, or *facendo il moroso* ("playing the lover"), as one contemporary accuser put it.[45] In 1617, Polo Loredan was charged with visiting the convent of La Celestia in order to further his relationship with "a nun from the Pisani family, who is a little lame but young and beautiful." It was reported that "he was seen kissing the nun, and that she was standing at the window of the parlour with his cock in her hand."[46] Such deeds were often standardized in the trials as "kissing" or "touching." For example, two nobles, Gerolamo Giustinian and Gerolamo Dolfin, visited the parlor of San Sepolcro in order to "carouse and touch the nuns."[47] Sexuality could also be expressed in less physical terms, as in an engaging incident when a man named Santo was found in the parlor passing a rose to a nun through the grate.[48]

The three strands of motivation governing the behavior of men who sought the attention of nuns could intertwine, and often did. Andrea Fiorelli was probably spurred on by all three to frequent La Celestia: He enjoyed behaving indecorously at the convent and flirting with the nuns, as well as reaping the benefits of being looked after by them. In 1619, he was denounced as "a foreign gentleman," "who goes continually to the parlours of La Celestia, speaking and creating an uproar with those nuns." Moreover, "He was at the grated window in the church, or at the little open balcony, and he was laughing with a nun, and he was kissing her." When interviewed, Andrea denied the kissing, but he was happy to admit that "I was there because I was taking my collars to be bleached by the nuns."[49]

All this is not to suggest that nuns were never involved in more developed sexual relationships, or indeed that laymen were always so restrained in their attentions. Glimpses of sexual scandals involving nuns *do* sometimes emerge, and their comparative rarity among the records of the magistrates may in part result from the success of damage-limitation policies. That the authorities were not above suppressing information has already been remarked. But the loss or survival of documents may result from more random factors. For whatever reasons, a number of verdicts survive, recording the conclusions of trials whose records are no longer extant.[50] Among this set of records, two documents of November 30, 1608, and January 31, 1609, stand out.[51] They are copies of the lists that were published in the Great Council bearing the names of men who had broken the laws relating to nunneries, and they bring to light a cluster of startling crimes.

Ten men were named in the first list and a further five in the second. Fourteen out of the fifteen names were noble, the exception being one Hieronimo Padavin, principal notary of the *Avogadori di Commun* (the attorneys of the Venetian state).[52] In accordance with the law, the identity of the convents was withheld, but the nature of each man's crime was specified.[53] Eight of the fifteen men, it is clearly stated, had had "carnal commerce" with nuns. Four more had attempted to have sex with nuns. The remaining three had taken nuns from the convent and enjoyed some sort of improper "practice" with them, although they had refrained from actual or attempted sexual intercourse. In these cases, the sexual element of the transgressions was given a central position. Those who had actually succeeded in having sex with nuns received the severest punishments. Those who had failed were treated more leniently, despite the fact that no doubt regarding their intentions is left. For example, Alvise Mocenigo, whose name appeared on the November list, was accused of taking a nun back to his home "where, locked up with her, he was determined by any means to have carnal commerce with her, notwithstanding the fact that she resisted him." Like Marco Giustinian and Almoro Dolfin, who were each accused of having "attempted with every power to conjoin carnally" with nuns, Alvise was banished to distant Venetian territory for twelve years.[54] The six nobles who were accused at the same time of "carnal copulation" with nuns were relegated for fifteen years. Among the three cases where sexual intercourse had not been attempted, two of the three nobles condemned were sentenced to ten years' banishment, and the third was exiled for twelve years (the rationale behind this distinction is not clear). In general, however, within this set of cases a hierarchy of transgressions was established, headed by fornication with nuns.

Contrary to the pattern discernible where the trial records are complete, here the sexual nature of the transgressions is clearly given pride of place over the issue of rupturing enclosure. On the other hand, although the severity of punishment corresponds to the extent of carnal engagement with the nun, there is not a very great difference between the fifteen years' banishment for successful fornicators and the ten or twelve years for those who did not attempt to have sexual intercourse. The details of how the convent walls came to be crossed are consistently supplied in the records, and we learn of how the men commonly entered the nunnery at night via the cellar, led the nuns away in a boat, then took them home or to a friend's house in order to try their luck. The following account dates from January 1609:

> Ser Galeazzo Simitecolo, son of the late Zorzi, has again contravened the laws of the said Council in the parlours of a convent of nuns in this City, procuring a friendship with a nun, doing his utmost to entice the same to accept others into her friendship, bringing her gifts and presents in the name of his friends, and commissioning portraits to send to her. And having gone in the company of others in boats, at night-time, to the canal which runs alongside this convent in order to take her away, he lifted the said nun into a little boat, and brought her to a small and concealed lodging, where she had carnal copulation with the person who was waiting for her there. And, on another occasion, he took the nun to the same place along with another nun who was pregnant, leading her into the lodging where a midwife was waiting for her in order to advise her on how to get rid of the baby. And while the midwife and the pregnant nun were together, he tried everything to get the other nun to commit carnal commerce with him.[55]

In this case, we see rather more literal parallels between the nunnery and the whorehouse. There was nothing innocent about the "gifts and presents" brought to the nuns by Galeazzo in his role as procurer. Not only did he fix up nuns with his friends, but he also, when necessary, fixed up an abortionist; and, undeterred by the risk of pregnancy, he tried to rape one nun while her friend sought advice on how to get rid of her baby. With regard to the fourteenth century, it has been remarked that "the rape of nuns was a popular diversion, especially for the nobility."[56] By the sixteenth century, a tough judicial line seems to have reduced the popularity of this pastime—but not to have eradicated it altogether.

These cases bring to light the persistence of sexual transgressions involving nuns long after the " 'golden century' of convent sexuality" had supposedly ended.[57] The density of the crimes is striking—fifteen serious cases in the space of only two months. While the anonymity of the convents involved is carefully maintained in these records, the identity of the nunnery at the center of the first set of verdicts is revealed in a gossipy letter of the English ambassador to Venice, Henry Wotton, dated November 14, 1608, which commented upon

> the apprehension of so many persons (whereof nine were gentlemen of principal houses) accused to have lasciviously haunted the Nunnery of St Anna, and thence to have transported those votaries to their private chambers, and up and down the town in masking attire at festival assemblies.[58]

So the convent in which Arcangela Tarabotti would spend her days was, a few years before her arrival, gathering a reputation which recalls Aretino's parody, with its lascivious feasts, erotic paintings and conveniently crannied walls. But the reality was probably darker. The prominence of violence among the descriptions of the crimes committed here raises important questions about whether the nuns were agents or victims in this sexual riot.

In considering the allure of nuns, it is worth bearing in mind the limited sexual possibilities that were available to Venetian men. The only strictly reputable place for sexual relations was the marriage bed. This applied, in theory, to men and women; in practice, a double standard operated, and it was easier for men than women to find sexual satisfaction outside marriage. Celibacy was enjoined on women who did not marry, whether they were sent to convents or lived their lives as pious spinsters. But although chastity was central to the roles prescribed for unmarried women, the possibilities for unmarried men were less tightly circumscribed. Of course men, too, could enter the religious life and take vows renouncing sexual activity—joining a category of male which was, as we shall see, frequently to be found within the ambit of the convent. But in Venice, fewer men than women took monastic vows, and they tended to come from a less elevated social background than their female counterparts. The noble class, in which policies of marriage limitation for men were most marked, produced relatively few priests, monks and friars; military and political careers were more favored, and the *fratellanza* (brotherhood) provided the alternative household to which unmarried men commonly belonged.

It has been estimated that nearly half of male nobles who reached adulthood in the fifteenth century appear to have remained bachelors.[59] Judging from the well-stocked convents of the next two centuries—a direct result of strategies of marriage limitation among the male nobility—the proportion of bachelors remained high into the sixteenth and seventeenth centuries.[60] Although it is not always possible to judge the marital status of the men who were involved with nuns, it is possible to speculate that nuns helped to fill the sexual gap in these bachelors' lives.

In his analysis of sexual transgressions involving nuns in the early Renaissance, Guido Ruggiero gives special attention to the scandal-prone community of Sant'Angelo di Contorta, which was finally shut down by the pope in 1474. He observes that the convent provided "a significant feature of Venice's culture of illicit sex," and suggests that among the attractions of the nuns were their "higher social and perhaps intellectual levels."[61] This, and the fact that they came cheap, may have made nuns more desirable than prostitutes for the man seeking extramarital contact with women. Although the concentration of sexual transgressions committed by nuns at Sant'Angelo during the fourteenth and fifteenth centuries was unheard of in the following two centuries, Ruggiero's perception of nuns contributing to a "culture of illicit sex" has certain resonances for the later period. Even if nuns did not trade in sex, many offered company and sociability to men with time on their hands.

Most men who visited nuns, even those who transgressed the regulations governing such visits, did not go there in order to rape or to seduce. Most were not even motivated by the expectation that a nun might take "his cock in her hand." Yet the patterns that have been revealed in the conduct of nuns and laymen were, if not overwhelmingly carnal, nevertheless sexually charged. The players in these relationships, both male and female, were aware of the erotic potential of the situations in which they found themselves, and this awareness added a further dimension to their transactions, however mundane they often were. The repressed, all-female world of the nunnery was a fascinating place for men to visit.

10. Between Celibates

On a memorably grim day in November 1561, a priest named Giovanni Pietro Lion was led to the scaffold in Piazza San Marco. Following the Venetian custom, he was accompanied by members of a religious confraternity whose special calling was to give Christian succor to the condemned. Having been offered their comforts, Lion placed his head on the block and felt the hatchet being moved into position on his neck. Then the executioner struck the hatchet with his cudgel more than eight times, but the head refused to roll. Moved by pity for the priest, one of Lion's comforters seized the executioner's instrument, and with all his force gave him four or five more blows. Still the head remained attached to the body. The executioner took back his bludgeon and inflicted several more strikes upon the battered and lacerated neck, all to no avail. One of the guards who was standing by supplied him with a knife, and with this, eventually, he finished off the job.

Present among the crowd of onlookers to this grisly scene was the papal nuncio to Venice, Ippolito Capilupi. For him, the bungled execution bore a spiritual message. God had deemed the punishment of decapitation too light for "the most wicked man in the world," and so had intervened to prolong the agonies of the condemned. It is to Capilupi that we owe our most detailed (if perhaps, on occasion, embroidered) account of Lion's misdeeds.[1]

Giovanni Pietro Lion, forty-three years old at the time of

his execution, and a native of Valcomonica (an Alpine valley
northwest of Venice), was confessor to the Convertite nuns,
who resided in a large and impoverished convent on the extreme western edge of the Giudecca—a marginal position be-
fitting their marginal status. Le Convertite was the convent
established just one decade previously to accommodate repentant prostitutes and other sexually dishonored women—a
convent dedicated to Christ's beloved sinner Mary Magdalene,
and where the chaste ideal was at once of special significance
and particular fragility. But, in a tale involving unparalleled
hypocrisy, depravity and abuse, an institution designed as a
spiritual refuge for vulnerable women was transformed into a
pleasure ground for their perverted priest. Capilupi summed
up Giovanni Pietro's objective simply:"He gave himself to sating all the uncontrolled appetites of his lust." Appointed to a
job that gave him authority over "400 nuns, for the most part
young and beautiful," he used his monopoly as provider of the
sacraments in order to gain sexual access to the women:[2]

> And he carried on in this manner, so that when he con-
> fessed one of the nuns whom he liked, in the very act of
> confession, he would try to draw her to his will with
> some pre-prepared speech, and by placing his hands
> upon her in order to excite the carnal appetite in her
> more readily; and if he found her at all opposed to his
> advances he would praise her greatly for her strength
> and constancy, and would seek to have her understand
> that he was moved to try her as a test of her goodness.[3]

Those who resisted their confessor's advances did not enjoy praise for long:

> A few days after the assault, perpetrated in the confes-
> sional, the priest would take advantage of whatever light

cause, and would put the nun in prison and beat her and torment her cruelly in diverse ways; and through cruelty he would often succeed in having what he could not gain with words alone, because some of the nuns, conquered by continual torments, gave in to his desires in order to be free of their irons and chains; others, refusing to give in to him, but too delicate to withstand the discomfort of prison and the cruelty of the torments, killed themselves by eating and drinking deadly things.[4]

The enclosed world of the convent offered the unscrupulous confessor unrivaled access to a large number of unprotected women.[5] Those nuns who were complicit would not talk; those who refused to be involved could be shut away. The convent walls, supposedly shielding the nuns from corruption, also shielded them and their seducer from exposure.

In the words of Capilupi, the errant confessor "was alone, like a great Turk in his seraglio." Surrounded by subservient nuns who looked after him and gratified his sexual desires, he lived a life of luxury: He dined on "pheasants and partridges and precious wines, and his room was full of sweets and restoratives and a thousand recipes designed to strengthen him in battle."[6] Nor were his lusts undiscriminating. In order to ensure that he did not end up in the embraces of a nun who failed to attract him, he wanted first of all to see them naked. To this end, he instituted a bizarre sort of nude beauty parade so that he might take his pick:

And so, during the summer, he made the nuns undress and go down to the covered area of sea water, where the gondola is kept; and having considered the women at leisure, and having selected in his head the most beautiful and finest nuns according to his judgement, he

endeavoured by both his usual methods to bring them
round to his dishonest desire.[7]

The confessor's audacity knew no bounds.

As the papal nuncio mused on the events that had taken
place, he emphasized two qualities that had enabled Giovanni
Pietro Lion to achieve such heights of debauchery and corruption during his employment at Le Convertite—"art" and
"tyranny." Capilupi tells how, across the course of nineteen
years, the confessor had successfully duped the city of Venice,
"covering up his vices with miraculous art" and projecting an
image of piety and self-abnegation. This was no ordinary
priest, but one "learned in the Greek and Latin languages, and
knowledgeable in Holy Scripture." He used his learning to secure contacts in high places.

> He enjoyed the friendship of persons of good repute,
> and in particular of Don Geremia, formerly the
> favourite of Pope Paul III; he was loved by the most
> Serene prince [the doge of Venice] and by all the great
> men of the dominion, and he always spoke with them
> about his holy and religious works.[8]

He also used his learning to manipulate the nuns, telling those
of them who had doubts about taking communion without
first being absolved from their sins that "he had studied and
that he knew better than them what he could do."[9] But while
some could be won over by persuasion and trickery, others
called for tyranny.

> He had contracted the closest friendship with the
> Abbess and also with some of the other nuns, in order to
> make himself a tyrant of all the women in a brief space

of time, and to conserve the command which he had acquired over them. He did not allow them to be confessed by anyone except himself, even if he were away from the city or if he were ill and consequently unable to confess them himself, because he feared that during the course of confession to other priests they might reveal his wickedness, on account of which it happened many times that a nun died without being confessed.[10]

Lion's relations with the nuns were founded on power and exploitation. Making use of his privileges as confessor, he held the souls of these women hostage. Meanwhile, their worldly goods as well as their bodies were at his disposal: He stole from convent funds and from the earnings brought in by the nuns. As Capilupi proclaimed, "In short, he was the owner of the bodies, souls, goods and actions of these poor women."[11]

The power of priests and other male ecclesiastics to manipulate nuns is a recurring issue. Even outside the vulnerable environment of the nunnery, priests were thought to have easy access to the pleasures of women. From a case of 1618, we learn how a Paduan dyer donned a friar's habit in order to gain the affections of nuns and other "simple women." The convent magistrates received the following denunciation concerning the fraudulent friar:

Throughout Venice and Murano, a Paduan dyer is going about in the habit of a religious hermit; he has left his wife and children, under the pretext of living according to his own ways with every liberty; and what is of greater scandal is that he goes to the churches and parlours of nuns; today, for example, he has been to San Bernardo di Murano, where having been arrested by me, on account of the prohibitions of the ecclesiastical laws, and of the Senate, he has dared to respond that, not

> knowing any superior authorities to God . . . he can do
> what he wants; and he has given the simple women to
> understand that he is a virgin, and without sin.[12]

The supposed purity of priests and friars gave them a head start when talking their way into nunneries. It could also protect them from accusations. When certain women eventually fled from the wiles of Giovanni Pietro Lion at Le Convertite, they found that their word was worth little against the saintly reputation of their confessor.[13]

Male clergy were, however, far from being immune from prosecution. They regularly found themselves before the convent magistrates (from whose authority they enjoyed no exemption) for breaking the rules intended to keep them separate from nuns. Priests and friars were central among the accused in 58 of the 263 "criminal and disciplinary trials" that passed before the magistracy in the period 1550–1650.[14] There is nothing in this body of evidence to rival the depravities of the Lion case. But in their less shocking substance, these trials richly document the day-to-day interactions of men and women sworn to celibacy.

Like laymen, male clergy were attracted to the convent for food, flirtation and the sheer thrill of transgression. But for them the attractions were thrown into sharper relief. Intimacy between nuns and priests (or monks and friars) was doubly subversive, for both parties—male and female—were supposed to have shut themselves off from the charms of the other sex. Just as nuns cherished their links with the outside world, so monks and friars sought a life beyond their religious community. Spiritual and administrative functions gave clergy access to Christ's brides. Theirs, one might say, was a match made in heaven.[15]

Many a transgression of the Venetian laws relating to nunneries seems to have been motivated by boredom. Nowhere is this clearer than in the cases involving priests and friars who, in general, appear to have been a somewhat underemployed social group. Thoroughly typical was a denunciation of 1618 against the parish priest of San Lio, employed at the convent church of La Celestia to carry out regular redemptive masses.

> He frequents the convent of the reverend nuns of La Celestia every Wednesday and Friday, in order to officiate at mass; but before he goes into the sacristy he goes to the grated window in order to speak to one of the mothers, and once he has finished mass, before leaving, he stays for a good hour chatting at the grate; and he dared to go there during the prohibited hours, that is before None [the fifth office of the day], notwithstanding the fact that he has been condemned and admonished; and, what is more, he receives presents from one of the nuns every day, and he brings her gifts, and they exchange letters too.[16]

Similarly, it was reported in 1620 that Andrea, the chaplain at Santa Maria Maggiore, came to the church to say mass every morning and that he spent the rest of the day idling in the company of nuns.[17]

The same chaplain also enjoyed sociable relations with the unenclosed *converse*. Besides chatting with them, the priest was charged with taking them on outings away from the convent in a boat. Given their greater freedom to leave the enclosure and, in particular, to oversee affairs in the "exterior church," it is unsurprising that Prete (priest) Andrea should have forged his most extensive contacts with these nuns. But there may also have been a closer class affinity between the run of male clergy (rarely of high social background) and *converse* than with the fully professed and predominantly noble choir nuns. We learn of priests consorting with *converse* at other convents. Francesco

Strata, chaplain of San Moro di Burano, could not resist the pleasures of a boat trip, and it was reported that "he goes out in a gondola with the *converse*."[18]

Monks, priests and nuns retained aspects of their lay identity that sometimes came to the fore in their interrelations. Friendships were renewed in the parlor that had once existed in the lay world. This is explicit in the case of Fra Daniel del Grafignana (from the male house of San Sebastian), who was accused of frequenting the parlors of three different convents. One witness explained how Fra Daniel had gained an introduction to the nuns of Santa Chiara through Suor Giacinta (this time a choir nun), "having known her in the secular world, and having been friends with her previously."[19]

For these men and women sworn to celibacy, flirting with worldliness was a valuable release. Playing at having sexual relationships, through courtship and dalliance, enabled religious celibates of both sexes to experience something of the life generally denied them. Their exchanges of letters and gifts were frequently noted during the trials by the convent magistrates. According to a record of 1617, the priest Gerolemo Grandi from Santa Trinità wrote regularly to Suor Giustignana at San Daniel and on one occasion "put a ring in with the letter." He also employed a friend to pen "a beautiful love sonnet" to send to a nun at San Sepolcro who had written him a love letter. And he was believed to be courting another nun at San Daniel for whom he had supposedly commissioned a portrait of himself bearing the arms of her family.[20] The exchange of sentimental tokens was a conspicuous feature in the contemporary trial of another priest, Francesco Dei, arising from his relationship with the *conversa* Suor Barbara.[21] Brought before the magistrates were a number of incriminating exhibits. There was a prayer book—the Office of the Blessed Virgin— which belonged to Francesco and contained pressed flowers sent by Suor Barbara, as well as written allusions to the nun. There were also love letters written by Barbara, and a missive in the priest's own hand, prefaced by a madrigal: "Love me little Barbara/Love my heart that longs/To love only one who loves it . . ."

The case of Francesco and Barbara reveals much that was characteristic about the restricted and unconsummated relationships that existed between nuns and priests across the barrier of enclosure. Francesco was dismissive about the letters he had received from Barbara. He insisted that "she sent them to me, and she wrote to me of her humours without expecting anything in return"; "she had this mad habit of writing 'dear heart' and other similar things."[22] As for the writings in his own hand, he admitted to being their author but claimed that he had had no intention of sending them. Given that they were found in his possession rather than in Barbara's, this is technically feasible, if not altogether probable.[23] Confronting Francesco with his own words, the magistrates made the following inference: "This letter and this madrigal suggest that obscene dealings took place: because it is difficult to say in a letter to a loved one, 'I kiss you,' if one has not really kissed her previously." But Francesco would have none of it. "I never kissed her," he asserted.[24] In fact, elsewhere, he claimed never even to have seen Suor Barbara, let alone kissed her, having only spoken to her in darkness at the convent *ruota;* nor, he protested, had he ever seen her, but had only heard her voice.[25] This state of affairs was more or less confirmed by the convent confessor, whose aim was to condemn rather than to excuse, but who nevertheless claimed that Francesco's conversations with Suor Barbara had taken place across the wheel in the sacristy.[26] In one of Barbara's letters to Francesco, she informed him of forthcoming services in the church in order that they might "see each other at a distance."[27] Perhaps Francesco was not straying far from the truth when he implied that the hottest aspects of their relationship were confined to the written word.

Yet in their dealings with nuns, some clerics evidently indulged in fantasies more erotic than sentimental. As we have seen, Gerolemo Grandi nursed a voyeuristic desire regarding one of the nuns at La Celestia. It was he who asked his friend Signor Nicolò Cressi for "a change of men's clothes in order to dress up . . . a *conversa* called Suor Lucia."[28] A denunciation from Le Convertite of 1624 complained that the priest Francesco Montenegro "has sent one of our nuns a chest with a portrait of a naked man on it."[29] Once again the subversive thrill of introducing sexuality into the sacred world of the nunnery is apparent.

Unsurprisingly, the attraction of the convents for male clergy often had a rather more practical basis. In a number of trial records, nuns are reported cooking, washing and mending for priests and friars. Even reports of illicit sexual liaisons between religious men and women are almost always accompanied by evidence of nuns providing these practical, domestic and traditionally female services to their lovers. The phenomenon is neatly encapsulated by a witness in the case against Fra Marc'Antonio Cazzano, brought before the magistrates in 1617. Apparently, Cazzano was accustomed to sending to the convents "now sheets to be washed, now messages and love-letters."[30] Significantly, the word used to describe untoward intimacy between nuns and male clergy was often *dimestighezza,* suggesting a *domestic* familiarity.

So the enduring stereotype of the hapless male, unable to cook or look after himself, was well established in Venetian religious communities. The propensity of priests to keep concubines may have resulted from a desire to ensure the provision of domestic services as much as sexual ones. It was common for clergy who lacked a live-in partner and could not afford to employ a permanent housekeeper to turn to nuns for assistance of this kind. In a perfectly innocent example, we learn of how the nuns of Malamocco took care of Prete Pietro Christiani. A neighbor testified in 1626 about how her daughters were employed to run errands for the nuns: "The mother prioress often sent my little girls with meat or cooked fish, because the said priest had nobody at home to cook for him."[31] *Converse* given the freedom to leave the convent could supply a helping hand within the priest's own home. In a trial that predates the restrictions imposed by Trent on the movements of *converse,* it was reported at San Giovanni Lateran "that suor Paula and suor Ganzenua, *converse,* go to the house of the said confessor and do services for him, and that suor Paula stays the night at his place."[32] That *converse* continued to supply priests with services of this sort even after the enforcement of enclosure may be seen from a case of 1614 from San Bernardo di Murano against Prete Zuane Bertoluzzi: "Suor Bernarda, a *conversa* from San Bernardo, frequents the house of the aforementioned prete Zuane at all hours of the day . . . causing the greatest scandal and rumours among everyone."[33] Interviews with neighbors make it clear that Bernarda went to the priest's house not at night, to bring him sexual favours, but first thing in the morning, to bring him food for the day.

Just as nuns' magnanimous treatment of friends and relatives could threaten the economic stability of a convent, so the determination of some nuns to shower favorite priests and friars with food meant that their fellow sisters had to go without. Male clergy, on occasion, clearly exploited nuns. In the case against Francesco Dei at San Daniel in 1617, this emerged as a significant aspect of his relationship with Suor Barbara. Throughout his defense, Francesco stressed his poverty and his family commitments: "I am poor and burdened with family";

"I had to mend my poverty and to maintain my family, that is my mother and two sisters, one unmarried and the other a widow with children."[34] Through his aunt, the *conversa* Suor Concordia, Francesco's relationship with the nuns dated back to his boyhood, and he seemed to consider it his birthright to take food from the convent: "I was brought up as a little boy on crumbs of bread given to me by the nunnery."[35] But although Francesco saw Suor Barbara's gifts to him as his rightful "charity and alms," there were suggestions that he was taking advantage of her. As one witness remarked, "He eats everything that she has; she works day and night in order to feed that priest."[36] The exploitation of the nuns at Santa Chiara di Murano by their male Franciscan counterparts at San Francesco della Vigna was more wholesale: "Those friars are the ruin of this convent, and they eat the food which was meant for the poor nuns, reducing them to extreme misery and penury."[37]

The final chapter of this book will address the question of why nuns laid themselves open to exploitation of this kind—why they played along with the sexual fantasies of frustrated priests and were such easy prey for parasites. But before shifting the focus to the aspirations and motives of the nuns, two more trials are worthy of examination, for they shed further light on how the celibate community tried to compensate for their exclusion from marital relations.

The first dates from 1570 and was brought against a group of male Augustinians from two Venetian houses, Sant'Antonio and San Salvador. They were charged with intruding upon the nuns of San Servolo. Their behavior, as described in the accusations, fits the patterns of conviviality and recreation we have already identified. The friars were accustomed to come to the nunnery for "banquets," a term that probably referred to desserts of fruit, nuts and sweetmeats, rather than full-blown meals. After they had eaten (and the witnesses are unclear as to whether the nuns partook of the food, though they doubtless provided it), the friars and nuns played cards and dice together. Notwithstanding their vows of poverty, bets were placed and money changed hands. (Indeed, it was rumored that Don Fedrigo, the prior of Sant'Antonio, had lost his community some eight hundred ducats in the course of these evenings of recreation.) As was also typical, the nuns sent food parcels to their favorite friars, and gladly took in their clothes and sheets to be washed and mended. Suor Giacoma, a *conversa* from San Servolo, obligingly called on the friars of San Salvador "and brought them sheets and other items which the friars had given them to sew and to wash."[38]

These exchanges give weight to the view that celibates of both sexes were keen to create situations in which they could mimic heterosexual and heterosocial relationships. But this case is also revealing of the terms on which more *personal* relationships between particular nuns and friars were conducted. First of all we hear of certain friars from San Salvador having "spiritual daughters" at the convent: "Don Tranquillo has for his spiritual daughter a nun called Suor Regina, Don Concordio's, I believe, is called Suor Helisabetha [. . .] Don Paulo Hebreo has a *conversa* [for his spiritual daughter]; her name is Suor Costanza." The witness who provides this information—himself a member of San Salvador—goes on to say that "almost all of the friars of San Antonio frequent the convent," and that they are forever boasting about their "spiritual daughters." Moreover, it was rumored that when Don Concordio began to show "friendship and favour" toward a nun at the Dominican convent of Corpus Domini, Suor Helisabetha at San Servolo "entered into a state of desperation for him."[39]

Other accounts of the events that went on at San Servolo go further, and we learn of "marriages" taking place between the friars and their "spiritual daughters." Don Apollinario of

Ravenna, another witness from San Salvador, recalls how he heard that one Don Gregorio

> was conducted to San Servolo by Don Concor-
> dio . . . and he was given a nun as his spiritual friend,
> and apparently he gave her a ring, and they carried out
> certain ceremonies.

Don Apollinario also relates another occasion of this sort:

> Last Epiphany, or around this time, Don Tranquillo led
> Don Cornelio from Venice to San Servolo in order to
> give him a spiritual daughter, and throughout the house
> it was said, "Don Tranquillo is marrying Don Cornelio"
> [in the sense that a priest "marries" a couple] and he has
> led him to San Servolo to this end.[40]

The choice of vocabulary in these depositions is worthy of note: The terms spiritual daughter and spiritual friend seem designed to hold at bay the implicit but never-quite-articulated idea of the spiritual wife. It is little wonder that the friars hung on to the adjective *spirituale* in explaining the relationships that took place between their brothers and the nuns at San Servolo. It gave an air of decency and religious justification to intimacies that were, in fact, well beyond the bounds of acceptability. On the other hand, there is no evidence to suggest that these pseudomarriage rituals led to sexual liaisons. What *is* clear is that a definite sense of possession went with these formalized relationships. Friars boasted that such and such a nun belonged to them. Suor Helisabetha became "desperate" because Don Concordio had grown close to another nun in a different convent. These are themes that recur in the remarkable case of Domenego Zon and the nuns of Santa Maria degli Angeli on the island of Murano.

Domenego Zon had been expelled in 1614 from his chap-
laincy at this convent because of misconduct, and in 1619 he
was brought before the magistrates as a reoffender for continuing to visit the nuns. The initial denunciation of this trial sets
out the nature of the charges:

> That a certain priest, Domenego Zon . . . a man of
> wicked life and evil nature . . . persists in going to the
> convent of the Angeli di Murano, in order to visit the
> nuns there, performing dishonest acts . . . touching and
> kissing them shamefully. And he has carnally used more
> than one of these nuns, scaling the walls of the nunnery
> several times at night.[41]

In fact, these sexual allegations are not as clear-cut as they
might be, since the prime witness against Domenego, a priest
named Nicolo Baruzzi, turned out to have committed perjury
on a grand scale. But even though some of the most incriminating details of the case were called into question, it is
nonetheless valuable historical evidence in two respects. First,
significant aspects of the priest's relationships with particular
nuns are borne out by the statements of more reliable witnesses. Second, the false or dubious information given by Prete
Nicolo Baruzzi gives us insights into another priest's fantasies
about nuns.

During his time as a chaplain in the church of the Angeli,
Domenego became intimate with four nuns in particular. Two
of these, Suor Gaspara and Suor Gieronima, were unenclosed
converse, aged about fifty. They abused their freedom to roam
by making a habit of visiting Domenego at his home in Venice
after he had been forced out of his job on Murano. Then there
was Suor Elena Bragadin, a professed nun, also in her fifties, or
thereabouts, of noble birth and some fortune. Finally, there was

the young and beautiful Suor Tecla, another *conversa,* who was not, however, afforded the same freedoms to leave the convent as those enjoyed by Gaspara and Gieronima.

While it is impossible to know from the web of false or exaggerated depositions exactly what Domenego and these four nuns got up to, we can unravel something of the priest's motivation. For the nuns brought Domenego more than just themselves. Suor Elena—seemingly the most smitten of the four and the one with the greatest personal wealth at her disposal—was notorious for sending the priest gifts and money, all of which Domenego meticulously noted down.

> She gave him beds, mattresses, sheets, blankets . . . clothes, shirts, handkerchiefs . . . 50 or 60 ducats at a time, and every edible delicacy, and all this Domenego recorded in a notebook.[42]

As for Gaspara and Gieronima, they did not have their own funds to draw upon, but were accused of embezzling money in order to provide material assistance to Domenego. Thus bequests to the convent intended to pay for votive masses ended up in the pockets of the corrupt priest. Only Suor Tecla was free from accusations of having given financial aid to Domenego (though she was the nun most implicated in the allegations of sexual misconduct). According to one witness, Domenego once admitted that he preferred Suor Tecla to Suor Elena "because she was the younger and more beautiful."[43] An alternative view on the matter came from Valerio Bognolo, the brother-in-law of Suor Tecla, who claimed of Domenego, "I believe that he has the most affection for those who can do him the most good." Valerio—who was doubtless trying to protect the honor of his kinswoman—pointed out that Tecla was just a poor *conversa.*[44] Yet, although this witness had his own reasons for wanting to shift attention away from Tecla and onto Elena, it is apparent that Domenego was indeed in pursuit of cash as well as youth and beauty.

Domenego exploited his relations with the nuns masterfully, managing to attain the authority of both husband and confessor. Suor Elena and Suor Tecla both received the dubious honor of being styled "wives" by him. Each was kept in ignorance of the other, and when Elena eventually discovered the truth (because a letter meant for Tecla accidentally fell into her hands), she berated the traitor who had deceived her for so long. For a period of five or six years, Suor Elena failed to mention her relationship with the priest whenever she made her confession. But, in the year of the Jubilee—a time of plenary indulgence proclaimed periodically by the Catholic Church—she wrote to Domenego saying that "she wanted to make a general confession, and to deliver herself from the hands of the Devil." He promptly wrote back with the following response, "It was sufficient for her to write down her sins for him to see, since he was a priest who had cure of souls, and that he would absolve her of whatever sins she had committed." Further, on no account should she mention *his* deeds to anyone else, including those he had committed "as a husband to his wife." Finally, Domenego told her that "as his wife she should obey him and that she should leave to him the care of her soul."[45]

The account is reminiscent of the spiritual tyranny exercised by the confessor Giovanni Pietro Lion at Le Convertite and brought to light in the 1561 scandal. But with his claim to husbandly authority, Domenego managed to pull out all the patriarchal stops at once. Underpinning the priest's tactics was his need to secure material support, not just for himself but also for the many nieces who were entrusted to his guardianship. Evidently perceiving his dutiful role as an uncle as a point in his defense, Domenego was himself willing to admit that the nuns had assisted him with providing for his wards. Giving a bizarre twist to his confusion of the spiritual and the domestic, he proudly testified

> that my home has always been a little nunnery of young virgins; I have married off 12 of my sisters and nieces, and among my little girls not one of them has ever been of bad reputation.[46]

So, in Domenego's topsy-turvy world, the real nuns became his imaginary "wives," and their money enabled his imaginary "nuns" at home to enter into real marriages. Financial need was a regular characteristic of priests who courted the affections of nuns, but rarely was it described in such warped terms!

Despite the regulations that insisted on the separation of female nuns and male clergy, priests and friars had a knack of finding their way into the convents. In material terms, visiting the nunnery could be well worth their while: They regularly received hospitality from the nuns, as well as baskets of food to take home and even financial handouts. Nuns also provided invaluable domestic assistance. But, alongside the social and domestic arrangements that existed between nuns and clergy, there was also often a sexual dimension to their interactions. These multiple strands, interwoven, created relationships that aped marriage. The process was sometimes even solemnized, as in the "marriages" that took place at San Servolo. Less formally, the exchange of rings and other love tokens, or the use of the terms husband and wife, allowed religious celibates to experience something of the world from which they were excluded. In an extraordinary detail, which formed part of Prete Nicolo Baruzzi's accusations against Domenego Zon, lies the suggestion that male and female celibates might even have shared their fantasies about procreation and parenthood with one another. Baruzzi claimed that Zon

> had a shirt of the said nun [Suor Tecla], and he put it on in the evening . . . and if there occurred pollutions, whether voluntary or involuntary, he sent the shirt to her saying, "These are the tears of your baby," and she did the same vice versa, having a shirt that belonged to the said prete Domenego.[47]

This lurid charge may have had no basis in truth (Domenego, of course, denied it). It is certainly extreme. But it is nevertheless powerfully indicative of the terms in which relationships between nuns and male clergy were more generally perceived.

11. Chastity and Desire

IN 1614, SCANDAL HIT that most aristocratic of all Venetian convents, San Zaccaria. Two nuns, Laura Querini and her friend the *conversa* Zaccaria (who had presumably taken the name of her convent as she embarked on the religious life), were discovered to have made a hole in the nunnery walls, and to have allowed two men into the sacred enclosure in order to pursue sexual relations with them. Interrogated across an iron grille by the patriarch himself, Laura Querini told her story from the very beginning:

> I came to this convent as a little girl during the time of the plague . . . and then I was sent to board at the convent of San Vido in Burano where I spent five or six years until I was accepted as a nun back at this convent—I must have been fifteen years old. I took my initial vows at the ceremony of clothing, and later I made my profession; but I spoke with my mouth, and not with my heart. I have always been tempted by the devil to break my neck.[1]

The plague of which Laura spoke was the devastating epidemic of 1575–77. Forty-five years old at the time of the trial, Laura's life at San Zaccaria had begun when she was only six or seven. In common with most noble nuns, Laura was dispatched to a convent with family connections; her maternal aunt Suor Honesta was a nun there.[2]

Laura first met her lover, whom she called by the pseudonym Zuanne Cocco, six years before her fall into scandal. He was introduced to her by a woman called Donna Cipriana, who over the years had supplied the noble nun with a series of "friendships." Laura stated that during the course of these liaisons, "I never did anything wicked, that is, I never lost my virginity."[3] But with Zuanne, a young man about twenty years her junior, things were different. Not satisfied by their occasional meetings in the convent parlor, Laura pursued Zuanne with absolute determination:

> I fell in love with him, and I induced him to love me. I used every means to make him love me, including diabolical methods, that is, spells and superstitious prayers invoking devils, and I paid Donna Cipriana to provide me with these things.[4]

Young Zuanne, however, was wary of the risks he ran. It was less than a decade since the Venetian government had passed the stern new law that prescribed capital punishment for any man found guilty of visiting a nun illegally.

Dangerous as the situation was, Laura devised a plan to enable the lovers to consummate their relationship. She identified a small storeroom on the canal side of the convent and, with the help of Suor Zaccaria, set about bashing a hole in the wall. The nuns were both resourceful and committed. They wrenched a piece of iron from the window grille of Laura's cell and used it as a crowbar. It took them more than a month to break their way through the wall, which was six stones deep.[5] In order to obscure the gaping hole in the convent wall, the nuns pulled a large stone across the outside and smeared it with terra-cotta; on the inside, they used black-and-white lime to fill in the cavity.[6] At last, the two nuns achieved their goal, and they were rewarded by the arrival of Zuanne Cocco and his cousin Zorzi, who would be Zaccaria's lover.

> The two men came in a boat, and put a plank across. We unblocked the hole, and they entered through it, and they stayed with us for two or three hours, while they had intercourse with us.[7]

Underlining the supremely sacrilegious nature of this encounter was the fact that it took place in Lent, the time of year expressly designated by the Catholic Church for fasting and sexual abstinence. Using language heavy with sexual overtones, Laura told of how Zuanne returned alone, after Easter, to penetrate the convent once more:

> The said Cocco entered through the same hole, and he concealed himself within the storeroom for ten or twelve days, nor did he ever leave that place; meanwhile, I went around the public spaces of the convent, ensuring that I was seen by the other nuns; and then when everyone was asleep, I went alone to be with him. Nor did I ever take lunch or dinner with him, except on just one occasion, but of course I brought him his food.[8]

With almost gratuitous honesty, Laura added, "And all those nights that Cocco stayed in the nunnery, he had intercourse with me."[9]

Behind a façade of openness, Laura Querini sought to conceal the identity of her lay accomplices. Only under threat of torture—a quite extraordinary measure never in the event implemented—did she admit the true name of her lover: "It was Andrea Foscarini . . . and I beg you to forgive me for not naming him earlier, for I did not want to be the cause of his ruin."[10] At the same time, she was forced to reveal the involvement of a serving woman named Antonia and her husband Zulian, a carpenter at the Arsenal, who had acted as go-betweens in the affair. The consequences of Laura's admissions were serious indeed. The nuns' lovers, Andrea Foscarini and Alvise Zorzi, who failed to attend the trial, were sentenced to exile from Venice and all its territories for twenty years. If either of them broke the ban, the death penalty awaited them. Zulian and Antonia also received harsh sentences for having "cooperated in the amorous affairs of the nuns and of Foscarini and Zorzi." Zulian was particularly condemned for having gone to the convent at nighttime in order to take Foscarini away in his boat.[11] He was sentenced to eight years on the republic's galleys or, if deemed physically unfit, to eight years' imprisonment and the severing of his more valued hand. Antonia was to be flogged from San Marco to the Rialto; if she was ever found in a nunnery or convent church again, she was liable to have her nose and ears cut off. As for Laura and Zaccaria, we do not know exactly how they were punished, though records held in the Vatican reveal that the Venetian patriarch sought permission from Rome to absolve the two nuns.[12] Like all the city's convent women (as we have seen), Laura and Zaccaria were exempt from the jurisdiction of the secular authorities, and their fates rested in the hands of the patriarch and their abbess. In fact, the options for punishing nuns—who, by definition, were already deprived of property and liberty—were limited. For these two women, a life sentence within the walls of San Zaccaria was probably punishment enough.

The events at San Zaccaria show two nuns acting with extraordinary daring and boldness. For some, then and now, such behavior is easily explained: Sexual transgression is the inevitable consequence of enforced celibacy. The fourteenth-century satirist, Giovanni Boccaccio, in his celebrated narrative cycle *The Decameron,* mocked the naïveté of those men and women,

> who are so stupid as to believe that when the white veil
> is placed on a girl's head, and her body covered in a
> black habit, she is no longer a woman and does not feel
> the feminine appetites, as if in becoming a nun she had
> been turned into stone. And if, by chance, they hear
> anything to confound their belief, they are greatly
> shocked, as if a great and terrible evil had been commit-
> ted against nature.[13]

Boccaccio's view of the matter was simple: Sexuality will out.
It cannot be stifled by habit and wimple; to repress it will only
result in scandal. The statement precedes the tale of Masetto da
Lamporecchio who, pretending to be deaf and dumb, takes a
job as a gardener in a convent. Duped into believing that he
cannot spread rumors about them, the nuns enjoy repeated or-
gies with their new employee, while Masetto silently basks in
the success of his ruse. Aretino alludes to the novella in his dialogue between Nanna and her fellow prostitute Antonia: The
story is depicted on one of the walls of the painted parlor
shown to Nanna on her guided tour of the convent.[14] And
Aretino also echoes Boccaccio's sentiments about the ill-fated
attempts of those who seek to impose chastity on women. It is
Antonia who voices the attack on the "mad mothers" and
"simple-headed fathers"

> who believe that girls who become nuns do not have
> teeth to gnaw with like those who marry; what a sorry
> life! They should realize that nuns too are made of flesh
> and bone, and that there is nothing which stimulates
> desire more than denial. For myself, I die of thirst when
> there is no wine in the house.[15]

Boccaccio and Aretino, of course, had their own agenda in exposing the hypocrisy surrounding sexuality in the convent. Their avowals justify the inclusion of what would otherwise appear to be gratuitously salacious passages. But the view that nuns were flesh and blood just like everyone else, that their repressed sexual desires were bound to burst out, found widespread support.

Nunneries had always been deemed to serve an important function in containing the lusts of women.[16] But it was well known that even the highest and most secure walls could be penetrated and that enclosure failed to obliterate sexuality in the convent. The phenomenon of forced vocations added another dimension to the problem. For if the adoption of chastity was not voluntary, then the chances of the vow being kept were lessened further. Girolamo Priuli wrote of Venetian noblewomen who became nuns: "Because they want to be married and to have a man, they behave in whatever way they can."[17] Arcangela Tarabotti, in contrast, blamed the parents who forced their daughters into convents for the resulting scandals.[18]

Historians have also assumed a direct link between forced vocations and disciplinary transgressions of various kinds, not least instances of sexual misconduct.[19] Nuns have been portrayed as fizzing with unsatisfied desires, desperate to give vent to their lusts; their crimes have been understood as the "natural" response to unnatural restrictions.[20] Despite the legal constructions of the crime of sacrilege, which focused on the violators of nuns' chastity rather than on the nuns themselves, sexual offenses in the convent have been represented as a female affair. As a result, there has been a tendency to class convents as virtuous or vicious according to the frequency with which they appeared in prosecutions against men.[21] (One historian goes so far as to provide a league table of "Leading

Convents in Sex Crimes."[22]) Yet the sexual experiences of nuns were not always self-determined. As we have seen, in the most extreme cases, sexual transgressions involving nuns amounted quite simply to rape.

We cannot generalize about the sexual urges of women sworn to chastity. Nuns themselves were sometimes the most assiduous in protesting against scandalous occurrences that threatened the honor of their convents. One subversive nun could wreck the integrity of an entire community. Following the pregnancies of the two "wicked" Corner sisters at San Maffio di Mazzorbo in 1564, many of the nuns were concerned about distancing themselves from the taint of sexual immorality.[23] We should be wary of inadvertently adopting the clichés of Boccaccio and Aretino about the irrepressibility of female lusts and their inevitably heterosexual turn.

Perhaps the most obvious place to seek the physical manifestations of nuns' sexuality is within the convent walls.[24] Here, relationships were harder to restrict, and physical intimacy did not have to take place across a parlor grate. The risk was recognized, and patriarchal visitors made a regular point of inquiring about the sleeping arrangements of the nuns; but they also revealed lapses in the code of conduct governing nuns' relations with one another. At Santa Marta in 1594, certain "significant love affairs" existing between nuns and boarding girls were exposed.[25] In 1595, at Santa Croce della Giudecca, it was recorded that "sensual practices take place among some nuns."[26] Suor Fiorenza was the prime object of concern at San Iseppo in 1626. The patriarchal visitors instructed:

> Let the nuns be interrogated concerning the life that Suor Fiorenza leads: if she goes to the parlour, and with whom, and if those she meets are family or relatives; if

the nuns have ever seen or heard tell (and, if so, by whom) that Fiorenza was found in the parlour with Suor Elena and Suor Chiara, and that they had their skirts lifted and their hands in their undergarments; whether the said nuns were kissing, or if other filthy acts of a similar kind took place.[27]

Such reports give rare glimpses of same-sex relationships within the convent. Largely undetected by outside authorities, the sexual nature of relations between nuns is tantalizingly elusive of historical investigation.

There was also scope for sexual engagement between nuns and laywomen. To the case of Suor Raphaela Balbi, who smuggled a former boarding girl into her cell at San Bernardo di Murano, or that of Felicità and her coterie of disobedient nuns at Sant'Andrea de Zirada, might be added the flirtations of the prostitute Malipiera Malipiero, who, as related earlier, showered the nuns of Spirito Santo with "many kisses."[28] The rules governing nuns' contact with laywomen were less strict than those relating to men, giving potential for sexual relationships to develop on the edges of enclosure.

If the Boccaccian assumptions of modern historians can blind us to obvious possibilities such as those offered by homosexual relationships, they also obscure the quirks and particularities of cases such as that of Laura Querini. For, far from depicting a woman out of control, driven by the helpless impulses of lust, Laura's story reveals a nun exercising her own agency in order to fulfill her long-cherished desires. Her determination to attain bodily consummation of her relationship with Andrea Foscarini puts her outside the common run of cases dealt with by the convent magistrates. Other nuns sought different kinds of experience and fulfillment from their "friendships" with outsiders, and it is often within the context of less physical relationships that religious women found a space in which to prove their self-determination and follow their desires.

One nun whose longings and aspirations contrast markedly with those of Laura Querini is Suor Deodata, who was the object of a patriarchal inquiry at San Iseppo in 1571. Deodata first attracted the attention of the authorities in January of that year during an investigation into the convent confessor and his brother, Gasparo, carried out by the magistrates.[29] She was the prime informant against the confessor—in particular shedding light on the "great boldness and familiarity" that he enjoyed in his relations with the prioress, Suor Cipriana Moresini—as a result of which Suor Deodata earned herself a good deal of unpopularity in the convent, and several months in its prison. Consequently, in August 1571, Patriarch Giovanni Trevisan was driven to investigate her case.[30] (We are lucky in that a transcript of this trial was sent to the magistrates, hence its survival.) The case offers insights into the division and infighting that could split a community of female religious. It also allows us to focus on the mental and emotional state of one particular nun.

Suor Deodata was the daughter of Piero da Lesina, captain of a ship belonging to the nobleman Hieronimo Mocenigo; she had been at San Iseppo since 1553.[31] In the hostile statements made against her, she was described as having "little brain" (though attempts by the magistrates to identify her handwriting revealed that she was the best in the nunnery at writing).[32] More convincingly, she was singled out as a busybody. The prioress complained that "one can do nothing in this house without her knowing about it; she speaks ill of everything, and is always grumbling." She was consistently noted for her sharp tongue and bad language (she cursed her parents, she insulted the confessor); one elderly nun told the investigator: "Let God twist her tongue, as she has twisted everyone else."[33] But for all these negative appraisals, the independence and tenacity of Deodata's campaign against the confessor mark her out as a free spirit, whose individuality refused to be subsumed beneath the interests of her community.

Unsurprisingly, the prioress and the various other nuns who enjoyed the entertainments afforded by the company of the priest and his fun-loving brother did not welcome Deodata's interventions. Nor could the confessor himself be expected to brook the nun's verbal assaults gladly. According to an anonymous statement addressed to the magistrates, Deodata first confronted the confessor in the confessional itself. With a splendid contempt for hierarchy, she chastised him about his relationship with the prioress and her niece and for his other misdeeds:

> It was one of the principal religious feasts on which the nuns were accustomed to be confessed. Suor Deodata came to give her confession to the said confessor, and when the confessor asked her if she had grumbled about anybody, she replied, "Yes, father, I have indeed been grumbling." He then asked her about whom she had grumbled, to which she responded, "About you." "Why do you complain about me?" he asked. And she said, "Because you bring your mother and niece into the confessional to eat with you, and—as you well know—you come right into our convent . . . and you do things that our previous fathers have never done."[34]

Deodata then proceeded to threaten the priest: "You had better take action; otherwise, I shall write to your superiors."[35] This nun was prepared to pursue her case to the highest authorities. According to the prioress, Deodata had boasted, "I have power at my disposal, even if I'm not a gentlewoman; I shall go to the Patriarch, to the heads of the order, and, if needs be, I shall apply to Rome."[36] (Her inferior social status may well have contributed to the tensions at San Iseppo.) Since Deodata was clearly not one to be dissuaded from her course of action, the confessor and his friends turned their efforts to undermining her credibility. They stressed that she was out on a limb in her opposition to the priest. Most of the nuns closed ranks and praised the confessor fulsomely. In the words of the sixty-five-year-old Suor Benedicta Gratarola, "We could say that he is a saint on this earth. Whoever speaks ill of this man speaks ill of the Lord God."[37] As for Deodata, she was almost unanimously condemned as "our ruin." But there were more concrete ways of injuring Deodata's reputation. And in a series of counterattacks, the confessor and his allies determined to tell the patriarchal authorities all about Deodata's relationships with a group of male clergy.

The prioress, Suor Cipriana Moresini, claimed that Deodata's campaign against the confessor was motivated solely by revenge "because he reproved her and stopped the friars from visiting her."[38] The friars to whom she referred came from the Augustinian houses of Sant'Antonio and San Salvador and, as we have seen, had recently been the object of another trial on account of their involvement with the nuns of San Servolo. In particular, Deodata enjoyed close relations with Fra Illuminato and Fra Bastian, with whom she exchanged presents. The excessive magnanimity of the nun toward her clerical acquaintances is consistently reiterated throughout the witnesses' statements. Suor Cipriana provided the following summary of Deodata's gifts to them:

> It would take a long time to tell you everything that she has given them: she has sewn a great number of surplices (to my knowledge, she has made more than

twenty for one of the friars), and she has sewn some stu-
pendous items for the other friars. I have seen her
sewing handkerchiefs for them as well as shirts, collars,
false sleeves, hats stupendously embroidered with gold
and silver, for she works miraculously with pearls and
jewels; and she also sends them baskets of cakes and biscuits.[39]

A secular priest, Mathio de Castello, was also mentioned as
having been the recipient of "a fine robe" made by Deodata.
The disciplinary implications of Deodata's gift giving were not
primarily related to the impropriety of her consorting with
male clergy; rather, they arose from her pursuit of personal
whims at the expense of community interest. Suor Seraphina
(aged seventy-six) saw Deodata's transgressions in economic
terms: "She has never been subject to obedience, she has always
lived slackly, she has always worked for herself in order to make
personal earnings."[40]

If Deodata was not contributing much to the convent
economy, her generous impulses toward her friar friends were
at least self-funded. Asked how Deodata obtained her money,
Suor Innocentia Gambarella testified "that her sister gave and
sent her money, and that she earnt money from her work that
she did for herself, because she never worked for the convent."[41] Deodata herself admitted to spending a considerable
amount of time and money in sewing for the friars (though
she stressed that Illuminato was her cousin). For some of the
jobs, she claimed to have been paid, or at least to have been
provided with the materials. From within the confines of the
nunnery, she established her own business.

Asked whether she sewed surplices for other friars, she
responded: "I sewed a surplice in return for payment for

one old friar from the order, and I sewed one as a gift for fra Illuminato who is my kinsman, and fra Sebastian paid me with so much linen." Asked who had bought the cloth for the said surplices, she replied, "They (that is fra Illuminato and fra Sebastian) gave me the cloth; if you ask father Mathio at Le Vergini, he gave the order to have the cloth made." Asked if she bought fine thread, she replied, "Yes, sir, I bought it myself with money that I had drawn out."[42]

Interviews with Anzolo Bressan, who was employed to do shopping for the convent, reveal further complicated transactions relating to Deodata's sewing enterprise, for he was also central in promoting her operations. He testified: "Several times she gave me money with which to buy two or three pieces of silk, and also gold and silver thread from a woman who was called 'the Catalan.' "[43] Besides sewing and cooking for the friars, Deodata also took in washing for them. From Suor Gratiosa's testimony, we again learn of the resentment the other nuns felt concerning Deodata's efforts to detach herself from the community: "She has always insisted on doing her laundry separately from everybody else's, and whenever she washed her own clothes, she also washed the surplices of the friars."[44]

Deodata pursued the tasks she undertook with almost obsessive determination. With characteristic obstinacy, she resolutely continued with her work even while she was sick and confined to the infirmary. This disgruntled account of Deodata's behavior was given by one of the nurses who looked after her during her illness:

Since I entered the convent twelve years ago, I have never heard a good word from her. . . . When I was working in the infirmary and I was looking after her she was never content, she always cursed what we did for her. We had to take off her shoes, to warm up her bed in the middle of August, to put her into bed, and keep the light burning for her work all night long, for she claimed that she could not sleep, and was always sighing and making surplices for the friars.[45]

Deodata's single-mindedness might be viewed as an aspect of her personal instability. She was not happy at San Iseppo and had once tried to escape. It was said that she cursed her parents for having made her take the veil, and one nun implied that a lack of true vocation had turned Deodata bad: "She has never lived a good life, because she has never embraced the religious life."[46] Her period of illness is frequently referred to in the statements, though witnesses were silent as to the physical symptoms of her condition. We know that she refused to eat "unless the doctor forced her," and it seems likely that the cause of Deodata's suffering was at least partly emotional.[47] One nun, Suor Augustina de Rafinis, was asked why she called Deodata *povereta* (poor thing), to which she replied, "Because she is sick, and because she has little brain."[48] Some pitied the nun, but others blamed her. It is clear both that she flouted the conventions of conventual life and that she was victimized. She described in some detail her months spent in the convent prison: Her quest for individual identity and independence had ended in enforced isolation. As she heard the lock being fixed on the door, she wept.[49]

Despite the alacrity with which the other nuns cast aspersions on Suor Deodata, they never described her relationships with friars and priests as being primarily sexual. The prioress claimed that she enjoyed "an intimate friendship" with Fra Bastian, calling him "my good, my life, my soul . . . and many similar words," a charge that other nuns backed up, and that

Deodata denied.[50] It was also said that the doting nun stood on the balcony outside her cell "in order to see the friars in their bell tower."[51] The friars were easier to bring into the gutter than was their admirer. One of the *converse,* Suor Veronica, told a bizarre story against Fra Bastian:

> One episode I found particularly scandalizing . . . because he came here and said certain words which it is shameful to relate. . . . He told of how he had gone to watch the regatta, an occasion which had given him great pleasure, that he had been a spectator at the women's race, that they were nude and had their fronts half uncovered, as was necessary for rowing women; he urged us to think what he could see.[52]

Suor Catherina had this tale to add:

> Once Don Illuminato asked me, in the presence of Don Bastian, if I knew how to make babies, and I replied that I had never done it in all my life, and Don Bastian said to me, "He is asking you, because he would like to teach you how to do it."[53]

Don Illuminato and Don Bastian were a pretty scurrilous pair. (It was subsequently reported that the latter had "cast off his habit and left the religious life.")[54] But while the friars evidently liked making suggestive remarks to nuns, Deodata's conduct was far more demure. She made them cakes, she sewed their surplices, and she admitted to having presented Fra Bastian with "a gilded picture, showing scenes from the Passion."[55]

Isolated and persecuted by the other nuns, Suor Deodata achieved self-expression and individuality through gift giving. Alienated from her own family as well as from the other mem-

bers of her community, she clung desperately to her relationships with these none-too-salubrious members of the clergy.
Making presents for the friars and for Prete Mathio gave her
life purpose. As Suor Maria Celestia Pisani commented,

> She has pursued this life for around 14 years, always
> working for herself and for her loved ones, and giving to
> understand that she was working for her sister, and for
> her family, when all the time she was working in order
> to earn money which she spends on making presents for
> the friars.[56]

Deodata's behavior was obsessive, all-consuming and intense, but scarcely physical; nevertheless, her contemporaries
might have interpreted her conduct as being charged with
erotic implications. That much is suggested by a detail of the
case from which the investigation of Deodata sprang—the trial
of the convent confessor, and his brother, Gasparo. When one
of the convent employees was asked for his opinion on
whether the prioress's niece, Suor Anzola, desired Gasparo, he
responded:

> Considering that she sends presents to him and that he
> sends presents in return and that he sends his salutations
> to her in the convent, I believe that she must desire him
> because these are the signs of love.[57]

If we are to understand the lives and loves of Renaissance
nuns, we shall have to learn to read their *segni d'amore,* as alien
and unfamiliar as they will undoubtedly seem.[58]

Cloistered women satisfied their desires in a variety of
ways; some with sex, others with surplices. Whatever their
goals, their actions demonstrate the inadequacy of the Boccac-

cian model of carnal desire, in which women's dealings are dictated—knee-jerk style—by the flesh. The contrasting relationships pursued by Laura Querini and Deodata Lesina were both conscious responses to the conditions of life in the enclosed convent. Through their brazenly individualistic conduct, both women purposefully defined themselves against the strictures and demands of the community. Although their actions far surpassed the ordinary, their dealings with noblemen or friars were an extension of the sociable contacts that most nuns sought to nurture across the convent walls. Laura smashed through those walls with an iron railing torn from her own cell window. Deodata set up complex networks of exchange, dispatching hats and hankies as her ambassadors to the outside world. Like so many other nuns whose stories we have heard, both women were determined above all to satisfy their lust for communication.

Epilogue

THE DOOR stands open and the sunshine floods in. It lights a scene of gaiety: an elegant and airy room peopled with well-dressed nobles, and with servants carrying great platters of cakes and other delicacies—one waiter is poised with a live bird. From the wigs and costumes, it is not hard to guess that this is an eighteenth-century scene. The mood is relaxed and cheerful. Indeed, one could mistake the place for an assembly room or a salon were it not for the bleak images of the stations of the cross adorning the far wall, or the cagelike grilles that separate the noble visitors from their hosts. For this is, in fact, the parlor of San Lorenzo, as depicted in an engraving of 1722.

It is impossible to find visual records from earlier than the eighteenth century of this liminal space, which has been so central to the accounts of nuns' experiences offered in this book. But the Dutch engraver of the San Lorenzo piece, Petrus van der Aa, appears to have initiated something of a genre with it. Giovanni Antonio Guardi and Gian Domenico Tiepolo both painted scenes of convent parlors showing nuns crowding at the iron grates in order to speak with their relatives and enjoy the merriments. And what merriments there were to be had! Both paintings have as their focal point a puppet theater, evidently intended for the amusement of all present.[1]

From the onset of the Counter-Reformation to the Enlightenment not much had changed in the convent parlors. Nuns had consistently encouraged laypeople to visit, and had relied on the enticements of food, drink, music and theater in order to maintain their connections with the wider world. Certainly, in interpreting the visual evidence, we must allow for considerable artistic license. That the iron bars on the parlor windows are so widely spaced is perhaps a contrivance to allow the clear representation of the women who stood within. The presence of a Punch-and-Judy show among the nuns' guests was possibly more fanciful than realistic. And yet contemporary trial evidence suggests that the artists' representations were grounded in fact. A band of musicians consisting of eight men—referred to in the documents rather grandly as an academy—came to the parlor of Sant'Alvise twice in June 1750 in order to play to the nuns and their guests, in recitals which had been arranged at the expense of one of the *converse,* Maria Gioconda.[2]

And so the convent magistrates continued to prosecute infractions of enclosure, and nuns persisted in their strategic socializing. The directives of the Counter-Reformation had certainly left their mark on conditions in the nunnery, but they had not succeeded in severing religious women from the society in which they were so firmly embedded.

The convents of Venice might have continued in this way into the modern era, had it not been for a further set of "reforms," fit to rival the ruthlessness of Henry VIII's in their expediency and suddenness. When Tiepolo and Guardi were at work, the days of the ancient republic of Venice were numbered. The year 1797 would see the introduction of the radical but short-lived regime of the Democratic Municipality, which was followed by a series of dominations by foreign powers. The Austrian Hapsburgs arrived for the first time in January 1798; in 1805–06, they were driven out by Napoleon. French rule continued until 1814, when the Austrians returned to Venice. Their renewed domination lasted for more than half a century, with a brief revolutionary interlude in 1848–49, when the popular government of Daniele Manin seized power. Finally, in 1866, Venice became part of the newly unified Italian state.

Of all the changes wrought by these successive governments, those imposed upon the church were among the most radical. Uneasy with the sprawl and power of the city's religious institutions, each regime had attempted to rationalize ecclesiastical organization, with varying degrees of respect for those whose lives would be affected. The most hostile phase of reform was that instigated by the Napoleonic government. Ecclesiastical property was confiscated, over three hundred confraternities were closed down, and many of the educational functions of the church were removed from its control.[3]

Most significant of all, however, was the decree of 1810, which commanded the systematic suppression of monasteries and convents throughout the Venetian lands, now ruled as part of Napoleon's satellite Kingdom of Italy. In the patriarchate of Venice alone, sixty religious houses were closed during the Napoleonic period. Of the monks and friars, 507 were cast out of their communities and either sent back to their places of origin (if they came from outside the Veneto) or forced to relinquish the religious life. Still more devastating was the impact on the far larger population of nuns: 1,130 women were expelled from their enclosed convents. It was expected that they would seek refuge with their families; they were prohibited from reestablishing any kind of community and from wearing the religious habit. Although state pensions were provided, in recompense for the conventual dowries that had been lost, many nuns—particularly the old—must have found returning to the world hugely traumatic. And for women from families that had once used the nunnery to unburden themselves of responsibility for their daughters it cannot have been easy to come home.[4]

The fates of these women are tantalizingly obscure. It is

much easier to trace the histories of the institutions they left behind. Soon after the suppressions, some convents were razed to the ground with little regard for their architectural value. Those that escaped demolition were ransacked by the state. They yielded paintings and treasures that decked out palaces and museums in Paris and Milan or, more commonly, were sold off to fill the coffers of the government.[5] As for the empty shells that remained, with their dormitories built to accommodate scores of nuns, their lofty refectories and high-walled courtyards, these were often converted effortlessly into military barracks.

Walking around Venice today, it is not easy to visualize the thirty-odd nunneries that once constituted such a sizable presence in the city. Many of the surviving convents are removed from public view. Spirito Santo and San Iseppo are now schools; San Zaccaria is the headquarters of the *carabinieri,* the police section of the Italian army; San Lorenzo is a home for the elderly. Sant'Anna, the convent that had once shut in an embittered Arcangela Tarabotti, lies in semidereliction, awaiting redevelopment. But could she return to Venice today, the seventeenth-century nun would doubtless be struck more by the fates of Le Convertite (once the convent that accommodated penitent women) and Santa Maria Maggiore. The former has become the women's prison; the latter is the city's main gaol. The urge to confine and separate lives on—so too, no doubt, the power of human relationships to undermine the walls of enclosed institutions.

Acknowledgments

My first debt is to my parents, Doreen and Peter Laven, who introduced me to the delights of Venice when I was very small indeed, and who have helped me with this project from start to finish. They have been the core of a veritable army of family, friends and colleagues without whose advice and encouragement this book would not have been possible.

Nick Davidson supervised my research in its earlier incarnation as a doctoral thesis, and I am immensely grateful for his wise and liberal guidance. Chris Black, David Gentilcore and Brian Pullan read drafts of the whole manuscript; Daniela Hacke, Bridget Heal and Filippo de Vivo commented on shorter sections. Their suggestions have proved invaluable. For vital advice and references, thanks are due to Tricia Allerston, Deborah Howard, David Laven, Margaret Meserve, Letizia Panizza and Julia Poole. Ian Agnew solved all my map problems at the drop of a hat, and Franco Gazzari generously made time to show me round the restoration site at San Lorenzo.

I might not have survived my first research trips to Venice had it not been for the friendship of Maria Fusaro, Alessandra Petrina, James Shaw and the Habibi-Minelli family. Social sustenance back home came from housemates, friends, and fellow graduates in Cambridge; from my friends at the Warburg Institute (especially Dorigen Caldwell and Margaret Meserve); and later, from the Fellowship of St. John's College. During the last three years, the period in which this book has finally taken shape, my colleagues at Jesus College, Cambridge, have been a solace. Among many friends there, John Cornwell deserves special mention for finding my nuns interesting and for encouraging me to do more with them. I also owe an immeasurable debt to Keith and Eva Wrightson for their support over the course of many years. Their capacity to restore bruised egos is unparalleled.

I am grateful for the financial assistance of several institutions. The University of Leicester granted me a three-year studentship, and I received travel bursaries from the Society for Renaissance Studies, the Gladys Krieble Delmas Foundation, St. John's College and Jesus College, Cambridge. Thanks too to Cambridge University Press for granting permission to reproduce material from my article "Sex and Celibacy in Early Modern Venice," *Historical Journal* 44 (2001), 865–88.

My editors, Juliet Annan and Kate Barker, have not only transformed this book for the better, they have also given me a lasting lesson in how to write history. Elisabeth Merriman, my copy editor, has done much to improve the text. All have treated me with great tact and kindness. I am also grateful to Clare Alexander for setting the ball rolling.

I am embarrassed to reflect on the number of times that Jason Scott-Warren has put aside his own work in order to help me with the research and writing of this book. He read and criticized my every word with unswerving alertness. More remarkably, he turned out to have astounding reserves of humor and patience that never flagged as he helped me out of countless messes of my own making.

This book is dedicated to my dear friends Nubar Gianighian and Pallina Pavanini. Patron saints of anglophone historians lost in the wilderness of the Venetian State Archives, they have mocked and celebrated me in equal measure, and have been an endless source of mirth and hospitality.

Notes

NOTE: The full bibliographical details of works cited here are to be found in the Bibliography.

ABBREVIATIONS USED IN NOTES WHEN REFERRING TO ARCHIVAL SOURCES:

ACPV = Archivio della Curia Patriarcale di Venezia
  Vis. past. = *Visite pastorali a monasteri femminili*
ASV = Archivio di Stato di Venezia
  PSM = *Provveditori sopra monasteri*
ASVat = Archivio Segreto Vaticano
BMC = Biblioteca Museo Correr, Venezia
  Cod. Cic. = *Codice Cicogna*
BNM = Biblioteca Nazionale Marciana, Venezia
B = *busta* (bundle of documents)
Cons. X = Consiglio di Dieci (Council of Ten)
m.v. = *more veneto* (Venetians began the year on March first; all dates in January and February according to the Venetian calendar have been converted to their modern equivalent in the text.)

INTRODUCTION

1. D. S. Chambers and B. Pullan, *Venice,* pp. 338–39.
2. R. Calimani, *Ghetto* (New York, 1987), p. 39; D. S. Chambers and B. Pullan, *Venice,* p. 326.
3. B. Ravid, "Curfew Time in the Ghetto."
4. See further C. Monson, *Disembodied Voices.*
5. For an analysis of these developments, see R. Sennett, *Flesh and Stone,* pp. 212–51. The historian R. Derosas sees such policies as part of a program of "moral cleansing" undertaken by the Venetian state; see his "Moralità e giustizia," pp. 433–528 (esp. 445–46).

6. Machiavelli, *Discorsi,* Bk. 2, Ch. 30; quoted in W. Bouwsma, *Venice and the Defense of Republican Liberty,* p. 99.

7. G. Benzoni, *Venezia nell'età della controriforma,* p. 19.

8. Venice was (and is) divided into six administrative units known as *sestieri:* Cannaregio, Castello, San Marco, San Polo, Dorsoduro and Santa Croce; the island of the Giudecca was usually administered as part of Dorsoduro.

9. Contemporary maps and plans give some idea of the vast tracts of space absorbed by the nunneries; see G. Cassini, *Piante e vedute prospettiche.* In surveying the land occupied by the nunneries, we need to remember that most Venetians lived and worked in the most cluttered conditions, attaching a great deal of status to a roof terrace or a private garden; see D. Thornton, *The Scholar in His Study,* p. 19, on the pressure of space in the city.

10. In the city itself, census information indicates that in 1581 there were 2,508 women living in nunneries, out of a total population of nearly 135,000. By 1642, the number of nuns had risen to 2,905, although the city's population had dropped to approximately 120,000. BMC, MS P.D. 230 b-II: "Descrition de tutte le aneme che sono in la cita fata l'anno 1581"; ASV, *Miscellanea Codici* I, Storia Veneta, filza 128: "Ristretto delle anime che sono nella città di Venezia." It is probable that the figure for 1581 incorporated all women living in the city's nunneries, including *educande* (girls who lodged at convents before marrying or themselves becoming nuns). The 1642 figure is explicitly broken down into choir nuns (1,991), *converse* (599) and *putte* (girls) (315). Both totals relate only to the convents of Venice and exclude the island communities. Statistical information is sparse regarding the number of nuns living in the island convents, which belonged to the diocese of Torcello rather than to the patriarchate of Venice. But the number of women living in those seventeen convents must have run into the hundreds.

11. G. Priuli, *I diarii,* vol. 4, pp. 33–39, 115.

12. Benzoni, *Venezia nell'età della controriforma,* pp. 63–64.

13. Ibid., p. 69.

14. E. Muir, *Civic Ritual,* pp. 228–30.

15. An early landmark in the feminist historiography of nunneries is L. Eckenstein, *Women Under Monasticism.* More recent contributions include P. Ranft, *Women and the Religious Life,* and J.A.K. McNamara, *Sisters in Arms.* For a renowned study of a lesbian nun, see J. C. Brown, *Immodest Acts.*

16. E. Arenal, "The Convent as Catalyst for Autonomy," p. 149.

1. BEHIND CLOSED DOORS

1. ACPV, *Vis. past.*, Vendramin, 1609–18, S. Zaccaria, 1609. At the end of the visitation, Vendramin chastised the nuns for their failure to institute various reforms ordered by Priuli in 1596, and gave them eight days in which to accomplish them.

2. On the nature and uses of inquisitorial and visitation records, see C. Ginzburg, "The Inquisitor as Anthropologist," and P. Burke, *Historical Anthropology*, pp. 40–47 ("The Bishop's Questions and the People's Religion").

3. ACPV, *Vis. past.*, 1452–1730, SS. Biagio e Cataldo, 1593; testimony of Suor Eufemia. Ibid., S. Daniel, 1604, fo. 7v, where the nuns made do with only two eggs a day.

4. ACPV, *Vis. past.*, Priuli, 1592–96, Miracoli, 1595, fo. 369r; ibid., S. Sepolcro, 1595, fo. 397r.

5. ACPV, *Vis. past.*, Vendramin, 1609–18, S. Andrea, 1609.

6. ACPV, *Vis. past.*, Vendramin, 1609–18, Ogni Santi, 1610.

7. ACPV, *Vis. past.*, Vendramin, 1609–18, S. Andrea, 1609.

8. ACPV, *Vis. past.*, misc., 1452–1730, SS. Biagio e Cataldo, 1593. See also, ACPV, *Atti patriarcali riguardanti le monache*, "Decretorum et mandatorum monialium," 1591–92, fos 38v–40r, for the three-day moratoria for the removal of dogs issued to S. Servolo, S. Lorenzo, S. Anna and S. Iseppo in 1593.

9. ACPV, *Vis. past.*, Vendramin, 1609–18, S. Andrea, 1609.

10. ACPV, *Vis. past.*, Vendramin, 1609–18, S. Daniel, 1610; ibid., S. Girolamo, 1609.

11. ACPV, *Vis. past.*, Priuli, 1592–96, S. Croce della Giudecca, 1595, fo. 494v; ACPV, *Episcopato di Torcello, Criminalia monialium*, 1600–89, S. Maffio di Murano, 1623.

12. D. O. Hughes, "Sumptuary Law and Social Relations"; S. Chojnacki, "La posizione della donna"; R. C. Davis, "The Geography of Gender," pp. 32–36.

13. ACPV, *Vis. past.*, misc., 1452–1730, SS. Biagio e Cataldo, 1593.

14. ACPV, *Vis. past.*, Vendramin, 1609–18, S. Andrea, 1609.

15. The standard phrases used by the patriarchs to describe the circumstances in which nuns could draw on their funds was *per bisogni* or *nelle necessità loro*. In records of the visitations carried out during Priuli's patriarchate (ACPV, *Vis. past.*, Priuli, 1592–96, lists of nuns' personal incomes are provided for the following convents: S. Marta, SS. Rocco e Margarita, S. Alvise, S. Croce della Giudecca, S. Iseppo, S. Lucia, Corpus

Domini, S. Zaccaria, Le Vergini, La Celestia, Spirito Santo. For example, at S. Alvise, in 1595, forty of the nuns were named as receiving personal allowances that ranged from one to twenty-five ducats per annum. Elsewhere, the allowances were even larger. At S. Zaccaria, in 1596, one nun, Suor Bianca Loredan, was paid fifty ducats per annum.

16. ACPV, *Vis. past.*, misc., 1452–1730, S. Andrea, 1596.

17. ACPV, *Vis. past.*, Priuli, 1592–96, S. Andrea, 1592, fo. 37r: nuns condemned for having embroidered bed linen and rugs. ACPV, *Vis. past.*, Tiepolo [Patriarch 1619–30], 1620–27, S. Sepolcro, 1622: ordered to remove from the cells "certain privately owned paintings depicting women in lascivious poses."

18. ACPV, *Vis. past.*, misc., 1452–1730, S. Daniel, 1604, fo. 8r; ACPV, *Vis. past.*, Priuli, 1592–96, Corpus Domini, 1595, fo. 558r. On nuns' bequests, see S. Evangelisti, " 'Farne quello che pare e piace. . . .' "

19. ACPV, *Vis. past.*, Priuli, 1592–96, SS. Rocco e Margarita, 1594, fo. 237v. ACPV, *Vis. past.*, Vendramin, 1609–18, S. Anna, 1609. ACPV, *Vis. past.*, misc., 1452–1730, S. Andrea, 1596.

20. ACPV, *Vis. past.*, Priuli, 1592–96, Corpus Domini, 1595, fo. 558r.

21. ACPV, *Vis. past.*, Priuli, 1592–96, Spirito Santo, 1596, fo. 616r.

22. ACPV, *Vis. past.*, misc., 1452–1730, S. Daniel, 1604. ACPV, *Vis. past.*, Priuli, 1592–96, SS. Rocco e Margarita, 1594, fo. 237v.

23. ACPV, *Vis. past.*, Vendramin, 1609–18, S. Anna, 1609. Ibid., S. Servolo, 1610, for evidence of nuns taking away leftovers from the common table. Cf. ACPV, *Vis. past.*, Priuli, 1592–96, S. Zaccaria, 1596, fo. 577r.

24. ACPV, *Vis. past.*, 1452–1730, S. Andrea, 1596.

25. ACPV, *Vis. past.*, Priuli, 1592–96, S. Iseppo, 1595, fo. 514v.

26. ACPV, *Vis. past.*, Priuli, 1592–96, S. Zaccaria, 1596, fo. 576v.

27. On the continuance of family identity within the convent see G. Zarri, "Monasteri femminili e città," pp. 386–98.

28. For a definition of *converse*, see *Dizionario degli istituti di perfezione,* sub "*Converso.*" According to Pius V's bull, simple vows should be taken by all nuns at their clothing; solemn vows should be taken by *monache da coro* only at their profession. For a full discussion of the implications of the *Circa Pastoralis* bull for *converse*, see R. Creytens, "La riforma," pp. 75–79. The theological distinction between simple and solemn vows is explained in *New Catholic Encyclopedia,* sub "Vow." Simple and solemn vows differ in their effects: Solemn profession renders acts contrary to the vows invalid as well as illicit; simple vows make contrary acts illicit, but not invalid. Thus, marriage attempted by one in solemn vows is invalid; marriage for one in simple

vows is illicit but valid. However, it would be foolish to assume that such subtle distinctions were necessarily understood and adhered to.

29. ACPV, *Vis. past.*, misc., 1452–1730, SS. Biagio e Cataldo, 1593; ACPV, *Vis. past.*, Priuli 1592–96, S. Zaccaria, 1596, fo. 576r.

30. ACPV, *Vis. past.*, Tiepolo, 1620–27, Corpus Domini, 1625; ibid., S. Girolamo, 1627.

31. ACPV, *Vis. past.*, Priuli, 1592–96, S. Servolo, 1594, fo. 168r.

32. ACPV, *Vis. past.*, Priuli, 1592–96, S. Maria Maggiore, 1594, fo. 283r–v.

33. A. Grimani, *Constitutioni*, cap. VIII. Antonio Grimani, author of this book on discipline for nuns, was bishop of Torcello, with authority over the convents on the lagoon islands.

34. ACPV, *Vis. past.*, Priuli, 1592–96, S. Iseppo, 1595, fo. 514v.

35. For this distinction, see *Dizionario degli istituti di perfezione*, sub "Abbadessa." In this book "abbess" is used generically to mean the superior of the convent, whether technically known as abbess or prioress. Usually, nuns adhering to the Augustinian rule (Dominicans included) were presided over by prioresses. An exceptional case in Venice was S. Maria delle Vergini. This Augustinian house was governed by an abbess, whose lifelong appointment was approved by the doge and confirmed by the pope. Benedictine communities often referred to their second in command as prioress.

36. ACPV, *Vis. past.*, misc., 1452–1730, S. Andrea, 1596.

37. A. Grimani, *Constitutioni*, cap. VII.

38. ACPV, *Vis. past.*, misc., 1452–1730, S. Maffio di Mazzorbo, 1564.

39. ACPV, *Vis. past.*, Priuli, 1592–96, Vergini, 1596, fo. 588v; cf. ibid., S. Alvise, 1595, fo. 425r.

40. One Venetian example was Cecilia Ferrazzi, a woman too poor to enter a convent who nevertheless made a name for herself through her ostentatious piety, including visions and stigmata, and her vocation to provide refuge for unmarried girls whose honor was in jeopardy. Her devotional excesses brought her before the Inquisition in 1664, and in 1665 she was sentenced to seven years' imprisonment, for "holding and believing that it is licit for a Catholic Christian to make herself a saint"; C. Ferrazzi, *Autobiography*, p. 16.

41. A. Grimani, *Constitutioni*, cap. LX.

42. ACPV, *Atti patriarcali riguardanti le monache*, reg. 5, fo. 16; S. Zaccaria, April 18, 1638.

43. A. Grimani, *Constitutioni*, cap. LXIII.

44. Ibid., cap. LV.

45. On communion and confession, see ibid., cap. LXI; N. Tanner, *Decrees,* vol. II, pp. 779–80, sess. 25, cap. X. Grimani reiterates the ruling of the Council of Trent, but praises the custom of taking the sacraments three or more times a month. See also ACPV, *Vis. past.,* misc., 1452–1730, SS. Biagio e Cataldo, 1593, for Patriarch Priuli's endorsement of more frequent communion. At San Zaccaria in 1596, it was noted that "some nuns desire communion and preaching at least every Sunday right through the year"; ACPV, *Vis. past.,* Priuli, 1592–96, fo. 576r. In midseventeenth-century Naples, nuns were expected to take communion at least twice a month and to confess as often as three times a week; C. Russo, *I monasteri femminili,* pp. 113–14. On the ambivalent attitude of the Counter-Reformation church to the frequent confession of nuns, and the perceived volatility of the relationship between confessor and female penitent, see S. Haliczer, *Sexuality,* especially p. 89.

46. ACPV, *Vis. past.,* misc., 1452–1730, S. Andrea, 1596. Although it was not embraced by all communities, the centrality of self-mortification within the nuns' regimen deserves comment on two counts. First, because—far from being a prominent feature of popular devotion—flagellation was in decline among Venetian confraternities during the sixteenth century. Second, because "the discipline" was and always had been overwhelmingly associated with male devotion. Flagellation required the baring of the back and shoulders, and was generally viewed as an unseemly activity for women. But the privacy and all-female environment of a nunnery provided the perfect circumstances for the practice. The keenness of Venetian prelates to promote the use of the scourge among nuns may have been inspired by Cardinal Carlo Borromeo (1538–84), the reforming archbishop of Milan, who attempted to revive this ascetic practice among confraternities within his diocese. Borromeo viewed the pain of flagellation as a means of atoning for the sins of the world and as an integral part of the *imitatio christi,* the process of recalling Christ's suffering on the cross. More generally, historians have identified a shift in the perception of flagellation during the fourteenth century, when it moved from being an act of penance to a reenactment of the Passion. The presence of the fifteenth-century *Imitatio Christi* by Jean Gerson on the sparse list of books prescribed by Grimani to the nuns in his diocese suggests the importance attributed to this aspect of devotion. See J. Henderson, "The Flagellant Movement"; B. Pullan, *Rich and Poor,* pp. 51–52; R.F.E. Weissman, *Ritual Brotherhood;* C. F. Black, *Italian Confraternities.*

47. A. Grimani, *Constitutioni,* cap. XVII.

48. ACPV, *Vis. past.*, Priuli, 1592–96, S. Croce della Giudecca, 1595, fo. 494r; cf. A. Grimani, *Constitutioni,* cap. LXXVI.

49. ACPV, *Vis. past.*, Priuli, 1592–96, SS. Rocco e Margarita, 1594, fo. 237r; ibid., S. Giustina, 1595, fo. 470v.

50. ACPV, *Vis. past.*, misc., 1452–1730, SS. Biagio e Cataldo, 1593 (Suor Laurentia, *conversa*).

51. ACPV, *Vis. past.*, Trevisan [Patriarch 1559–90], 1560–89, fos 47v–48r; C. Monson, *Disembodied Voices;* R. L. Kendrick, *Celestial Sirens.*

52. On the question of whether nuns could actually see the art in their convent churches, see J. Hamburger, "Art, Enclosure, and the *Cura Monialium,*" p. 120; J. Gardner, "Nuns and Altarpieces," pp. 50–51; G. M. Radke, "Nuns and their Art."

53. A. Grimani, *Constitutioni,* cap. LXVIII.

54. On art in the enclosed nunnery, see M. A. Winkelmes, "Taking Part." Hidden from public view, the full extent of Venetian nuns' patronage of art only became apparent in the early nineteenth century when inventories were drawn up following the suppression of the convents. The fullest survey of art once belonging to the convents of Venice is A. Zorzi, *Venezia scomparsa,* vol. II.

55. Ibid., p. 489.

56. ACPV, *Vis. past.*, misc., 1452–1730, SS. Biagio e Cataldo, 1593: The appointed priests were named as "the Reverend Archdeacon, Father Confessor of the convent of Santa Giustina, and the Reverend priest Brother Eliseo of the order of Saint Dominic."

57. A. Grimani, *Constitutioni,* caps XXXIX, LXIII; *Alcuni avertimenti nella vita monacale,* cap. XII.

58. A. Grimani, *Constitutioni,* cap. LXXVI.

59. ASVat, *S. C. Episc. et reg.,* I, Positiones: 1620, lett. T–V; January fourteenth petition from Suor Lucrezia Morosini of S. Croce della Giudecca, who complained that the nuns' present confessor was "old, in poor health, gouty, and incapable of performing his duties"; she requested instead the services of Zorzi Polacco, an energetic reforming cleric who would later be appointed the patriarch's vicar in charge of the convents. See also, in the same dossier, a petition from the abbess of S. Croce requesting permission for a Franciscan friar to be allowed to visit and offer spiritual guidance to a certain Suor Dionora, who was refusing to take the sacraments and had tried to commit suicide.

60. ACPV, *Vis. past.*, misc. 1452–1730, S. Andrea, 1596.

61. ASV, *PSM, B.* 265; S. Sepolcro, 1618.

62. For a discussion of the ritual calendar, see E. Muir, *Ritual in Early Modern Europe,* pp. 55–80.

63. ASV, *S. Bernardo di Murano,* B. 4: 1 May 1614. *Staro* or *staio* was a measure of capacity, equivalent to approximately eighty-three liters; *mastello* was a measure of liquid capacity, equivalent to approximately seventy-five litres; A. Martini, *Manuale,* p. 818.

64. ACPV, *Vis. past.,* misc., 1452–1730, SS. Biagio e Cataldo, 1593; testimony of Suor Eufemia, *conversa.*

65. Ibid.; testimony of Suor Helisabet Moresini.

66. ACPV, *Vis. past.,* misc., 1452–1730, S. Maffio di Mazzorbo, 1575.

67. ACPV, *Vis. past.,* misc., 1452–1730, SS. Biagio e Cataldo, 1593; testimony of Suor Eufemia, *conversa.*

68. ACPV, *Vis. past.,* Priuli, 1592–96, S. Sepolcro, 1595, fo. 396v, for evidence of bread shortages; ACPV, *Vis. past.,* Tiepolo, 1620–27, Corpus Domini, 1625, for complaints of bad wine.

69. ACPV, *Vis. past.,* Priuli, 1592–96, S. Chiara, 1594, fo. 338r–v.

70. Ibid., fo. 339r.

71. ACPV, *Vis. past.,* Priuli, 1592–96, S. Zaccaria, 1596, fo. 578r.

2. BECOMING A NUN

1. A. Tarabotti, *Inferno,* p. 71.

2. G. Badoer, *Ordo rituum,* p. 7. Cf. F. Vendramin, *Ordo rituum,* and B. Buommattei, *Modo di consecrar le vergini.*

3. G. Badoer, *Ordo rituum* p. 5. On the symbolic death signified by profession, see A. Molho, " 'Tamquam vere mortua.' " For literary representations of the drama of the nun's rites, see P. Aretino, *Sei giornate,* p. 11; D. Diderot, *The Nun,* p. 25; J.A.K. McNamara, *Sisters in Arms,* p. 537; K. O'Brien, *Land of Spices,* p. 7.

4. BMC, *Cod. Cic.* 2570, pp. 299–304 (Letter to the doge and Senate), p. 303.

5. H. Wotton, *Life and Letters,* vol. I, pp. 438–39 (Letter of November 14, 1608, to Sir Thomas Edmondes).

6. S. Chojnacki, "Dowries," p. 575; V. Cox, "The Single Self," pp. 532–33. For a broader discussion of women's inheritance rights in Renaissance Italy, and especially the principle of *exclusio propter dotem,* see T. Kuehn, *Law, Family and Women,* pp. 13 and 238–41.

7. For discussion of the socioeconomic factors behind female vocations in Venice, see J. C. Davis, *Decline,* pp. 62–67; P. Paschini, "I monasteri femminili," p. 58; G. Spinelli, "I religiosi," p. 194; S. Chojnacki, "Dowries," p. 576;

A. F. Cowan, *The Urban Patriciate,* p. 148; D. S. Chambers and B. Pullan, *Venice,* p. 192; V. J. Primhak, "Women in Religious Communities," p. 30; V. Hunecke, "Kindbett," pp. 460–61. For comparative evidence on Florence see R. B. Litchfield, "Demographic Characteristics," p. 203; R. Trexler, "Le Célibat"; and A. Molho, " 'Tamquam vere mortua,' " p. 137. On Bologna, see C. Monson, *Disembodied Voices,* p. 8. On Genoa, see M. Rosi, "Le monache," pp. 67–74.

8. G. Zarri, "Monasteri femminili e città," p. 366: "filias in monasteriis carcerare, cum dignis lacrimis et plantibus ipsarum."

9. S. Chojnacki, "Dowries," p. 572. Two further Senate decrees set maximum limits for marital dowries at four thousand and five thousand ducats, respectively: ASV, *Senato Terra,* Reg. 28, 1535, April 29; ibid, Reg. 37, 1551, March 23.

10. In 1532, the diarist Marin Sanuto recorded that the contract for a high-society marriage alliance had been concluded ("between the second daughter of Ser Hironimo Bragadin, son of the late Vetor, son-in-law of Messer Jacomo Negron, the richest Knight in Cyprus, and Lorenzo Justinian, son of Lunardo who is *capitanio* [one of two governors] of Verona") with a dowry of eight thousand ducats; M. Sanuto, *Diarii,* LVI, col. 33. For further figures, see V. J. Primhak, "Women in Religious Communities," p. 30; D. S. Chambers and B. Pullan, *Venice,* p. 223. Medioli suggests that in the first half of the seventeenth century, marriage dowries could be as high as forty thousand ducats; A. Tarabotti, *Inferno,* p. 113. According to S. Chojnacki, "Dowries," it is difficult to gauge the relationship between rising dowries and all-round inflation (p. 573).

11. J. G. Sperling, *Convents,* p. 24, stresses this point.

12. G. Spinelli, "I religiosi," p. 195.

13. N. Tanner, *Decrees,* vol. II, pp. 781–82; sessio 25, cap. XVIII. The Council pronounced excommunication on anyone guilty of forcing a woman to become a nun. The same penalty was prescribed for anyone hampering the true vocation of a woman to enter a nunnery.

14. Ibid., cap. XVII.

15. Ibid., cap. XV.

16. Ibid., cap. XVI. The implications of this ruling on *converse,* who only took the first "simple" vows, are unclear.

17. A. Grimani, *Constitutioni,* caps XV on clothing and XIX on profession. For comparative evidence, see E. Cattaneo, "Le monacazioni forzate," pp. 164–66. He provides extensive discussion of the *Regole appartenenti alle monache cavate da i concili provinciali di Milano,* published by Carlo Borromeo in 1583.

18. A. Grimani, *Constitutioni,* cap. XV.

19. Cited in P. Paschini, "I monasteri femminili," p. 58.

20. BMC, *Cod. Cic.* 2570, pp. 299–304 (Letter to the doge and Senate), p. 303.

21. A. Tarabotti, *Inferno,* p. 93: "Pregiudicar la multiplicità delle figliole alla Ragion di Stato." The concept of *ragion di stato* also occurs in a report of 1644, issued by the Genoese magistracy in charge of female monastic affairs. It stated, "Not all nuns are consecrated to their spouse by reason of vocation, but rather on account of personal interests and Reason of State"; M. Rosi, "Le monache," p. 73.

22. A. Tarabotti, *Inferno,* p. 35.

23. Quoted in E. Zanette, *Suor Arcangela,* p. 93.

24. A. Tarabotti, *Inferno,* p. 44.

25. Ibid., p. 37.

26. Ibid., p. 35.

27. Ibid., pp. 32–33.

28. Ibid., p. 71.

29. Ibid., p. 39.

30. Ibid., p. 27.

31. Ibid., p. 93.

32. ACPV, *Vis. past.,* misc. 1452–1730, SS. Biagio e Cataldo, 1593.

33. J. G. Sperling, *Convents,* p. 25.

34. A. Tarabotti, *Inferno,* p. 47.

35. M. Rosi, "Le monache," pp. 70–71, and C. Russo, *I monasteri femminili,* p. 60, comment on the pressure exerted by nuns to persuade girls to enter the convent.

36. A. Tarabotti, *Inferno,* pp. 31–32.

37. Ibid., p. 44.

38. BNM, MS it. IX–173: 6282, fos 36v–37r.

39. See, for example, the case of Laura Querini, discussed in my concluding chapter. Sent to the nunnery as a little girl, Laura passed her entire childhood between the convents of San Vido di Burano and San Zaccaria. When the time came for her to take her religious vows, she spoke "with her mouth, but not with her heart"; ASV, *PSM,* B. 265, 1614, S. Zaccaria, fo. 9r.

40. ASV, *PSM,* B. 263, 1555, S. Giovanni Lateran, fo. 18v, Suor Faustina de Polo: "mi hanno posta per forzza in monastier"; ibid., 1566, S. Andrea, Suor Vittoria: "non mi ho mai contentà de star in la religion"; cf. ASV, *PSM,* B. 265, 1618, Convertite, testimony of Suor Maria Isabella Franceschi.

41. ASV, *PSM,* B. 263, 1561 [m.v.], Spirito Santo, fo. 12v.

42. ASV, *PSM,* B. 263, 1555, Giovanni Lateran.

43. Ibid., fo. 18v.

44. On this alternative view of the vow-taking ceremonies, see C. Monson, *Disembodied Voices*, pp. 184–5, and K. J. P. Lowe, "Secular Brides."

45. ASV, *Comp. Leggi*, B. 288, fo. 405; Senate decree, 26 July 1602. ASV, *Spirito Santo*, B. 1; "Registro dei Capitoli et altro (1534–1805)." On dowries paid to San Lorenzo, see O. Battiston, *Un piccolo regno*, pp. 72–73.

46. G. F. Loredan, *Delle lettere*, vol. 2, p. 201.

3 . BLOOD OF THE REPUBLIC

1. M. Sanuto, *Diarii*, XXXI, col. 162; August 2, 1521. M. P. Pedani, "L'osservanza imposta."

2. M. Sanuto, *Diarii*, XXXI, cols 276–77; August 21, 1521.

3. Ibid., XXXI, col. 384; September 10, 1521.

4. Ibid., XXXI, cols 398–99; September 13, 1521. In an age when rebels and rioters regularly made the civic granary the focus of their protests, the nuns' attack on the convent's flour store carried particular significance.

5. Ibid., XXXI, cols 423–24; September 17, 1521; I. Giuliani, "Genesi."

6. Sanuto, *Diarii*. XXXI, col. 276; August 21, 1521.

7. J. Burckhardt, *The Civilization of the Renaissance*, p. 40.

8. B. Pullan, *Rich and Poor*, p. 22.

9. For a discussion of the causes of popular acquiescence to the state, see E. Muir, *Civic Ritual*, pp. 42–44.

10. ACPV, *Vis. past.*, misc. B, 1452–1730, SS. Biagio e Cataldo, 1593.

11. ACPV, *Vis. past.*, Trevisan, 1560–89, Corpus Domini, 1560, order 29. On Venetian marriage rituals, see P. Labalme and L. S. White, "How to (and How not to) Get Married," p. 44.

12. The figures collected by Vendramin are as follows: S. Zaccaria, 1609, seventy choir nuns of whom seventy were noble (100 percent); S. Andrea, 1609, forty-five choir nuns, forty-three noble (96 percent); SS. Rocco e Margarita, 1609, thirty-four choir nuns, eighteen noble (53 percent); Ogni Santi, 1610, fifty-three choir nuns, thirty-one noble (58 percent); S. Chiara, 1611, forty choir nuns, eleven noble (28 percent); Spirito Santo, 1611, thirty-five choir nuns, thirty-three noble (94 percent); S. Alvise, 1612, eighty-nine choir nuns, eighty-six noble (97 percent); S. Lucia, 1613, fifty-nine choir nuns, twenty-four noble (41 percent); S. Caterina, 1616, one hundred choir nuns, ninety-nine noble (99 percent); S. Iseppo, 1618, sixty-seven choir nuns, thirty-five noble (52 percent). The mean proportion of noble nuns within these convents is 72 percent. Roughly in keeping with these figures is J. G. Sperling's estimate (*Convents*, pp. 26–29) for the late sixteenth century that

74 percent of all nuns were noble, based on information from the 1586 census about all the Venetian convents. However, her figure is even more impressive than it seems, since the census figures for the overall number of nuns include *converse*. My figures exclude *converse*, on the grounds that (i) visitation records tend not to provide their family names; (ii) *converse* were almost by definition nonnoble. The exceptionally low proportion of noble nuns at S. Chiara in 1611 suggests that, in the ninety years that had passed since she made her protests, the fears of Anzola Boldù had been fulfilled.

13. ACPV, *Vis. past.*, Trevisan, 1560–89, Corpus Domini, 1560, order 12.

14. ACPV, *Vis. past.*, Trevisan, 1560–89, fo. 21r (undated).

15. ACPV, *Vis. past.*, Priuli, 1592–96, S. Zaccaria, 1596, fo. 576r.

16. On the elite character of convents throughout Italy and Europe, see L. Roper, *Holy Household*, p. 209; O. Hufton, *Prospect*, p. 65; M. E. Wiesner, *Gender, Church and State*, p. 50; C. Russo, *I monasteri femminili*, pp. 69–71; G. Zarri, "Monasteri femminili e città," pp. 368–72; L. Fiorani, "Monache," p. 70.

17. ACPV, *Vis. past.*, Vendramin, 1609–18; S. Servolo, 1610, on the "vain" and "indecent" custom whereby nuns call one another "Signora"; ACPV, *Atti patriarcali*, reg. 1, fos 8r–9r; April 8, 1591, S. Anna, detailing a dispute between two nuns regarding order of precedence.

18. These data testify to the failure of ecclesiastical measures to limit the concentration of blood relatives in particular houses; see for example A. Grimani, *Constitutioni*, cap. XV. Venetian families regularly petitioned Rome for the relaxation of these rules; see permissions granted to Marietta Grimani, Lucretia Falier and Felicita Genova to enter San Maffio di Mazzorbo, where each already had two blood sisters; ASVat., *S. C. Episc. et reg.*, I Positiones, 1620, lett. T–V.

19. ASV, *PSM*, B. 267; S. Iseppo, 1626.

20. ACPV, *Vis. past.*, Tiepolo, 1620–27, S. Iseppo, 1622; thirty-two of the sixty-four choir nuns came from Venetian noble families.

21. G. Priuli, *I diarii*, IV, p. 34.

22. G. Zarri, "Monasteri femminili e città," p. 378.

23. ASV, *PSM*, B. 265, Celestia, 1614; B. 268, convent unknown, 1631.

24. ASV, *PSM*, B. 268, S. Lorenzo, 1642.

25. D. S. Chambers and B. Pullan, *Venice*, p. 206.

26. BMC, *Cod. Cic.* 2570, pp. 299–304; undated letter to the doge and Senate (p. 303).

27. Cf. L. Roper, *Holy Household*, p. 224.

28. Using the records of tax assessments, Sperling has pointed to the impressive gains in income and property achieved by nearly all Venetian con-

vents during the period 1564–1769. Among those that made the most dramatic increases in their land ownership were S. Maria degli Angeli, which extended its rural holdings by 713 hectares or 276 percent, and S. Maffio di Murano, which acquired its entire farmland of 536 hectares after 1564. The Carmelite house of S. Teresa, founded in 1647, was remarkably quick to develop its agricultural estates, acquiring about 500 hectares in the Verona area during the course of the seventeenth century. The highest increases in total revenues, however, came more predictably from the two oldest convents in the city of Venice, S. Zaccaria and S. Lorenzo, whose position at the head of the wealth tables had long been secure. Apart from the general increase in real estate, another noticeable feature of the investment portfolios of the nunneries is the rise in revenues from urban property. This widespread tale of expansion flew in the face of the state's efforts to limit the amount of land in the hands of ecclesiastical institutions, including the tough-talking mortmain law of 1605, which attempted to end the acquisition of real estate by ecclesiastical institutions throughout the republic of Venice; J. G. Sperling, *Convents,* pp. 200–201, 219, 224–27.

29. A. Grimani, *Constitutioni,* cap. XLII, fo. 41v.

30. ACPV, *Vis. past.,* 1452–1730, SS. Biagio e Cataldo, 1593.

31. A. Grimani, *Constitutioni,* cap. XVI, fos 18v–19r.

32. Ibid.; cf. ACPV, *Vis. past.,* misc., 1452–1730, SS. Biagio e Cataldo, 1593.

33. ACPV, *Vis. past.,* misc., 1452–1730, S. Andrea, 1596.

34. On the self-perpetuating system of rule by the old in Venice, see R. Finlay, "The Venetian Republic as Gerontocracy."

35. ACPV, *Vis. past.,* Priuli, 1592–96, S. Servolo, 1594, fo. 168r; the instruction to change offices annually or biennially (according to the convention of the nunnery) is reiterated throughout the visitation reports of Priuli's patriarchate.

36. *Bullarium diplomatum,* VIII, pp. 404–405; Pope Gregory XIII's decree of 1583, "Abbatissae et aliae praefectae monasteriorum in Italia triennium tantummodo eligantur." See ASV, *Comp. Leggi,* B. 288, fo. 385 ff., for a series of supplications from Venetian convents protesting at the introduction of triennial (as opposed to perpetual) abbesses.

37. On this issue, see K. J. P. Lowe, "Elections of Abbesses."

38. A. Grimani, *Constitutioni,* cap. VI, Here, Grimani was adopting the Tridentine legislation (sessio 25, cap. VII; N. Tanner, *Decrees,* pp. 778–79).

39. A. Grimani, *Constitutioni,* cap. VI, fo. 5r.

40. *Nunziature,* I, pp. 123–24.

41. Ibid., p. 96.

42. ASV, *PSM*, B. 263, 1567, S. Sepolcro, fo. 1r. Although this was evidently a very full investigation, the middle section between fo. 12 and fo. 51 has been lost.

43. ASV, *PSM*, B. 263, 1567, S. Sepolcro, fo. 3v.

44. Ibid., fo. 4r.

45. Ibid., fo. 7r.

46. Ibid., fo. 52r.

47. Ibid., fo. 61v–62r.

48. Ibid., fo. 65r.

49. Ibid., fo. 57v.

50. Ibid., fo. 58r.

51. Ibid., fo. 68r. The biblical reference—"noli tangere christos meos"— is to 1 Chronicles 16:22.

52. For a survey of the extensive literature on the myth of Venice, see D. E. Queller, *The Venetian Patriciate*, Ch. 1; for a lucid account of the antimyth, see D. Wootton, "Ulysses Bound?".

53. Ibid.; on the *broglio*, pp. 354, 357–58.

54. F. C. Lane, *Venice*, pp. 109–11.

4. SACRED AND PROFANE

1. ASV, *PSM*, B. 264; S. Maria Maggiore, 1612; on Venetian ceremonies to mark Candlemas, see E. Muir, *Civic Ritual*, pp. 135–56.

2. O. Hufton, *Prospect*, p. 301; L. Roper, *Holy Household*, pp. 101–2.

3. ASV, *PSM*, B. 264; S. Maria Maggiore, 1612.

4. U. Franzoi and D. Di Stefano, *Le chiese*, p. xix; according to an arcane medieval convention, the parishes were officially grouped beneath five "mother-churches," which held a monopoly over marriages and baptisms: S. Maria del Giglio, S. Maria Formosa, S. Silvestro, S. Marco and S. Pietro.

5. B. Pullan, *Rich and Poor*, p. 34; cf. C. F. Black on women in confraternities.

6. ACPV, *Vis. past.*, Vendramin, 1609–18; from these visitations, we learn that there were ten priests at Ogni Santi (1610); twenty-one at SS. Biagio e Cataldo (1610); seventeen at S. Caterina (1616); nineteen at S. Iseppo (1618).

7. Counter-Reformation rulings discouraged marriages and baptisms in convent churches. ACPV, *Vis. past.*, misc., 1452–1730, SS. Biagio e Cataldo, 1593; orders regarding the *chiesa esteriore*.

8. M. Sanuto, *La Città di Venetia*, pp. 46, 163–64.

9. F. Corner, *Ad Ecclesias Venetas*, 15, pp. 165–72.

10. U. Franzoi and D. Di Stefano, *Le chiese*, p. 519: QUESTA CAPELA ET

ALTAR/FU FATTO PER VOTO/DELLE MAESTRANZE/DELL'ARSENAL/NEL TEMPO DELLA PESTE/DELLI LORO BENI/L'ANNO MDCXXXI/MARANGON CALAFAI/REMERI E SEGADORI.

11. O. Battiston, *Tre monasteri scomparsi,* pp. 42–43.

12. For an in-depth study of the Arsenal workers, see R. C. Davis, *Shipbuilders.* The Arsenal chapel, Beata Madonna dell'Arsenale, was situated at the heart of the community, in Campo dell'Arsenale; the parish church of S. Martin was sometimes referred to as "the Arsenal church" (pp. 86–87). Davis makes no mention of S. Anna. On the drinking habits of the Arsenal workers, see R. C. Davis, "Venetian Shipbuilders."

13. ASV, *S. Croce di Venezia,* B. 3, "Testamenti sec. XVII–XVIII," March 5, 1601: Zuane di Mascaroni. In 1550, the *Maggior Consiglio* had passed a law obliging all notaries to ask testators if they wished to leave money to Le Convertite, which was then a recent foundation; ASV, *Comp. Leggi,* B. 288, fo. 324, March 19, 1550. Whatever personal connections Zuane may have had with S. Croce and Le Convertite, both would have been viewed by contemporary Venetians as highly worthy objects of charity.

14. ASV, *S. Croce di Venezia,* B. 3, "Testamenti sec. XVII–XVIII," June 21, 1608: Contarina Capello (legacy of 2 ducats per annum indefinitely to each convent); November 18, 1629: Giovanni Busca (legacies of 250 ducats to S. Maria Maggiore, 200 ducats to S. Croce, 150 ducats to S. Chiara di Murano, and 100 ducats to S. Sepolcro).

15. Ibid., February 19, 1600 [m.v.]: Lucretia Corner.

16. ASV, *Notarile Testamenti,* B. 1246, testament 683, July 25, 1602: Sebastian Capello.

17. ASV, *S. Iseppo,* B. 5, July 27, 1644: Angela Caristo, whose executor and principal beneficiary was the nun Suor Fede Priuli at San Iseppo; ASV, *S. Croce di Venezia,* B. 3, "Testamenti sec. XVII–XVIII," August 18, 1605: Viena Bianchi, who appointed the nuns of S. Croce and S. Giustina, along with the male procurators of each convent, to act as her executors.

18. T. Coryat, *Coryats Crudities,* p. 255.

19. ASV, *S. Croce di Venezia,* B. 3, "Testamenti sec. XVII–XVIII," August 18, 1605: Viena Bianchi: "I wish to be buried in the convent of the Reverend nuns of Santa Croce in Venice, dressed in their habit and accompanied by *converse* . . . and to these nuns shall be given five ducats for the habit in which I am to be buried"; ibid., October 21, 1622: Franceschina Littegato named two *converse* whom she wished to dress her body, Suor Anna and Suor Catterina; they were to be paid one ducat each besides the cost of the habit.

20. ACPV, *Atti patriarcali,* reg. 1, fos 29v–30v.

21. On the intercessory power of nuns, see D. S. Chambers and B. Pullan, *Venice,* p. 114; a Senate decree of April 17, 1464, issued at a time of plague, instructed the patriarch "to have prayers recited unceasingly in all convents and religious houses for the deliverance of this our city from the sudden assaults of such a dangerous disease." Compare R. Trexler, "Le Célibat," p. 1329; the Florentine nuns of San Piero Martire cast their "continual prayers" as a military advantage, arguing in a fiscal declaration of 1478 that they were "more useful than two thousand horses," "coming as they do from persons of such great religion."

22. ASV, *PSM,* B. 266; S. Chiara di Murano, October 7, 1620.

23. From the fifteenth century, when the traditional immunity of ecclesiastical institutions was abolished, convents paid tax on the rental value of their properties. The *decima del clero,* the primary tax on clerical wealth, was first imposed in 1463, and soon assumed the character of an ordinary and regular exaction, yielding about 18,000–20,000 ducats a year. The frequency with which this tax was levied, without recourse to papal permission, caused resentment in Rome, and when Venice was in a diplomatically weak position after its defeat at Agnadello in 1509, Julius II took the opportunity to renounce the government's right to tax the church. Responding to the Turkish threat in 1523, Adrian VI relented and the *decima del clero* was levied anew. In 1535, the menace of the "infidel" was once again sufficient to boost the claims of the Venetian treasury. And so the state continued to tax the church throughout the sixteenth and seventeenth centuries, with varying degrees of efficiency, hampered by Rome and by the historical exemptions claimed by certain institutions. In 1564, Pope Pius IV gave permission for the Venetian government to carry out a reappraisal of ecclesiastical wealth for the purposes of taxation. This major concession came only months before Venice's recognition of the decrees of Trent, and represented a high point of cooperation between the republic and the papacy. The tax law required all properties and their incomes in cash or kind to be declared, along with the revenue from other capital investments: *livelli,* forced loans made to government funds known as *monti,* and *procuratie* (trust funds); only government bonds were exempt. These returns testify to the extent of assets managed by female religious houses; they also suggest the potential of the convents as a source of tax revenue for the government. But that potential was only partially realized. For example, the richly endowed convent of San Lorenzo, with "taxable" revenues estimated at 2,644 ducats in 1564, was, in fact, exempt from all ecclesiastical taxes. Although the state managed to squeeze some financial support out of San Lorenzo, in the form of *decime laiche* (the lay property tax extended to the clergy in 1472), this imposition covered only a fraction of the real es-

tate actually owned by the convent. Moreover, a substantial part of the nuns' income, in many convents, came in the form of material support from their families (dowries, annuities and cash supplements), from nuns' earnings, and from government bonds, none of which was liable to taxation. G. Del Torre, *Venezia e la terraferma dopo la guerra di Cambrai: fiscalità e amministrazione (1515–1530)* (Milan, 1986); pp. 85–98; J. G. Sperling, *Convents,* pp. 196–98, 200–201, 222; O. Battiston, *Un piccolo regno,* p. 74.

24. ASV, *S. Andrea de Zirada,* B. 21, 1196, fo. 12r: 1610, 12 June, "formenti menudi della serenissima signoria." In total, 653 *stara* of wheat were distributed among 52 institutions. Of these, 39 were nunneries situated in Venice or on the surrounding lagoon islands, which together took 480 *stara.* The donations received by convents ranged from 36 *stara,* the amount allotted to the Franciscan houses of Santa Croce di Venezia, Santa Chiara di Murano, San Sepolcro and Santa Maria Maggiore, to 2 *stara* (approximately 167 lires), given to a variety of less needful or deserving houses. In 1581, responding to a series of supplications, the government ruled that the annual subsidy of wood supplied to the convent of Santa Marta should be increased threefold from 8 to 24 *cara;* ASV, *S. Marta,* B. 7.

25. ASV, *Comp. Leggi,* B. 288, fo. 444, November 17, 1607. In response to this petition from the "poor nuns" of Santa Chiara di Murano, who sought to be released from a debt to the Venetian water authority of seventy-nine ducats and nineteen denari (outstanding since 1580), the Senate wiped out both the capital debt and the interest "in segno della pietà, et benignità della Signoria nostra."

26. ASV, *Comp. Leggi,* B. 288, fo. 592, 1627, June eleventh.

27. ACPV, *Atti patriarcali, reg.* 1 (February 14, 1591–October 16, 1599), fos. 102r–103r, April 26, 1597 (fo. 102r).

28. On the relationship between the doge and the nuns of S. Zaccaria, see U. Franzoi and D. Di Stefano, *Le chiese,* pp. 390–490. Marin Sanuto mentions the doge's annual visit to the convent in *La Città di Venezia,* p. 181.

29. I. Fenlon, "Lepanto," p. 29. L. Roper, *Holy Household,* p. 228, comments on the prominent role of nuns in the civic ritual of Augsburg, which was anomalous given the exclusion of laywomen from official ceremony.

30. E. Muir, *Civic Ritual,* p. 127; Francesco Sansovino mentions the ceremony in the 1581 edition of *Venetia città nobilissima,* fo. 4v: "il Principe, ceremonialmente sposa in persona, la Badessa nuova, in ricognitione dell'antica sua preminenza."

31. See E. Muir, *Civic Ritual,* pp. 103–05, 119–34, for a full account of the mythology surrounding these events.

32. BMC, MS Correi 317, "Cronica del Monistero delle Vergini di Venetia," fo. 1r–v.

33. Here I disagree with E. Muir, *Civic Ritual,* p. 128: "The monastic nuptials and the crediting of their origin to Pope Alexander, of course, closely paralleled the Sensa and signified a similar relationship: the husband was to be *padrone* of the wife."

34. E. Cicogna, *Delle iscrizioni veneziane.* For a full account of the investiture of Sofia Malipiero in 1598, including the "beautiful" and much praised oration given by Aurelia Querini in her honor, see Giovanni Stringa's updated and revised edition of F. Sansovino (Venice, 1604), fos. 126v–128r.

35. According to M. Sanuto (*Diarii,* vol.VI, col. 353), five hundred guests were invited to the banquet following the investiture of Margarita Badoer in 1506.

36. G. Zarri, "Monasteri femminili e città," p. 375.

37. T. Coryat, *Coryats Crudities,* p. 278. See also the oration of Luigi Groto, published in 1570, which depicted Venice as a virgin, nestling in the arms of its other protector, Saint Mark the Evangelist, untouched by the violations of tyrants; cited in R. Goffen, *Piety,* p. 145.

38. For a discussion of the prominence of the Virgin within Venetian civic culture, see ibid., pp. 138–54; J. G. Sperling, *Convents,* pp. 12–14.

5. THE BOUNDARIES OF REFORM

1. For a survey of the Protestant assault on nunneries, see J.A.K. McNamara, *Sisters in Arms,* pp. 419–51.

2. Ibid., p. 442; M. E. Wiesner, *Gender, Church and State,* p. 51. Particularly celebrated is the case of Caritas Pirckheimer, abbess of the Nuremberg house of Saint Clara, who defended her nuns against a concerted campaign of intimidation by the Council and the townspeople. Local men and women (especially women, Caritas noted) threatened to burn down the convent, threw stones and tried to drown out the nuns' singing with their profane songs. Meanwhile, the nuns were deprived of their priests and subjected to Protestant preaching, and their servants found it difficult to buy food for the community. Eventually, the abbess was forced to release some of her nuns, as they were dragged from the convent by their families. In a carefully choreographed drama, she bade them tearful farewells, ceremoniously removing their sacred vestments and dressing them in worldly clothes: L. Roper, *Oedipus and the Devil,* pp. 41–42; M. E. Wiesner, "Nuns, Wives and Mothers," p. 10; J.A.K. McNamara, *Sisters in Arms,* pp. 437–39, 441–43, 451; P. S. Datsko Barker, "Caritas Pirckheimer."

3. On the Protestant propaganda surrounding the closure of the nunneries, see S. Ozment, *When Fathers Ruled*, pp. 9–25; L. Roper, *Holy Household*, pp. 231–33.

4. See especially L. Roper, *Holy Household*, and M. E. Wiesner, "From Spiritual Virginity to Family as Calling," in *Gender, Church and State*, pp. 36–46. Whereas historians like Roland Bainton and Steven Ozment, who pioneered an interest in the gender implications of the Reformation, tended to see the religious changes as beneficial to women, stressing the new possibilities for spiritual equality and companionate marriage, more recent work by Roper and Wiesner has revealed the fundamentally conservative agenda of mainstream Protestantism.

5. For this insight and for discussion of the Virgin Mary's changing role in Reformation Germany, see B. Heal.

6. Erasmus criticized the church's stand against clerical marriage and argued, controversially, that chaste marriage was a higher state than virginity; see his *Encomium matrimonii* (first published 1518, though written, Erasmus claimed, some twenty years earlier as a rhetorical exercise) and *Institutio christiani matrimonii* (1526). For a full discussion of Erasmus's views on marriage and celibacy see D. Erasmus, *Collected Works*, vols 39–40 (1997), pp. 279–85. In 1538, a commission of leading churchmen, appointed by Pope Paul III, published a document advocating reforms, *Consilium de emendanda ecclesia*. This included the recommendation that the religious orders be abolished, but maintained a commitment to celibacy within the priesthood; see H. C. Lea, *History*, p. 450.

7. Ibid., p. 464; M. E. Wiesner, *Christianity and Sexuality*, pp. 102–40.

8. R. Creytens, "La riforma," especially pp. 49–52, for the hurried treatment of monastic reform by the Council; N. Tanner, *Decrees*, II, pp. 776–84.

9. My citations of Tridentine decrees follow N. Tanner, *Decrees*, and use Tanner's translations with minor modifications; II, p. 776; decree on regulars and nuns, Ch. 1.

10. Ibid., p. 778; Ch. 5.

11. Cited in J. T. Schulenburg, "Strict Active Enclosure," pp. 61–63.

12. For an excellent summary of developments in the theory and practice of enclosure, see Silvia Evangelisti's forthcoming book, *Beyond the Veil*.

13. U. Strasser, " 'Aut murus aut maritus?' "; G. S. Daichman, "Misconduct," p. 98, who quotes a different version of the same saying, "Aut virum aut murum oportet mulierem habere"; A. Tarabotti, *Inferno*, p. 112.

14. R. Creytens, "La riforma," pp. 52–53; N. Tanner, *Decrees*, II, p. 778. According to K. Gill, "*Scandala*," p. 177, the 1298 bull "did not constitute a dramatic turning-point [...] It neither reflected nor achieved a general

acceptance of strict enclosure as a necessary and validating feature of women's religious life." K. Norberg, "The Counter-Reformation," p. 134, refers to compulsory enclosure as "the great innovation of the Council of Trent."

15. See F. Medioli, "La clausura delle monache," pp. 253–55, for the early history of conventual enclosure. Medioli notes that there is a lack of clarity in dating the origins of enclosure, with some scholars tracing the first injunctions to the fourth century and others to the sixth.

16. R. Creytens, "La riforma," p. 53; K. Gill, "Open Monasteries," especially p. 17: She argues that the Counter-Reformation "struck a fatal blow" to open monasteries, whose active apostolate outside the convent walls depended on freedom of movement for their members. Ironically, the enclosure reforms were also to have troublesome effects for some of the new orders—supposedly models of Tridentine ideals; J. Delumeau, *Catholicism,* pp. 37–38.

17. R. Creytens, "La riforma," p. 54.

18. Ibid., pp. 63–64.

19. *Bullarium diplomatum,* VII, pp. 447–50. The rationale behind Pius's characteristically forthright decree was that profession implied the willing and total abdication of will. K. Gill has stressed the radicalism of the new drive for enclosure. In her view, it was *Circa pastoralis,* not the Council of Trent, that was "the real herald and agent of change": "*Scandala,*" p. 199. A series of bulls followed *Circa pastoralis;* these adhered to the principle of compulsory enclosure for all nunneries, and served to tighten up the details of the regulations: *Decori* (1570), *Deo sacris* (1572) and *Ubi gratiae* (1575). Gregory XIII issued a clarification of the last of these, known as *Dubiis,* in 1581. For texts, see *Bullarium diplomatum,* VII, pp. 808–10, VIII, pp. 28–32 and pp. 113–15.

20. ACPV, *Vis. past.,* misc., 1452–1730, SS. Biagio e Cataldo, 1593.

21. Cited in R. Creytens, "La riforma," p. 48.

22. ASV, *PSM,* B. 1, fos 25v–26r, 1551, November nineteenth; I. Giuliani, "Genesi," p. 161. In cases of particular importance, sentencing was to be reserved to the Council of Ten itself.

23. ASV, *PSM,* B. 1, fo. 27v, 1561 [m.v.], February twelfth, Cons. X.

24. ASV, *PSM,* B. 1, fo. 29v, 1569, June tenth, Cons. X.

25. ACPV, *Vis. past.,* misc., 1452–1730: S. Andrea, 1596.

26. ACPV, *Vis. past.,* misc., 1452–1730: SS. Biagio e Cataldo, 1593.

27. ACPV, *Vis. past.,* Vendramin, 1609–18, SS. Rocco e Margarita, 1609.

28. A. Grimani, *Constitutioni,* cap. XXI.

29. ACPV, *Vis. past.*, misc., 1452–1730, S. Andrea, 1596. ASV, *PSM*, B. 263: 1566, S. Andrea.

30. A. Grimani, *Constitutioni*, cap. XXI; see also ACPV, *Vis. past.*, misc., 1452–1730, SS. Biagio e Cataldo, 1593: "[The doors] must be strong and secure, locked with two different keys, and bolts."

31. A. Grimani, *Constitutioni*, cap. XXV.

32. L. Priuli, *Ordini* 1–7.

33. Ibid., *Ordine* 10.

34. P. Paschini, "I monasteri femminili," p. 44.

35. ACPV, *Vis. past.*, misc., 1452–1730, S. Maffio di Mazzorbo, 1564.

36. L. Priuli, *Ordine* 13.

37. A. Grimani, *Constitutioni*, cap. XXIII.

38. Ibid., cap. XXVI.

39. Ibid., cap. XXXI.

40. Ibid., cap. XXXIII.

41. ASV, *PSM*, B. 264, 1611, S. Anna. There is some uncertainty as to the date of this trial. The case is labelled 1611. So are the first three documents: a denunciation marked "Adi 2 April, 1611"; the order for Battista's arrest marked "A 11 ditto"; notice of his detention marked "A 12 ditto." Then follows the interrogation of the builder, which is headed "1612 à 13 di Aprile." It seems unlikely that the interrogation should have been delayed by a year and one day. Presumably this should read 1611.

42. ASV, *PSM*, B. 264: 1611, S. Caterina. The case is incorrectly labeled "Contra Francesco Rivoltela." The name of the accused is, in fact, Zuane [da] Rivoltela.

43. ASV, *PSM*, B. 264, 1612, S. Girolamo.

44. ASV, *PSM*, B. 264, 1611, S. Caterina.

45. ASV, *PSM*, B. 264, 1612, Ogni Santi.

46. ASV, *PSM*, B. 263, 1554, "Monache di Malamocco" (i.e., S. Maria dell'Orazione).

47. ASV, *PSM*, B. 263, 1569, Celestia.

48. The placard outside Spirito Santo dates from 1653; the example at S. Zaccaria is dated 1620. The text of the latter reads: "IN QUESTO CAMPO NELLA CLAUSURA ENTRO DELLI PORTONI SONO PROHIBITI TUTTI LI GIOCHI IL TUMULTAR STREPITAR DIR PAROLE OBSENE COMMETER DISONESTA FAR IMONDITIE METERVI ALBERI ANTENE ROTAMINE QUALSI VOGLIA ALTRA SORTE DI ROBBE SOTTO GRAVISSIME PENE ET E PER DECRETO DEL' ILLUSTRISSIMI ET ECCELLENTISSIMI SIGNORI ESSECUTORI CONTRA LA BIASTEMA DE XVI LUGLIO ET VIII AGOSTO M.DCXX." U. Franzoi and D. Di Stefano, *Le*

chiese, p. 403, speculate that the *campo* outside S. Zaccaria had a semiprivate character and was probably closed to the public at nighttime.

49. ASV, *PSM,* B. 267, 1621, S. Bernardo di Murano.

50. ASV, *PSM,* B. 264, 1611, Corpus Domini. No verdict survives for this case. In a contemporary trial, a Jew who was charged with singing and making music in a convent parlor was sentenced to two months' imprisonment; ASV, *PSM,* B. 12, January 21, 1611 [m.v.].

51. ASV, *PSM,* B. 264, 1611, S. Anna.

52. ASV, *PSM,* B. 264, 1611, S. Andrea.

53. ASV, *PSM,* B. 264, 1612, S. Maria Maggiore.

54. ASV, *PSM,* B. 264, 1612, S. Giustina.

55. ASV, *PSM,* B. 264, 1611 (case pertains to several convents).

56. R. Derosas, "Moralità e giustizia," especially pp. 433–46.

57. N. S. Davidson, "Theology, nature and the law," pp. 90–92.

58. R. Derosas, "Moralità e giustizia," p. 446.

6. SUSTAINING NETWORKS

1. A. Tarabotti, *Inferno,* p. 101.

2. A. Grimani, *Constitutioni,* cap. XLV.

3. ASV, *PSM,* B. 266, 1620, S. Marta, fo. 20r.

4. A. Grimani, *Constitutioni,* cap. XLV, emphasized the sexual risks of "particular" relationships, whether between nuns or involving outsiders of either sex: "This love and singular affection . . . usually has the worst possible consequence . . . and so you must look out for the signs of this most dangerous affection, called sensual by the saints, since it generally ends up being carnal."

5. ACPV, *Vis. past.,* Priuli, 1592–96, S. Iseppo, 1595, fos. 514v–516r.

6. ACPV, *Vis. past.,* Priuli, 1592–96, S. Giustina, 1595, fo. 471r; ibid., S. Lucia, 1595, fo. 537v.

7. ACPV, *Vis. past.,* Priuli, 1592–96, S. Sepolcro, 1595, fo. 397r. At Le Vergini, the failure of nuns to eat communally in the refectory was judged to be partly to blame for the lax devotional habits of the community: "During summer, the nuns do not go to compline in the evening because they eat in groups of five or six in their cells"; ACPV, *Vis. past.,* Priuli, 1592–96, Vergini, 1596, fo. 589r.

8. ACPV, *Vis. past.,* Vendramin, 1609–18, S. Andrea, 1609.

9. ACPV, *Vis. past.,* Vendramin, 1609–18, S. Zaccaria, 1609.

10. ACPV, *Vis. past.,* Priuli, 1592–96, S. Alvise, 1595, fo. 425v. *Donnette* is

the term used here to disparage those laywomen with whom the young nuns chatted.

11. ACPV, *Vis. past.*, Vendramin, 1609–18, S. Croce, 1611.

12. ACPV, *Vis. past.*, Priuli, 1592–96, S. Maria dei Miracoli, 1595, fo. 369r.

13. Cf. R. Trexler, "Le Célibat," pp. 1341–42, on the custom of sending more than one daughter to the same house, and A. Grimani, *Constitutioni,* cap. XV, on attempts to regulate kinship links in the convents of his diocese.

14. A. Tarabotti, *Inferno,* p. 32.

15. ACPV, *Vis. past.*, Priuli, 1592–96, Ogni Santi, 1594, fo. 261r. G. Zarri notes that nuns' cells were often arranged according to family groupings in her useful section on "Famiglie e 'sette' dentro al monastero," in "Monasteri femminili e città," pp. 386–98. Relevant here is S. Evangelisti, " 'Farne quello che pare e piace, . . .' " regarding nuns' efforts to control the transmission of their cells posthumously through testamentary instructions.

16. Tarabotti's life at S. Anna was rendered tolerable by her friendship with Regina Donà. The two nuns entered the convent simultaneously in 1617, and Tarabotti's letters reveal considerable distress after Regina's death in 1645 (E. Zanette, *Suor Arcangela,* pp. 21, 27).

17. For a full set of patriarchal regulations governing visits to nuns, see L. Priuli, *Ordini.* According to this, fathers, brothers and uncles were the only male relatives admitted to the *parlatorio.* This 1591 list had shrunk from that of 1558, when Vicenzo Diedo, the then patriarch, had named the permitted "degrees of kin" as "father, brothers, uncles . . . nephews, brothers-in-law . . . and cousins," BMC, *Cod. Cic.* 2570, pp. 167–68.

18. A. Tarabotti, *Inferno,* pp. 65–66.

19. ACPV, *Vis. past.*, Priuli, 1592–96, S. Croce della Giudecca, 1595, fo. 494r.

20. ACPV, *Vis. past.*, misc., 1452–1730, SS. Biagio e Cataldo, 1593.

21. ASV, *PSM,* B. 263, 1571, S. Iseppo. Here, several nuns were indignant in response to the lack of respect shown by Suor Deodata for her parents. One commented: "I've never heard her when she isn't speaking ill, and cursing the souls of her father and mother" (fo. 22r). Suor Deodata's case is discussed in full in Chapter 11.

22. ACPV, *Vis. past.*, Priuli, 1592–96, S. Zaccaria, 1596, fo. 577r.

23. BMC, *Cod. Cic.* 2583, 1554, November twenty-sixth: "Novitie non accedant ad Monasteria Monialium." This custom is described in F. Sansovino, *Venetia città nobilissima* (1581 ed.), fo. 153r, in the section entitled "Matrimonii."

24. ACPV, *Vis. past.*, Trevisan, 1560–89, Corpus Domini, 1560, fo. 2v. See

also the prohibition that "Neither weddings nor baptisms should take place in the convent church; nor should marriages be contracted in the convent parlour"; ACPV, *Vis. past.*, B. 1, 1593, SS. Biagio e Cataldo.

25. ASV, *PSM*, B. 265, 1616 [m.v.], S. Maffio di Murano. Another instance of this practice is noted in the case against Alessandro Branazzini, ASV, *PSM*, B. 265, 1618 [m.v.], S. Sepolcro, who apparently first came in contact with the nuns of S. Sepolcro on the occasion of his own wedding: "Accompanied by his bride, Ser Alessandro came [to the convent] in a gondola, and consequently nearly all the nuns came to the window in order to see the bride" (fo. 40r).

26. A. Tarabotti, *Inferno,* p. 66.

27. For example, at S. Zaccaria in 1596, the complaint was made that "certain *converse,* namely Suor Agata and Suor Cipriana, have made substantial wedding gifts to their sisters"; ACPV, *Vis. past.* B. 3, 1596, S. Zaccaria, fo. 578r.

28. ACPV, *Vis. past.,* B. 5, 1610, S. Servolo. Relevant here are the ideas of the anthropologist Marcel Mauss, as laid out in his celebrated "Essai sur le don." From his studies of primitive societies, Mauss observed how gift giving that appears at first to be voluntary, spontaneous and disinterested, reveals itself on closer inspection to be obligatory and self-interested. His ideas have proved influential for studies of this period; see especially N. Z. Davis, *The Gift.* For more on Venetian nunneries and the gift, see J. G. Sperling, *Convents,* passim.

29. ASV, *PSM,* B. 267, 1626, Celestia. Piero and Alvise Pisani transgressed by bringing into the parlor a third man, their friend Antonio Balanzan, who had no family connections at the nunnery; and by eating in the parlor, which was strictly forbidden. Sentenced on July 4, 1626, the two brothers were banned for one year from speaking to any nun from La Celestia, and from entering its parlors or church, without express written license; they were also fined thirty ducats. Antonio Balanzan was banned from going to the church or parlor of La Celestia for five years.

30. ASV, *PSM,* B. 267, 1626, S. Girolamo. See L. Priuli, *Ordine* 8, and A. Grimani, *Constitutioni,* cap. XXIII, for regulations against male religious visiting nuns, regardless of family ties.

31. ASV, *PSM,* B. 265, 1618, S. Anna.

32. ASV, *PSM,* B. 264, 1609, S. Maffio di Murano.

33. Ibid. Recognizing the relatively remote locations of some convents in his diocese, the bishop of Torcello conceded that minimal hospitality might be offered to close relatives of nuns in the convent guest house: here, the food should be consumed "modestly, without noise, or signs of vain gaiety"; A. Grimani, *Constitutioni,* cap. XVIII.

34. ASV, *PSM,* B. 265, 1616 [m.v.], S. Maffio di Murano. *Bozza* was a measure of liquid capacity, equivalent to approximately 2.7 litres; A. Martini, *Manuale,* p. 818.

35. ASV, *PSM,* B. 266, 1621, S. Maffio di Murano. See also *Notarile Testamenti,* B. 94, no. 164, 1646, September fourteenth, for the will of "Paulina Gozi, Relicta del quondam Signor Oratio Coreggio." Paulina made a point of remembering the many nuns to whom she was kin, including a bequest of ten ducats to Suor Crestina Coreggio at San Maffio. Showing her more general concern, she asked her son, Agostino, "to look after the nuns." See also *Notarile Testamenti,* B. 1268, no. 216, September 1, 1661, for the will of "Gio Donato Coreggio quondam Oratio," another of Paulina's sons. He also bequeathed ten ducats to Suor Crestina Coreggio, whom he described as "the natural daughter of Signor Zio Gio. Donato." In other words, one of the girls for whom Paulina was so concerned was the illegitimate daughter of her husband's brother.

36. See BMC, *Cod. Cic.* 2570, pp. 170–71, for Patriarch Trevisan's ruling of January 10, 1564 against eating in the parlor.

37. ASV, *Sant'Andrea de Zirada,* B. 23, fasc. 73; 1605, August twenty-fourth.

38. ASV, *PSM,* B. 265, 1616 [m.v.], S. Maffio di Murano.

7. THE CONVERSATION OF WOMEN

1. A. Valier, *La istituzione,* cap. XIX.

2. B. Sultanini, *Il puttanismo romano,* pp. 96–97.

3. BMC, *Cod. Cic.* 2570, pp. 169–70, 1564, February nineteenth.

4. In 1555, one Donna Andriana testified that once, while her husband was standing trial, she had taken up temporary residence in the convent of S. Giovanni Lateran, "in order to be closer to the judicial palace where she had to go to give witness for her late husband." ASV, *PSM,* B. 263, 1555, S. Giovanni Lateran. The nature of the husband's trial is not specified here. Presumably, the "palazzo" referred to was the Ducal Palace. On the common practice of laywomen receiving hospitality from Florentine convents in the late fifteenth and early sixteenth centuries, see K. J. P. Lowe, "Female Strategies," p. 219.

5. J. M. Ferraro, "The Power to Decide," cites two cases: Pasquetta Peregrini, in 1584, stayed at S. Maffio di Murano, and subsequently at S. Andrea de Zirada (p. 498); Faustina Gradenici retreated to the convent of S. Anna in 1637 (p. 508).

6. BMC, *Cod. Cic.* 2570, pp. 180–82; 1592, November second: "Ordini per le figliuole a spese." See also A. Grimani, *Constitutioni,* cap. XIV.

7. ACPV, *Vis. past.*, Priuli, 1592–96, S. Marta, 1594, fo. 184v.

8. V. Hunecke, "Kindbett," pp. 457–59, points to the proliferation of *educande* in Venetian convents during the seventeenth and eighteenth centuries. He argues that, by the eighteenth century, it was standard for noble girls to live in convents as *educande* prior to their marriage. P. Grendler, *Schooling,* pp. 96–100, notes the very basic nature of the education offered to *educande* and affirms that they could be a disruptive presence in the nunnery. On the other hand, he suggests that these girls were valued by the nuns for their "youthful joy and energy."

9. ACPV, *Vis. past.*, Vendramin, 1609–18, S. Servolo, 1610.

10. For example, in 1558 Suor Raphaela Balbi, a young nun at San Bernardo di Murano, was discovered to have admitted into her cell a Paduan girl, Laura Cumeni, previously a boarder at the convent. Fearful of punishment, Raphaela fled, making her way to the house of Madonna Helena Foscarini, another lay acquaintance who had also once lodged with the nuns; ASV, *PSM,* B. 263, 1558, S. Bernardo di Murano.

11. A. Grimani, *Constitutioni,* cap. XIV: "The custom of taking in boarding girls is an acceptable part of a convent's business."

12. B. Buommattei, *Modo di consecrar le vergini,* pp. 4–5.

13. ASV, *PSM,* B. 263, 1555, S. Giovanni Lateran. Following the escape of Suor Faustina from the convent, it was reported that "the door-keeper, who is a *conversa,* and who has had a husband, believes that Faustina is pregnant." The remark is revealing of the worldly knowledge that a widow might have been expected to possess.

14. G. Dominici, *Lettere,* pp. 295–330. The necrology covers the period 1394–1436.

15. *Bullarium diplomatum,* VII, pp. 447–50. *Converse* had in the past been given the option of taking either solemn vows or simple vows. This situation potentially contravened the doctrine now being espoused by Pius V that full profession (that is, the taking of solemn vows) necessarily entailed strict enclosure. In view of the practical need for convents to allow certain members occasional access to the outside world, *converse* were permitted to venture beyond the convent walls, but henceforth were not allowed to be professed (R. Creytens, "La riforma," pp. 75–79).

16. A. Grimani, *Constitutioni,* cap. XII.

17. ACPV, *Vis. past.*, misc., 1452–1730, S. Andrea, 1596.

18. ACPV, *Vis. past.*, Priuli, 1592–96, S. Alvise, 1595, fo. 426r.

19. ACPV, *Vis. past.*, Priuli, 1592–96, S. Sepolcro, 1595, fo. 397r.

20. ACPV, *Vis. past.*, Priuli, 1592–96, Corpus Domini, 1595, fo. 559r.

21. ACPV, *Vis. past.*, Priuli, 1592–96, S. Maria Maggiore, 1594, fos 282v–283r.

22. ASV, *PSM*, B. 263, 1565, S. Maria Maggiore.

23. ASV, *PSM*, B. 263, 1555, S. Giovanni Lateran, fo. 12r.

24. Ibid., fo. 7r.

25. ASV, *PSM*, B. 263, 1561 [m.v.], Spirito Santo.

26. ACPV, *Vis. past.*, Priuli, 1592–96, Vergini, 1596, fo. 588r–v.

27. Ibid., fos. 590r–591r.

28. ACPV, *Vis. past.*, Priuli, 1592–96, S. Chiara di Venezia, 1594, fo. 339r. In her study of Neapolitan nuns in the seventeenth century, C. Russo comments on the long-established custom of nuns giving away *cose di zuccaro* ("sugary things") and provides an extensive footnote on the various sweets produced by different convents; *I monasteri femminili*, p. 93.

29. S. Chojnacki, "Patrician Women," pp. 181–83; idem, "La posizione della donna," pp. 68–69.

30. ASV, *PSM*, B. 263, 1566 [m.v.], S. Andrea.

31. Ibid.

32. Ibid., fo. 2v.

33. Ibid., fo. 8r.

34. Ibid., fo. 2v.

35. C. Russo finds that disciplinary transgressions at Neapolitan convents often occurred literally on the edge of enclosure. At the convent of S. Maria Donnaregina, several illicit banquets were reported to have taken place involving nuns and lay folk; on one such occasion, the table was described as having been positioned "in the doorway that led into the convent, so that half of it was inside the enclosure and the other half outside"; *I monasteri femminili*, p. 103.

36. ASV, *PSM*, B. 263, 1566 [m.v.], S. Andrea; fo. 3r–v.

37. Ibid., fo. 13r.

38. ACPV, *Vis. past.*, Trevisan, 1560–89, Corpus Christi, 1560; see also ACPV, *Vis. past.*, Vendramin, 1609–18, SS. Biagio e Cataldo, 1610: "Let no nun dare to tell of the deeds of nuns, or speak of the convent, to members of the laity, not even to their relatives, but only to the prelate; under pain of being deprived of the parlours for six months." Note also ASV, *PSM*, B. 263, 1567, S. Sepolcro, fo. 54r: Following the removal of abbess Michaela Beltrame from office, Michaela's sister was imprisoned in her cell "because she went about telling everything to seculars."

39. A. Grimani, *Constitutioni*, cap. LXXX.

40. ASV, *PSM*, B. 263, 1566 [m.v.], S. Andrea; fo. 11v.

41. Ibid., fo. 2r.

42. Note also ASV, *PSM*, B. 264, 1612, Spirito Santo: Malipiera Malipiero, who frequented the parlor, was accused of kissing nuns and lending them clothes and jewelry during carnival.

43. ASV, *PSM*, B. 163, 1566 [m.v.], S. Andrea; fo. 12r.

44. ASV, *PSM*, B. 263, 1568, S. Andrea.

45. See also ACPV, *Vis. past.*, misc. B, 1452–1730, SS. Biagio e Cataldo, 1593. Here the women who served the convent all lived locally, and were the recipients of food from the nuns.

46. ASV, *PSM*, B. 265, 1617, S. Caterina.

47. ASV, *PSM*, B. 267, 1621, S. Servolo.

48. ASV, *PSM*, B. 264, 1612, Spirito Santo. In a more standard incident, a prostitute by name of Lugretia was charged in 1625 with speaking to nuns in the parlor of Le Celestia, and for "making an uproarious din"; ASV, *PSM*, B. 267, 1624 [m.v.], Celestia.

49. ASV, *PSM*, B. 267, 1626, S. Servolo.

50. The historian Dennis Romano has argued that "patrician men and women operated at the helms of two different patronage systems that were closely linked to notions of male and female space. Male patronage was citywide, highly institutionalized, and focused on the councils of government. . . . Female patronage, by contrast, was parochial, private and highly personal"; *Patricians and Popolani*, p. 120.

8. CARNIVAL IN THE CLOISTER

1. E. Muir, *Civic Ritual*, pp. 160–61.

2. Ibid., pp. 162–64.

3. For a broader picture of the Venetian Carnival, see ibid., pp. 156–81; P. Burke, *Historical Anthropology*, pp. 183–90; G. Ruggiero, *Binding Passions*, pp. 3–23.

4. ACPV, *Vis. past.*, Trevisan, 1560–89, 1588, fo. 83v.

5. At the convent of Corpus Christi in 1560, the nuns were instructed not to give presents within or without the convent on the feast of S. Martino; ACPV, *Vis. past.*, Trevisan, 1560–89, Corpus Christi, 1560, fo. 2v. Following a visitation of 1596 to Le Vergini, Priuli told the nuns "that they must cease to celebrate the September feast of the Birth of the Virgin with a lavish meal, on which they are accustomed to spend a large amount of money"; ACPV, *Vis. past.*, Priuli, 1592–96, Vergini, 1596, fo. 589r. In 1611, certain nuns of S. Marta themselves complained to the magistrates con-

cerning "the music-making which occurred on the evening of San Pietro, close to the said convent"; ASV, *PSM,* B. 264, 1611, S. Marta.

6. It is not possible to posit any more concrete statistical link since 1) not all transgressions occurring during Carnival would have been related to the festivities; 2) although we know the dates of the trials, sometimes there is ambiguity about the exact date of the disciplinary lapse; it might have taken time for the case to come to court. The variety of visitors, from close family to total strangers, attracted to convents during Carnival is indicated by Trevisan in his "Mandatum generale" of 1574, ACPV, *Vis. past.,* Trevisan, 1560–89, fo. 45r–v; banned from entering, eating, singing and dancing in the parlor were "fathers, mothers, brothers, sisters, masked revelers, clowns, singers, musicians and other similar sorts of people, on whatever pretext."

7. For the regulations concerning drama that were imposed on Italian convents elsewhere, see E. Weaver, "The Convent Wall," especially pp. 74–75.

8. BMC, *Cod. Cic.* 2570, pp. 182–83, 1593, January fifteenth. See also A. Grimani, *Constitutioni,* cap. XLVIII, for an even more grudging attitude to convent drama: "Regarding the plays which it is customary on occasion for nuns to put on, it would be much better if they abstained from them altogether, as we strongly exhort them to do; but if they have to admit them for honest recreation, we shall tolerate them, so long as they are stories from holy scripture, or from the lives of the saints; and no nun may presume to wear secular dress, whether male or female, nor is it permissible to wear masks or beards, under pain of the suspension of the abbess for one year."

9. ACPV, *Vis. past.,* Priuli, 1592–96, Miracoli, 1595, fo. 369r.

10. E. Weaver, "The Convent Wall," especially pp. 76, 83.

11. By contrast, E. Weaver comments of Tuscan nuns that "for the most part the audience was the convent community"; "Spiritual Fun," pp. 179–80.

12. ACPV, *Vis. past.,* Priuli, 1592–96, S. Sepolcro, 1595, fo. 398v.

13. ACPV, *Vis. past.,* Vendramin, 1609–18, S. Girolamo, 1609.

14. ASV, *PSM,* B. 263, 1570, S. Servolo, fo. 9r. This case is discussed in detail in Chapter 10.

15. Ibid., fo. 5v.

16. ACPV, *Vis. past.,* Tiepolo, 1620–27, S. Lorenzo, 1622.

17. ASV, *PSM,* B. 265, 1614, S. Zaccaria, fo. 5v.

18. Ibid., fo. 10v.

19. Ibid., fos. 12v–13r.

20. ASV, *PSM,* B. 265, 1616 [m.v.], Celestia.

21. N. Z. Davis, "Women on Top," provides insightful discussion of the cultural functions of sexual inversion and cross-dressing. She challenges the view that sexual inversion necessarily reinforced hierarchy, and perceives subversive possibilities for changing sexual status; see especially pp. 130–31.

22. ASV, *PSM,* B. 267, 1626, S. Maria dell'Orazione di Malamocco, fo. 4r.

23. ACPV, *Vis. past.,* Vendramin, 1609–18, S. Servolo, 1610.

24. In August 1575, the papal nuncio Giambattista Castagna complained that on holidays the Venetians "are accustomed to spend the day out with their wives and daughters on these little islands, where the only cover is a convent, and there they pursue their recreations in the cloisters and gardens," *Nunziature,* vol. 11, p. 401. These remarks probably referred to both male and female houses.

9. CRIMES OF SACRILEGE

1. P. Aretino, *Dialogues,* p. 11.

2. Ibid., p. 34.

3. G. Priuli, *I diarii,* II, p. 115; 1501, March twenty-first.

4. Ibid., IV, p. 34; 1509, June sixth.

5. Ibid., p. 115; 1509, June twenty-ninth.

6. Conversely, in the same period (at least in England and in Germany), "nunnery" and "nun" in slang could be used to refer to brothel and whore; see R. Levin, "More Nuns."

7. M. Sanuto, *Diarii,* I, col. 836.

8. Cited by P. Tacchi-Venturi, *Storia,* I, p. 81.

9. ASV, *PSM,* B. 263, 1564, S. Maffio di Mazzorbo. For a gloss on this passage, see G. Lorenzi, *Leggi,* p. 290, notes b and c.

10. ASV, *PSM,* B. 266, 1620, S. Servolo.

11. ASV, *PSM,* B. 266, 1620, S. Vido di Burano.

12. The Convertite and the Zitelle were both situated on the Giudecca; the Soccorso, reputedly founded by the poet Veronica Franco, was in Dorsoduro, on the Fondamenta di Santa Margarita.

13. G. Priuli, *I diarii,* IV, p. 34; 1509, June sixth.

14. ASV, *PSM,* B. 260, 1612, December third.

15. ASV, *PSM,* B. 1, fos 25v–26r, 1551, November nineteenth.

16. M. Ferro, *Dizionari,* pp. 287–91, especially pp. 289–90.

17. G. Ruggiero, *Boundaries,* pp. 70–88.

18. Ibid., p. 73. The accusation of incest (as Ruggiero explains, p. 74) was premised on the notion that God was both father to all men and the spouse

of all nuns: A man copulating with a nun would therefore be guilty of incest with his father's wife. G. S. Daichman, "Misconduct," p. 104, gives a
more limited definition of spiritual incest as "intercourse between persons
who were both under ecclesiastical vows and thus in the relation of spiritual father and daughter, or brother and sister." However, she goes on to
quote from a fourteenth-century source that undermines her own definition and rather endorses Ruggiero's: "He who corrupteth a nun com-
miteth incest for she is the bride of God, who is our Father." The Vianaro
case set the tone for the fifteenth century, a period in which stern legislation was followed up by action in the courts. In 1455 and 1486, the *Maggior
Consiglio* passed further legislation. See R. Canosa, *Il velo*, pp. 29–44, for a
whistle-stop tour of trials conducted against *monachini* during the fifteenth
century.

19. The first legislation against fornication with nuns was passed in 1349
and was drafted in conspicuously pious language, clearly invoking the concept of divine offense. It may be significant that this provision was made in
the wake of the Black Death of 1348.

20. M. Sanuto, *Diarii,* VIII, col. 454 and ff.

21. ASV, *PSM,* B. 1, fos 1v–4v; 1514, 9 August, Cons. X.

22. The 1509 laws may perhaps be construed as panic legislation, since
they followed so quickly after Agnadello. From 1514, in place of perpetual
banishment, those who fornicated with nuns were subject to a fine of two
hundred ducats, imprisonment for one year and two years' exile. Nobles
were then deprived from holding office for a further year, which was sub-
stituted by an additional year's exile for "cittadini o forestieri" ("citizens or
foreigners"—the absence of *popolani* is noteworthy). Those found guilty of
entering a convent were subject to the same penalties as above (instead of
the ten years' exile prescribed in 1509). Those who led nuns out of the convent were liable to a fine of one hundred ducats, one year's imprisonment
and a year's deprivation of office, or alternatively, two years' exile for citizens and foreigners. (According to the 1509 legislation, these transgressors
would have been subject to the same penalties as those guilty of *sacrilegio*.)
Boatmen guilty of transporting nuns from their convents were liable to a
more obvious increase in punishment: Instead of the six months' imprisonment laid down in 1509, they were to be fined one hundred "lire de pic-
coli" and banished for three years.

23. ASV, *PSM,* B. 1, fos 28v–29v; 1566, 29 March, Cons. X.

24. ASV, *PSM,* B. 1, fos 39r–41v; 1604, 7 February [m.v.], Cons. X.

25. A close analysis of trial records up to 1650 suggests that the death
penalty was never employed during this period for this crime.

26. See ASV, *PSM,* B. 347 and G. Lorenzi, *Leggi,* pp. 307–39, for the case of 1604 against Francesco Badoer, a nobleman, and Piero Pellegrini, secretary to the Council of Ten, accused of having unlawfully entered the convent of San Daniel. At the end of a lengthy trial lasting from March until September, the two men were absolved by the Council of Ten, presumably as a result of their political prominence and their connections. The concern of the Ten to avoid scandal was made clear by its decision to conceal the documentation: "The trials which were conducted against Ser Francesco Badoer and Ser Andrea and the circumspect and most faithful Secretary of this Council Piero Pellegrini, concerning the matter of the nuns of San Daniel of this city, shall—for reasons well known to this Council—be sealed and bound and put in the Office of the State Inquisitors, from which Office they may never be removed, nor at any time may they be unsealed nor seen, unless by a ruling of this Council, taken by ballot and requiring a two-thirds majority"; Lorenzi, p. 339.

27. See ASV, *PSM,* B. 264, for a cluster of cases around 1610 which crack down on minor breaches of enclosure.

28. ASV, *PSM,* B. 267. During the period 1625–26, there was a total of forty-seven trials, of which twenty-nine were directed against laymen, ten against laywomen, and four against clergy. Three out of four of the remaining cases were investigations into disorder at convents, and were not focused on particular individuals; the one other case concerned an attack on an official of the convent magistracy and did not involve nuns. Twenty-seven out of twenty-nine cases against laymen resulted from accusations of illicit contact with nuns. Of the remaining two, one case (1625) was against Giacomo Morato for failure to obtain a license for his niece's clothing ceremony at San Antonio di Torcello, and the other (1626), relating to San Maffio di Mazzorbo, was against "some men who had stolen chickens from the nuns."

29. ASV, *PSM,* B. 267, 1626, S. Caterina di Mazzorbo.

30. ASV, *PSM,* B. 267, 1626, Convertite.

31. Ibid.; 1625, S. Anna.

32. ASV, *PSM,* B. 267, 1625, S. Sepolcro; the event took place "in the little alley next to the convent of San Sepolcro, which runs down to the canal."

33. ASV, *PSM,* B. 267, 1625 [m.v.], S. Sepolcro.

34. R. Canosa, *Il velo,* p. 11.

35. Examples of reoffenders, all taken from ASV, *PSM:* Vicenzo Trevisan (B. 265, 1614, S. Antonio di Torcello; B. 267, 1621, S. Antonio di Torcello; B. 268, 1627 [m.v.], S. Antonio di Torcello) discussed below; Antonio Giustin-

ian (B. 265, 1617, S. Maria dell'Orazione; ibid., 1617, S. Servolo); Polo Loredan (B. 265, 1616 [m.v.], Celestia; B. 267, 1625, Celestia); Nicolo da Molin (B. 267, 1624, Celestia; ibid., 1624 [m.v.], Celestia); Marc'Antonio Santurini (B. 268, 1626 [m.v.], S. Sepolcro; ibid., 1626 [m.v.], S. Sepolcro; ibid., 1627, S. Sepolcro).

36. ASV, *PSM*, B. 264, 1608 [m.v.], S. Daniel.

37. ASV, *PSM*, B. 266, 1620, S. Giovanni Lateran.

38. ASV, *PSM*, B. 264. 1611, fos. 2v–3r.

39. ASV, *PSM*, B. 266, 1619, SS. Marco e Andrea.

40. ACPV, *Vis. past.*, Priuli, 1592–96,Vergini, 1596, fo. 589r.

41. ASV, *PSM*, B. 265, 1614, S. Antonio di Torcello, fo. 4v:Vicenzo Trevisan was accused of eating, drinking and dancing with the nuns of San Antonio di Torcello, as if the nunnery were "a public brothel."

42. ASV, *PSM*, B. 267, 1621, S. Antonio di Torcello.

43. ASV, *PSM*, B. 265, 1618 [m.v.], S. Sepolcro, fo. 18r.

44. Ibid., fo. 24v.

45. ASV, *PSM*, B. 267, 1624 [m.v.], S. Maffio di Murano. Of Zuan Paolo Horologio, a man of around thirty years old, it was claimed, "One evening during Carnival, he stayed until one hour after dark at San Maffio di Murano, playing the lover."

46. ASV, *PSM*, B. 265, 1616 [m.v.], Celestia.

47. ASV, *PSM*, B. 268, 1630, S. Sepolcro.

48. ASV, *PSM*, B. 268, 1627, S. Sepolcro.

49. ASV, *PSM*, B. 266, 1618 [m.v.], Celestia.

50. ASV, *PSM*, B. 12 contains a series of verdicts mostly deriving from trials otherwise undocumented. Ibid., B. 260 contains a number of denunciations for trials whose records no longer exist.

51. ASV, *PSM*, B. 12. The two documents are, in fact, dated—according to the Venetian calendar—November 30 and January 31, 1608.

52. On the *Avogadori di Commun,* see G. Ruggiero, *Boundaries,* p. 5.

53. According to laws of 1584 and 1617, the names of nobles who had transgressed the laws relating to nunneries were to be published in the *Maggior Consiglio;* citizens and *popolani* had their names displayed on the steps of San Marco and of the Rialto. Presumably, Hieronimo's name appeared alongside those of the nobles by virtue of his important official position. The same laws also stressed that the convents should not be identified.

54. ASV, *PSM*, B. 12, 1608, November thirtieth.

55. ASV, *PSM*, B. 12, 1608 [m.v.], January thirty-first.

56. G. Ruggiero, *Violence,* p. 169.

57. R. Canosa, *Il velo,* p. 226.

58. H. Wotton, *Life and Letters,* p. 438.

59. S. Chojnacki, "Subaltern Patriarchs," p. 78.

60. On the cultural impact of nonmarriage and late marriage on Venetian men, see G. Ruggiero, *Violence,* and S. Chojnacki, "Subaltern Patriarchs." A burgeoning literature on sexuality also helps to shed light on the bachelor experience, leaving us in little doubt that the sexual and emotional urges of Venetian men found vent in extramarital relationships, notably sex with prostitutes and sex with men. See N. S. Davidson, "Theology and the Law" and E. Pavan, "Police des moeurs."

61. G. Ruggiero, *Boundaries,* p. 80.

10. BETWEEN CELIBATES

1. G. B. Intra, "Di Ippolito Capilupi," pp. 102–107. Letters to Cardinal Borromeo, papal secretary, from Ippolito Capilupi, bishop of Fano and papal nuncio to Venice; November 9 and 15, 1561.

2. Ibid., p. 103. (The figure of 400 used in Capilupi's account is possibly an exaggeration. According to the 1581 census, there were 238 nuns at the Convertite (B.M.C., Ms. P.D. 230 b-II); at the time of the 1593 patriarchal visitation, there were apparently 214 choir nuns and 27 *converse* (ACPV, *Vis past.,* Priuli, 1592–96, fo. 84r). However, in a second letter to Cardinal Borromeo of November 15, 1561, Capilupi noted the expulsion of 90–100 nuns from the Convertite following the scandal, and although this figure may also be an exaggeration, a subsequent decline in numbers might be expected; G. B. Intra, p. 107.

3. Ibid., pp. 103–04.

4. Ibid., p. 104.

5. Stephen Haliczer's study of *Sexuality in the Confessional* in Spain during this period provides excellent analysis of the sexual hold confessors exercised over female penitents. He emphasizes the particular vulnerability of nuns to the advances of their confessors, and the heightened sexual tensions that resulted from the imposition of enclosure: "The pressure for strict enclosure meant that in many female houses the confessor was almost the only male figure with whom the nun could interact, apart from the occasional relative. The relationship between nun and confessor, moreover, was no ordinary one, as the nun revealed all her thoughts, feelings, and temptations to this man who, for his part, was presented as an exalted figure of learning and authority [. . .] This excessive familiarity [. . .] could transform the nature of the relationship from spiritual to sensual" (pp. 89–90).

6. G. B. Intra, "Di Ippolito Capilupi," p. 105.

7. Ibid., p. 104.

8. Ibid., p. 103.

9. Ibid., p. 104.

10. Ibid., p. 103.

11. Ibid., p. 105. On November 15, 1561, Capilupi wrote a postscript to this tale, relating how two days earlier ninety to a hundred nuns had left the convent (see above, note 2), with the consent of the Venetian government (p. 107). The prioress of the Convertite, Suor Petronilla, was subsequently put in the prisons of the *Capi dei Dieci* (Heads of the Ten). Her name appears in an Inquisition case of 1562, when she was questioned about her request that two Protestants be removed from the prison; ASV, *Santo Ufficio,* B. 18, "Gherlandi Giulio." I am grateful to N. S. Davidson for this reference.

12. ASV, *PSM,* B. 265, 1618, S. Bernardo di Murano and S. Giacomo di Murano.

13. G. B. Intra, "Di Ippolito Capilupi," p. 106.

14. Included in this total are a few cases where the priest was not the specific object of the trial, although his misconduct was, in fact, central to the investigation. For example, ASV, *PSM,* B. 267, 1624, Convertite, trial of Lucia, an employee of the nuns, who was brought before the magistrates for her role in conveying gifts from Prete Francesco Montenegro to one of the nuns.

15. In the year 1581, there were recorded as resident in the city of Venice, 2,508 nuns, 1,132 monks and friars, and 586 priests; B.M.C., MS. P.D. 230 b-II, "Descrition de tutte le aneme che sono in la Cita fata l'anno 1581." The figure of 1,132 is the sum of 945 *frati* and 187 *poveri mendicanti.* These statistics exclude religious men and women living on the lagoon islands.

16. ASV, *PSM,* B. 265, 1617 [m.v.], Celestia.

17. ASV, *PSM,* B. 266, 1620, S. Maria Maggiore.

18. ASV, *PSM,* B. 266, 1619, S. Moro di Burano.

19. ASV, *PSM,* B. 265, 1614, S. Chiara, SS. Rocco & Margarita, S. Maffio di Mazzorbo.

20. ASV, *PSM,* B. 265, 1616 [m.v.], Celestia, S. Daniel.

21. ASV, *PSM,* B. 265, 1616 [m.v.], S. Daniel.

22. Ibid., fos. 17v–18r.

23. Ibid., unnumbered folio. The complete madrigal and letter read as follows: "Love me little Barbara / Love my heart that longs / To love only one who loves it; / According to the law of loving / And amongst others the greatest / Is to return love for love. As my sweetest treasure, my one contentment, never have my eyes seen such another creature, who any-

where could equal your heavenly gifts; so at this time another rose similar to these I send you might seem to some. Enjoy them, therefore, my treasure, and remember that if they should wither in leaving my hand, yours, which wear them on your breast, will revive them to the state that they were in when they were with me, so they will serve to kiss you. Farewell my only treasure."

24. Ibid., fo. 30r.

25. Ibid., fo. 19v.

26. Ibid., fo. 3v.

27. Ibid., unnumbered folio.

28. ASV, *PSM,* B. 265, 1616 [m.v.], Celestia, S. Daniel.

29. ASV, *PSM,* B. 267, 1624, Convertite.

30. ASV, *PSM,* B. 265, 1617, S. Anna.

31. ASV, *PSM,* B. 267, 1626, S. Maria dell'Orazione di Malamocco, fo. 24r.

32. ASV, *PSM,* B. 1556, S. Giovanni Lateran.

33. ASV, *PSM,* B. 265, 1614, S. Bernardo di Murano.

34. ASV, *PSM,* B. 265, 1616 [m.v.], S. Daniel, fos. 18v and 39v.

35. Ibid., fo. 19r.

36. Ibid., fo. 12v.

37. ASV, *PSM,* B. 266, 1620, S. Chiara di Murano.

38. ASV, *PSM,* B. 263, 1570, S. Servolo, fo. 9v.

39. Ibid., fos. 1v–2r.

40. Ibid., fo. 8v.

41. ASV, *PSM,* B. 266, 1619, S. Maria degli Angeli, fo. 1r.

42. Ibid., unnumbered folio.

43. Ibid., fo. 15r.

44. Ibid., fo. 46r.

45. Ibid., unnumbered folio. This document constitutes the initial statement against Domenego, which is probably derived from the unreliable testimony of Nicolo Baruzzi.

46. Ibid., fo. 85r.

47. Ibid., fo. 7r.

II. CHASTITY AND DESIRE

1. ASV, *PSM,* B. 265, 1614, S. Zaccaria, fo. 9r.

2. ASV, *Notarile Testamenti,* Atti Nicolò Cigrini, B. 198, test. 112, 25 February 1574, for the will of Laura's mother, Beatrise Batagia.

3. ASV, *PSM,* B. 265, 1614, S. Zaccaria, fo. 9r–v.

4. Ibid., fo. 9v.

5. Ibid., fo. 3v.

6. Ibid., fo. 5v.

7. Ibid., fo. 10r.

8. Ibid.

9. Ibid., fo. 10v.

10. Ibid., fo. 39v. The exceptional reference to the possible use of torture to extract confessions from nuns is made in the following instruction, which emanated from the Council of Ten and was dated August 13, 1614: "Since it is necessary in the service of justice and for the continuation of the trial, undertaken by the *provveditori sopra monasteri,* regarding the events which took place at the convent of San Zaccaria, to have the persons of Suor Laura Querini, nun, and Suor Zaccaria, *conversa,* who however are to be found at this convent, let it be made known to the Patriarch by means of these same *provveditori* that it is the will of this Council that the aforementioned nuns be removed from there and placed at the disposal of the said *provveditori* who, with the assistance of the Most Reverend Patriarch or his vicar, will have to summon them again and, if necessary, torture them, in order to bring thoroughly to light those who have committed these crimes with them, in order that they might be given due punishment, offering to His Most Reverend Lordship the secular arm for the aforementioned examination"; ibid., unnumbered folio preceding 39r. In the event, torture was not used, nor were the nuns removed from their nunnery for questioning.

11. Ibid., unnumbered folio, September 15, 1614.

12. ASVat, *Nunziatura di Venezia,* B. 42A, fo. 130r.

13. G. Boccaccio, *Decameron,* p. 182 (terza giornata, novella 1).

14. P. Aretino, *Dialogues,* p. 16.

15. Ibid., p. 49.

16. On contemporary perceptions of female sexuality, and particularly the unruly lusts of women, see M. E. Wiesner, *Women and Gender,* pp. 46–56 (esp. 48); O. Hufton, *Prospect,* pp. 36–46 (especially 41, 45–6); L. Roper, *Oedipus and the Devil,* p. 93; A. Fletcher, *Gender,* pp. 48–59.

17. G. Priuli, *I diarii,* II, p. 115: 1501, March 21.

18. A. Tarabotti, *Inferno,* p. 71.

19. P. Tacchi-Venturi, *Storia,* p. 87; P. Paschini, "I monasteri femminili," p. 37; O. M. T. Logan, "Studies," p. 362; C. Russo, *I monasteri femminili,* p. 121; E. Cattaneo, "Le monacazioni forzate," passim; G. S. Daichman, "Misconduct," p. 98.

20. R. Canosa, *Il velo,* pp. 10–11.

21. I. Giuliani, "Genesi," p. 345; P. Paschini, "I monasteri femminili," p. 31.

22. G. Ruggiero, *Boundaries,* p. 78. G. Spinelli, "I religiosi," also attempts to rank convents according to the number of appearances they make in the trials, but importantly he concedes that often the nuns themselves were not accused: "spesso le monache non erano affatto imputate" (p. 197).

23. ASV, *PSM,* B. 263, 1564, S. Maffio di Mazzorbo.

24. See J. C. Brown, *Immodest Acts,* a study of Benedetta Carlini, abbess of a Theatine community in seventeenth-century Pescia. Her sexual acts with another nun were recorded in some detail in trial documents.

25. ACPV, *Vis past.,* Priuli, 1592–96, S. Marta, 1594, fo. 184v.

26. ACPV, *Vis past.,* Priuli, 1592–96, S. Croce della Giudecca, 1595, fo. 493v.

27. ACPV, *Vis past.,* Tiepolo, 1620–27, S. Iseppo, 1626.

28. ASV, *PSM,* B. 264, 1612, Spirito Santo.

29. ASV, *PSM,* B. 263, 1570 [m.v.], S. Iseppo.

30. A copy of the patriarchal trial may be found among the records of the magistrates; see ASV, *PSM,* B. 263, 1571, S. Iseppo.

31. ASV, *PSM,* B. 263, 1570 [m.v.], S. Iseppo.

32. ASV, *PSM,* B. 263, 1571, S. Iseppo, fo. 3r.

33. Ibid., fos. 3r–4r.

34. ASV, *PSM,* B. 263, 1570 [m.v.], S. Iseppo.

35. Ibid.

36. ASV, *PSM,* B. 263, 1571, S. Iseppo, fo. 2r.

37. Ibid., fo. 5r.

38. Ibid., fo. 1v.

39. ASV, *PSM,* B. 263, 1571, S. Iseppo, fo. 2r–v.

40. Ibid., fo. 6v.

41. Ibid., fo. 8v.

42. Ibid., fos. 12v–13r.

43. Ibid., fo. 19v.

44. Ibid., fo. 23v.

45. Ibid., fo. 90r–v.

46. Ibid., fo. 24r.

47. Ibid., fo. 47r.

48. Ibid., fo. 30r.

49. Ibid., fo. 115r.

50. Ibid., fo. 2r.

51. Ibid., fo. 39r.

52. Ibid., fos. 79v–80r.

53. Ibid., fo. 82r.

54. Ibid., fo. 103v.

55. Ibid., fo. 82v.

56. Ibid., fo 41r.

57. ASV, *PSM,* 1570 [m.v.], S. Iseppo.

58. The remarks of L. Faderman, *Surpassing,* on relationships between women prior to the twentieth century provide useful analogies. She argues that "romantic love and sexual impulse were often considered unrelated," and insists on the seriousness of relationships between women even when they were probably not genital. See especially pp. 18–19.

EPILOGUE

1. The attribution of the Guardi painting, held at the Museum of Ca' Rezzonico and thought to portray the parlor of San Zaccaria, is questionable. Art historians differ as to whether it is the work of Giovanni Antonio Guardi or of his younger brother Francesco. On Tiepolo's painting, see J. Gardner, "Nuns and Altarpieces," p. 56.

2. ASV, *PSM,* B. 278, S. Alvise, 1750.

3. F. Agostini, *La riforma napoleonica.* An earlier bout of suppressions had taken place in 1763, as part of the reforms initiated by the Venetian statesman Andrea Tron.

4. B. Bertoli, "La chiesa veneziana," p. 194.

5. D. Laven, *Venice and Venetia.*

List of Convents in Venice and the Lagoon
(in order of foundation)

V = Venice *sestiere*

Convent	Location	Order	Foundation
S. Giovanni Evangelista	Torcello	Benedictine	640
S. Zaccaria	V–Castello	Benedictine	809–827
S. Lorenzo	V–Castello	Benedictine	854
S. Eufemia	Mazzorbo	Benedictine	900
S. Secondo	island nr Mestre	Benedictine	1034; closed in 1521; nuns to SS. Cosma e Damiano
S. Servolo	island of S. Servolo; moved to Cannaregio in 1615	Benedictine	1109
S. Giacomo di Paludo	nr Mazzorbo	Cistercian	mid 12th century; closed in 1441; nuns to S. Margarita, Torcello
S. Maria degli Angeli	Murano	Augustinian	1187
S. Angelo	Ammiana	Benedictine	1195; closed in 1438; nuns to S. Eufemia, Mazzorbo
S. Adriano	Costanziaca	Benedictine	12th century; closed 14th century; nuns to S. Girolamo

Convent	Location	Order	Foundation
SS. Filippo e Giacomo	Ammiana	Benedictine	1210; closed mid 14th century; nuns to S. Antonio, Torcello
S. Mauro	Burano	Benedictine	1214
S. Maffio	Costanziaca; moved to Mazzorbo in 1298	Cistercian	1218
SS. Biagio e Cataldo	V–Giudecca	Benedictine	1222
S. Maria delle Vergini (Le Vergini)	V–Castello	Augustinian	1224
S. Chiara	V–S. Croce	Franciscan	1236
S. Maria della Celestia (La Celestia)	V–Castello	Cistercian	1237
S. Margarita	Torcello	Cistercian	before 1244; closed in 1521; nuns to S. Maffio, Mazzorbo
S. Antonio Abate	Torcello	Benedictine	1246
S. Maffio	Murano	Benedictine	1280
S. Maria della Valverde	Mazzorbo	Cistercian → Benedictine (14th century)	1281
S. Caterina	V–Cannaregio	Augustinian	1288
S. Caterina	Mazzorbo	Benedictine	1291
S. Anna	V–Castello	Benedictine	c. 1300
S. Chiara	Murano	Benedictine → Franciscan (1440)	c. 1300

Convent	Location	Order	Foundation
S. Marta	V–Dorsoduro	Benedictine → Augustinian (1520s)	1318
S. Croce	V–Giudecca	Benedictine	before 1328
S. Giacomo	Murano	Augustinian	1330
S. Andrea de Zirada	V–S. Croce	Augustinian	1347
S. Bernardo	Murano	Augustinian	1362
S. Girolamo	V–Cannaregio	Augustinian	1375
S. Alvise	V–Cannaregio	Augustinian	1388
Corpus Domini	V–Cannaregio	Benedictine → Dominican (1394)	late 14th century
S. Lorenzo	Ammiana	Benedictine	foundation unknown; closed 14th century; nuns to S. Marta
SS. Giovanni e Paolo	Costanziaca	Benedictine	foundation unknown; closed 14th century; nuns to S. Antonio, Torcello
SS. Marco e Cristina	Ammiana	Benedictine	foundation unknown; closed in 1432; nuns to S. Antonio, Torcello
S. Daniel	V–Castello	Augustinian	1437
S. Giustina	V–Castello	Augustinian	1448
S. Croce	V–S. Croce	Franciscan	1470
Ogni Santi	V–Dorsoduro	Cistercian → Benedictine (1494)	1472

Convent	Location	Order	Foundation
S. Angelo	Contorta (nr Giudecca)	Benedictine	foundation unknown; closed in 1474
S. Lucia	V-Cannaregio	Augustinian	1476
S. Maria dei Miracoli	V-Castello	Franciscan	1480s
SS. Cosma e Damiano	V-Giudecca	Benedictine	1481
Spirito Santo	V-Dorsoduro	Augustinian	1483
SS. Rocco e Margarita	V-S. Marco	Augustinian	1488
S. Sepolcro	V-Castello	Franciscan	1493
SS. Marco e Andrea	Murano	Benedictine	1496
S. Maria Maggiore	V-S. Croce	Franciscan	1497
S. Martin	Murano	Augustinian	1501
S. Giovanni Lateran	V-Castello	Augustinian → Benedictine (1551)	1505
S. Maria dell' Orazione	Malamocco	Augustinian	1511
S. Iseppo	V-Castello	Augustinian	1512
S. Vito	Burano	Benedictine	1516
Le Convertite	V-Giudecca	Augustinian	1551
S. Maria del Redentore	V-Cannaregio	Capuchin	1605
S. Giorgio dei Greci	V-Cannaregio	Basiliane	1609

Convent	Location	Order	Foundation
S. Maria delle Grazie	Burano	Servite	1619
Gesù e Maria	V–S. Croce	Augustinian	1623
S. Maria del Pianto	V–Castello	Servite	1646
S. Teresa	V–Dorsoduro	Carmelite	1647
S. Maria delle Grazie	island nr S. Giorgio Maggiore	Capuchin	1671
S. Maria delle Grazie	Mazzorbo	Capuchin	1685

Sources: Da Mosto, Franzoi and Di Stefano; cf Pullan, *Rich and Poor,* pp. 377–79, on the foundation of the Convertite, Da Carmignano on the Capuchins in Venice.

Bibliography

Primary Sources

Manuscript and Archival Sources

ARCHIVIO DELLA CURIA PATRIARCALE DI VENEZIA

Visite pastorali a monasteri femminili:
Miscellaneous, 1452–1730
Patriarch Trevisan, 1560–89
Patriarch Priuli, 1592–96
Patriarch Vendramin, 1609–18
Patriarch Tiepolo, 1620–27
Episcopato di Torcello, Criminalia monialium 1600–89.
Atti patriarcali riguardanti le monache.

ARCHIVIO DI STATO DI VENEZIA

Compilazione Leggi
Consultori in Iure
Miscellanea Codici
Notarile Testamenti
Provveditori sopra monasteri
Sant'Andrea de Zirada
San Bernardo di Murano
Santa Croce di Venezia
Santa Marta
Spirito Santo
Senato Terra
Santo Ufficio

BIBLIOTECA MUSEO CORRER, VENEZIA

Codice Cicogna 2570, "Raccolta di documenti relativi alla riforma dei monasteri di monache"; 2583, "Intorno chiese e clero veneto"; 3677, "Relazioni e memorie storiche di Venezia."
MS Correr 317, "Cronica del Monistero delle Vergini di Venetia."
MS P.D. 230 b-II: "Descrition de tutte le aneme che sono in la cita fata l'anno 1581."

BIBLIOTECA NAZIONALE MARCIANA, VENEZIA

MS it. IX-173: 6282.

ISTITUTO DI RICOVERO E DI EDUCAZIONE, VENEZIA

SOC. A1, *Capitolare* (1585?).

ARCHIVIO SEGRETO VATICANO

Nunziatura di Venezia (viewed on microfilm at the Fondazione Cini, Venice).
S. C. Episcoporum et regularium. Positiones 1573–1908.

Printed Works

Alcuni avertimenti nella vita monacale, utili et necessari à ciascheduna Vergine di Christo (Venice, 1575).
Aretino, P., *Sei Giornate,* ed. G. Aquilecchia (Bari, 1969).
———, *Aretino's Dialogues,* trans. R. Rosenthal (London, 1972).
Avertimenti monacali, et modo di viver religiosamente secondo Iddio per le Vergini, et Spose di Giesu Christo (Venice, 1576).
Badoer, G., *Ordo rituum et caeremoniarum tradendi velamina monialibus, Quae jam emiserunt Professionem, vel eodem tempore emittunt* (Venice, 1689).
Boccaccio, G., *Decameron,* ed. V. Branca (Florence, 1976).
Bolognetti, A., "Dello stato et forma delle cose ecclesiastiche nel dominio dei signori venetiani, secondo che furono trovate et lasciate dal nunzio Alberto Bolognetti," in A. Stella, *Chiesa e stato nelle relazioni dei nunzi pontifici a Venezia* (Vatican, 1964).
Bullarium diplomatum et privilegiorum sanctorum romanorum pontificum, 24 vols. (Turin, 1857–85).

Buommattei, B., *Modo di consecrar le vergini, secondo l'uso del pontifical Romano. Con la dichiarazion de' misteri delle Cerimonie, che in quell'azion si fanno* (Venice, 1622).

Constitutioni et regole della casa delle Cittelle di Venetia, eretta, & fondata sotto il titolo della Presentatione della Madonna (Venice, 1649).

Corner, F. (ed.), *Ecclesiae Venetae antiquis monumentis nunc etiam primum editis illustratae ac in decades distributae*, 18 vols. (Venice, 1749).

————, *Ad ecclesias Venetas et Torcellanas documentis illustratas indices duo alter chronologicus diplomatum et documentorum* (Venice, 1749).

Coryat, T., *Coryats Crudities* (London, 1611).

Diderot, D., *The Nun*, trans. L. Tancock (Harmondsworth, 1977).

Dominici, G., *Lettere spirituali*, eds. M. T. Casella and G. Pozzi (Freiburg, 1969).

Erasmus, D., *Collected Works* (Toronto, 1974—).

Ferrazzi, C., *The Autobiography of an Aspiring Saint*, ed. A. Jacobsen Schutte (Chicago, 1996).

Ferro, M., *Dizionari del dritto comune, e veneto*, 10 vols. (Venice, 1778–81).

Franco, G., *Habiti delle donne venetiane intagliate in rame, nuovamente da Giacomo Franco* (Venice, 1610; facsimile edn, Venice, 1990).

Grimani, A., *Constitutioni et decreti approvati nella sinodo diocesana, sopra la retta disciplina monacale* (Venice, 1592).

Loredan, G. F., *Delle lettere*, 2 vols. (Venice, 1687–93).

Lorenzi, G., *Leggi e memorie venete sulla prostituzione* (Venice, 1870–72).

Manzoni, A., *I promessi sposi*, ed. E. Bonora (Turin, 1972).

Nunziature di Venezia, 7 vols to date [I, II, V, VIII, IX, X, XI] (Rome, 1958–).

O'Brien, K., *The Land of Spices* (London, 1988).

Pellizzari, F., S.J., *Manuale regularium* (Lyons, 1653).

Priuli, G., *I diarii;* vol. 1, ed. A. Segre; vols 2 and 4, ed. R. Cessi *Rerum Italicarum Scriptores*, vol. 24, pt 3 (Città di Castello, 1912; Bologna, 1933 and 1938, respectively).

Priuli, L. *Ordini & avvertimenti, che si devono osservare ne' monasteri di monache di Venetia, sopra le visite et clausura* (Venice, 1591).

Sandi, V., *Principi di storia della repubblica di Venezia dalla sua fondazione sino all'anno di N.S. 1700*, 3 vols. (Venice, 1755–56).

Sansovino, F., *Venetia città nobilissima et singolare* (Venice, 1581); *Venetia città* [. . .] *Et hora con molto diligenza corretta, emendata, e più d'un terzo di cose nuove ampliata dal M.R.D. Giovanni Stringa Canonico della Chiesa Ducale di San Marco* (Venice, 1604).

Sanuto, M., *Diarii*, ed. N. Barozzi et al., 58 vols. (Venice, 1879–1903).

————, *De origine, situ et magistratibus urbis venetae ovvero la città di Venezia*, ed. A. Caracciolo Arico (Milan, 1980).

Sultanini, B., *Il puttanismo romano, nuovamente ristampato con l'aggiunta d'un dialogo tra Pasquino, e Marforio, sopra lo stesso soggetto, & insieme, con il nuovo parlatorio delle monache* (London, 1675).

Tanner, N., et al. (eds.), *Decrees of the Ecumenical Councils*, 2 vols. (London, 1990).

Tarabotti, A., *Paradiso monacale libri tre* (Venice, 1643).

————, *Lettere familiari e di complimento della signora Arcangela Tarabotti* (Venice, 1650).

————, *La semplicità ingannata di Galerana Baratotti* (Venice, 1654).

————, *L' "Inferno monacale" di Arcangela Tarabotti*, ed. F. Medioli (Turin, 1990).

————, *Che le donne siano della spezie degli uomini*, ed. L. Panizza (London, 1994).

Valier, A., *La istituzione d'ogni stato lodevole delle donne cristiane* (Padua, 1744).

Van der Aa, P., *Thesaurus antiquitatum* (Leiden, 1722).

Vendramin, F., *Ordo rituum et caeremoniarum suscipiendi habitum monialem, & emittendi professionem* (Venice, 1694).

Wotton, H., *The Life and Letters of Sir Henry Wotton*, ed. L. Pearsall Smith, 2 vols. (Oxford, 1907).

Secondary Works

Agostini, F., *La riforma napoleonica della chiesa nella repubblica e nel regno d'Italia 1802–1814* (Vicenza, 1990).

Arenal, E., "The Convent as Catalyst for Autonomy: Two Hispanic Nuns of the Seventeenth Century," in B. Miller (ed.), *Women in Hispanic Literature* (Berkeley, 1983), pp. 147–83.

Battiston, O. (ed.), *Tre monasteri scomparsi a Venezia: Sestiere di Castello* (Venice, 1991).

———— et al. (eds), *Un piccolo regno teocratico nel cuore di Venezia: Il monastero di San Lorenzo* (Venice, 1993).

Bell, R. M., "Telling Her Sins: Male Confessors and Female Penitents in Counter-Reformation Italy," in L. L. Coon et al. (eds), *That Gentle Strength: Historical Perspectives on Women in Christianity* (Charlottesville, 1990), pp. 118–33.

Benzoni, G., "Una controversia tra Roma e Venezia all'inizio del '600: La conferma del Patriarca,"20*Bollettino dell'istituto di storia della società e dello stato veneziano* 3 (1961), pp. 121–38.

————, *Venezia nell'età della controriforma* (Milan, 1973).

Bertoli, B., "La chiesa veneziana dalla caduta della Repubblica alle soglie del Novecento," in S. Tramontin (ed.), *Storia religiosa del Veneto 1: Patriarcato di Venezia* (Padua, 1991), pp. 189–218.

Black, C. F., *Italian Confraternities in the Sixteenth Century* (Cambridge, 1989).

Bolton, B., "Mulieres Sanctae," in D. Baker (ed.), *Studies in Church History* 10 (1973), pp. 77–95.

Bossy, J., "The Counter-Reformation and the People of Catholic Europe," *Past and Present* 47 (1970), pp. 51–70.

————, *Christianity in the West, 1400–1700* (Oxford, 1985).

Bouwsma, W., *Venice and the Defense of Republican Liberty* (Berkeley, 1968).

Brown, J. C., *Immodest Acts: The Life of a Lesbian Nun in Renaissance Italy* (New York, 1986).

————, "Monache a Firenze all'inizio dell'età moderna: Un analisi demografica," *Quaderni storici* 85 (1994), pp. 117–52.

Burckhardt, J., *The Civilization of the Renaissance in Italy* (1860), trans. S.G.C. Middlemore (London, 1965).

Burke, P., *The Historical Anthropology of Early Modern Italy* (Cambridge, 1987).

————, *Venice and Amsterdam: A Study of Seventeenth-Century Elites,* 2nd ed. (Cambridge, 1994).

Calimani, R., *The Ghetto of Venice,* trans. K. Silberblatt Wolfthal (New York, 1987).

Canosa, R., *Il velo e il cappuccio: Monacazioni forzate e sessualità nei conventi femminili in Italia tra 400 e 700* (Rome, 1991).

Cappelli, A., *Cronologia e calendario perpetuo* (Milan, 1906).

Cassini, G., *Piante e vedute prospettiche di Venezia (1479–1855)* (Venice, 1982).

Cattaneo, E., "Le monacazioni forzate fra cinque e seicento," in U. Colombo (ed.), *Vita e processo di suor Virginia Maria de Leyva, monaca di Monza* (Milan, 1985), pp. 147–95.

Cecchetti, B., *La repubblica di Venezia e la corte di Roma,* 2 vols. (Venice, 1874).

Chambers, D. S., and B. Pullan (eds.), *Venice: A Documentary History, 1450–1630* (Oxford, 1992).

Chojnacka, M., "Women, Charity and Community in Early Modern Venice: The Casa delle Zitelle," *Renaissance Quarterly* 51 (1998), pp. 68–91.

————, "Women, Men, and Residential Patterns in Early Modern Venice," *Journal of Family History* 25 (2000), pp. 6–25.

Chojnacki, S., "Patrician Women in Early Renaissance Venice," *Studies in the Renaissance* 21 (1974), pp. 176–203.

————, "Dowries and Kinsmen in Early Renaissance Venice," *Journal of Interdisciplinary History* 5 (1975), pp. 571–600.

————, "La posizione della donna a Venezia nel Cinquecento," in *Tiziano e Venezia: Convegno internazionale di studi, Venezia 1976* (Milan, 1980), pp. 65–70.

————, "Subaltern Patriarchs: Patrician Bachelors in Renaissance Venice," in C. A. Lees (ed.), *Medieval Masculinities: Regarding Men in the Middle Ages* (Minneapolis, 1994), pp. 73–90.

————, "Kinship Ties and Young Patricians in Fifteenth-Century Venice," *Renaissance Quarterly* 38 (1995), pp. 240–70.

————, *Women and Men in Renaissance Venice: Twelve Essays on Patrician Society* (Baltimore, 2000).

Cicogna, E., *Delle iscrizioni veneziane* (Venice, 1824–53).

Cohn, S. K., Jr, *Women in the Streets: Essays on Sex and Power in Renaissance Italy* (Baltimore, 1996).

Colombo, U. (ed.), *Vita e processo di suor Virginia Maria de Leyva, monaca di Monza* (Milan, 1985).

Cowan, A. F., *The Urban Patriciate: Lübeck and Venice, 1580–1700* (Cologne, 1986).

Cox, V., "The Single Self: Feminist Thought and the Marriage Market in Early Modern Venice," *Renaissance Quarterly* 48 (1995), pp. 513–81.

Creytens, R., "La riforma dei monasteri femminili dopo i decreti tridentini," in *Il Concilio di Trento e la riformatione* (Rome, 1965), pp. 45–84.

Da Carmignano di Brenta, M., *Le clarisse cappucine a Venezia* (Venice-Mestre, 1985).

Daichman, G. S., "Misconduct in the Medieval Nunnery: Fact, Not Fiction," in L. L. Coon et al. (eds.), *That Gentle Strength: Historical Perspectives on Women in Christianity* (Charlottesville, 1990), pp. 97–117.

Da Mosto, A., *L'archivio di stato di Venezia: Indice generale, storico, descrittivo ed analitico,* 2 vols. (Rome, 1937–40).

Datsko Barker, P. S., "Caritas Pirckheimer: A Female Humanist Confronts the Reformation," *Sixteenth Century Journal* 26 (1995), pp. 259–72.

Davidson, N. S., "The Clergy of Venice in the Sixteenth Century," *Bulletin of the Society for Renaissance Studies* 2 (1984), pp. 19–31.

————, *The Counter-Reformation* (Oxford, 1987).

————, "Theology, Nature and the Law: Sexual Sin and Sexual Crime in Italy from the Fourteenth to the Seventeenth Century," in T. Dean and K.J.P. Lowe (eds.), *Crime, Society and the Law in Renaissance Italy* (Cambridge, 1994), pp. 74–98.

Davis, J. C., *The Decline of the Venetian Nobility as a Ruling Class* (Baltimore, 1963).

———, *A Venetian Family and its Fortune, 1500–1900: The Donà and the Conservation of Their Wealth* (Philadelphia, 1975).

Davis, N. Z., "Women on Top," in idem, *Society and Culture in Early Modern France* (Stanford, 1975), pp. 124–51.

———, *The Gift in Sixteenth-Century France* (Oxford, 2000).

Davis, R. C., *Shipbuilders of the Venetian Arsenal: Workers and Workplace in the Preindustrial City* (Baltimore, 1991).

———, "Venetian Shipbuilders and the Fountain of Wine," *Past and Present* 156 (1997), pp. 55–86.

———, "The Geography of Gender in the Renaissance," in J. C. Brown and R. C. Davis (eds.), *Gender and Society in Renaissance Italy* (London, 1998), pp. 19–38.

Dean, T., and K.J.P. Lowe (eds.), *Crime, Society and the Law in Renaissance Italy* (Cambridge, 1994).

Del Torre, G., *Venezia e la terraferma dopo la guerra di Cambrai: fiscalità e amministrazione (1515–1530)* (Milan, 1986).

Delumeau, J., *Catholicism between Luther and Voltaire: a New View of the Counter-Reformation* (London, 1977).

Derosas, R., "Moralità e giustizia a Venezia nel '500–'600. Gli esecutori contro la bestemmia," in G. Cozzi (ed.), *Stato, società e giustizia nella repubblica veneta (sec. XV–XVIII)* (Rome, 1980), pp. 435–528.

Dizionario degli istituti di perfezione (Rome, 1974–).

Eckenstein, L., *Women under Monasticism: Chapters on Saint-Lore and Convent Life between A.D. 500 and A.D. 1500* (New York, 1963; first published Cambridge, 1896).

Evangelisti, S., "'Farne quello che pare e piace . . .': L'uso e la trasmissione delle celle nel monastero di Santa Giulia di Brescia (1597–1688)," *Quaderni storici* 88 (1995), pp. 85–110.

———, "Wives, Widows, and Brides of Christ: Marriage and the Convent in the Historiography of Early Modern Italy," *Historical Journal* 43 (2000), pp. 233–47.

Faderman, L., *Surpassing the Love of Men: Romantic Friendship and Love Between Women from the Renaissance to the Present* (London, 1985; first published New York, 1981).

Fenlon, I., "Lepanto and the Arts of Celebration," *History Today* 45 (1995), pp. 24–30.

Ferraro, J. M., "The Power to Decide: Battered Wives In Early Modern Venice," *Renaissance Quarterly* 48 (1995), pp. 492–512.

Finlay, R., "The Venetian Republic as Gerontocracy: Age and Politics in the Renaissance," *Journal of Medieval and Renaissance Studies* 8 (1978), pp. 157–78.

Fiorani, L., "Monache e monasteri romani nell'età del quietismo," *Ricerche per la storia religiosa di Roma* 1 (1977), pp. 63–111.

Fletcher, A., *Gender, Sex and Subordination in England 1500–1800* (New Haven, 1995).

Franzoi, U., and D. Di Stefano, *Le chiese di Venezia* (Venice, 1976).

Gardner, J., "Nuns and Altarpieces: Agendas for Research," *Römisches Jahrbuch der Bibliotheca Hertziana* 30 (1995), pp. 27–57.

Gehl, P. F., "Libri per donne: Le monache clienti del libraio fiorentino Piero Morosi (1588–1607)," in G. Zarri (ed.), *Donna, disciplina, creanza cristiana dal XV al XVII secolo* (Rome, 1996), pp. 67–82.

Gill, K., "Open Monasteries for Women in Late Medieval and Early Modern Italy: Two Roman Examples," in C. Monson (ed.), *The Crannied Wall* (Michigan, 1992), pp. 15–47.

————, "*Scandala*: Controversies Concerning Clausura & Women's Religious Communities in Late Medieval Italy," in S. Waugh and P. Diehl (eds.), *Christendom and Its Discontents* (Cambridge, 1996), pp. 177–203.

Ginzburg, C., "The Inquisitor as Anthropologist," in idem, *Myths, Emblems, Clues*, trans. J. and A. Tedeschi (London, 1990), pp. 156–64.

Giuliani, I., O.F.M., "Genesi e primo sec. di vita del magistrato sopra monasteri, Venezia, 1519–1620," *Le Venezie Francescane: Rivista storica artistica letteraria illustrata* 28 (1961), pp. 42–68, 106–69.

Goffen, R., *Piety and Patronage in Renaissance Rome: Bellini, Titian, and the Franciscans* (New Haven, 1986).

Grendler, P., *Schooling in Renaissance Italy: Literacy and Learning, 1300–1600* (Baltimore, 1989).

Grieser, D. J., "A Tale of Two Convents: Nuns and Anabaptists in Münster, 1533–35," *Sixteenth-Century Journal* 26 (1995), pp. 31–47.

Haliczer, S., *Sexuality in the Confessional: A Sacrament Profaned* (New York, 1996).

Hamburger, J., "Art, Enclosure, and the *Cura Monialium*: Prolegomena in the Guise of a Postscript," *Gesta* 31 (1992), pp. 108–34.

Heal, B., "Alone of All Her Sex or a Woman Like any Other? Devotion to the Virgin Mary in Reformation Germany," in E. Clark and M. Laven (eds.), *Women and Religion in the Atlantic World, 1550–1900* (forthcoming).

Henderson, J., "The Flagellant Movement and Flagellant Confraternities in

Central Italy, 1260–1400," in D. Baker (ed.), *Studies in Church History* 15 (1978), pp. 147–60.

Hierarchia Catholica, ed. C. Eubel et al., 8 vols (Regensburg & Padua, 1910–79).

Hills, H., "Cities and Virgins: Female Aristocratic Convents in Early Modern Naples and Palermo," *Oxford Art Journal* 22 (1999), pp. 29–54.

Hufton, O., *The Prospect before Her: A History of Women in Western Europe* (London, 1995).

Hughes, D. O., "Sumptuary Law and Social Relations in Renaissance Italy," in J. Bossy (ed.), *Disputes and Settlements: Law and Human Relations in the West* (Cambridge, 1983), pp. 69–99.

Hunecke, V., "Matrimonio e demografia del patriziato veneziano (sec. XVII–XVIII)," *Studi veneziani* n.s. 21 (1991), pp. 269–319.

———, "Kindbett oder Kloster: Lebenswege venezianischer Patrizierinnen im 17. und 18. Jahrhundert," *Geschichte und Gesellschaft* 18 (1992), pp. 446–76.

Intra, G. B., "Di Ippolito Capilupi e del suo tempo," *Archivio storico Lombardo* 20 (1893), pp. 76–142.

Kendrick, R. L., *Celestial Sirens: Nuns and their Music in Early Modern Milan* (Oxford, 1996).

King, M. L., *Women of the Renaissance* (Chicago, 1991).

Kirshner, J., and A. Molho, "The Dowry Fund and the Marriage Market in Early Quattrocento Florence," *Journal of Modern History* 50 (1978), pp. 403–38.

Klapisch-Zuber, C., *Women, Family and Ritual in Renaissance Italy* (Chicago, 1985).

Kuehn, T., *Law, Family and Women: Toward a Legal Anthropology of Renaissance Italy* (Chicago, 1991).

Labalme, P., "Venetian Women on Venetian Women: Three Early Modern Feminists," *Archivio veneto* 117 (1981), pp. 81–109.

——— and L. S. White, "How to (and How Not to) Get Married in Sixteenth-Century Venice. (Selections from the Diaries of Marin Sanudo)," *Renaissance Quarterly* 52 (1999), pp. 43–72.

Lane, F. C., *Venice: A Maritime Republic* (Baltimore, 1973).

Laven, D., *Venice and Venetia under the Habsburgs, 1814–35* (Oxford, 2002).

Lea, H. C., *History of Sacerdotal Celibacy in the Christian Church,* 2nd edn. (London, 1932; first published 1867).

Levin, R., "More Nuns and Nunneries and Hamlet's speech to Ophelia," *Notes and Queries* 239 (1994), pp. 41–42.

Litchfield, R. B., "Demographic Characteristics of Florentine Patrician Families, Sixteenth to Nineteenth Centuries," *Journal of Economic History* 29 (1969), pp. 191–205.

Logan, O.M.T., "Studies in the Religious Life of Venice in the Sixteenth and Early Seventeenth Centuries: The Venetian Clergy and Religious Orders, 1520–1630" (unpublished doctoral dissertation, University of Cambridge, 1967).

———, "The Ideal of the Bishop and the Venetian Patriciate: *c.* 1430–*c.* 1630," *Journal of Ecclesiastical History* 29 (1978), pp. 415–50.

———, *The Venetian Upper Clergy in the Sixteenth and Early Seventeenth Centuries: A Study in Religious Culture*, 2 vols. (Salzburg, 1995).

Lowe, K.J.P., "Female Strategies for Success in a Male-Ordered World: The Benedictine Convent of Le Murate in Florence in the Fifteenth and Early Sixteenth Centuries," in W. J. Sheils and D. Wood (eds.), *Studies in Church History* 27 (1990), pp. 209–21.

———, "Secular Brides and Convent Brides: Wedding Ceremonies in Italy during the Renaissance and Counter-Reformation," in T. Dean and K.J.P. Lowe (eds.), *Marriage in Italy 1300–1650* (Cambridge, 1998), pp. 41–65.

———, "Elections of Abbesses and Notions of Identity in Fifteenth- and Sixteenth-Century Italy, with Special Reference to Venice," *Renaissance Quarterly* 54 (2001), pp. 389–429.

McGough, L., " 'Raised from the Devil's Jaws': A Convent for Repentant Prostitutes in Venice, 1530–1670" (unpublished doctoral dissertation, Northwestern University, 1997).

McNamara, J.A.K., *Sisters in Arms: Catholic Nuns through Two Millennia* (Cambridge, MA, 1996).

Martin, R., *Witchcraft and the Inquisition in Venice, 1550–1650* (Oxford, 1989).

Martini, A., *Manuale di metrologia ossia misure, pesi e monete in uso attualmente e anticamente presso tutti i popoli* (Rome, 1976).

Mauss, M., "Essai sur le don: Forme et raison de l'échange dans les sociétés archaïques," *L'Année sociologique* n.s. 1 (1923–4), pp. 30–186.

Medioli, F., "Monacazioni forzate: donne ribelli al proprio destino," *Clio* 30 (1994), pp. 431–54.

———, "Monache e monacazioni nel Seicento," *Rivista di storia e letteratura religiosa* 33 (1997), 670–93.

———, "La clausura delle monache nell'amministrazione della congregazione romana sopra i regolari' " in G. Zarri (ed.), *Il monachesimo femminile in Italia dall'alto medioevo al secolo XVII* (Verona, 1997), pp. 249–82.

Molho, A., " 'Tanquam vere mortua': Le professioni religiose femminili nella Firenze del tardo medioevo," *Società e storia* 43 (1989), pp. 1–44.

Monson, C. (ed.), *The Crannied Wall: Women, Religion, and the Arts in Early Modern Europe* (Michigan, 1992).

———, "Disembodied Voices: Music in the Nunneries of Bologna in the Midst of the Counter-Reformation," in idem (ed.), *The Crannied Wall*, pp. 191–209.

———, *Disembodied Voices: Music and Culture in an Early Modern Italian Convent* (Berkeley, 1995).

Muir, E., *Civic Ritual in Renaissance Venice* (Princeton, 1981).

———, *Ritual in Early Modern Europe* (Cambridge, 1997).

New Catholic Encyclopedia, 15 vols. (New York, 1967).

Niero, A., *I patriarchi di Venezia* (Venice, 1961).

Norberg, K., "The Counter-Reformation and Women, Religious and Lay" in J. O'Malley (ed.), *Catholicism in Early Modern History* (St Louis, 1988), pp. 133–46.

Odorisio, G. C., *Donna e società nel seicento: Lucrezia Marinelli e Arcangela Tarabotti* (Rome, 1979).

Ozment, S., *When Fathers Ruled: Family Life in Reformation Europe* (Cambridge, MA, 1983).

Paschini, P., "I monasteri femminili in Italia nel '500'," in *Problemi di vita religiosa in Italia nel cinquecento* (Padua, 1960), pp. 31–60.

Pavan, E., "Police des moeurs, société et politique à Venise à la fin du Moyen Age," *Revue Historique* 264 (1990), pp. 241–88.

Pedani, M. P., "Monasteri di agostiniane a Venezia," *Archivio veneto* 125 (1985), pp. 35–78.

———, "L'osservanza imposta: i monasteri conventuali femminili a Venezia nei primi anni del cinquecento," *Archivio veneto* 144 (1995), pp. 113–25.

Perry, M. E., *Gender and Disorder in Early Modern Seville* (Princeton, 1990).

Pilot, A., "Una capatina in alcuni monasteri veneziani del '500'," *Rivista d'Italia* 13 (1910), pp. 49–72.

Primhak, V. J., "Women in Religious Communities: The Benedictine Convents in Venice, 1400–1550" (unpublished doctoral dissertation, University of London, 1991).

Prodi, P., "The Structure and Organization of the Church in Renaissance Venice: Suggestions for Research," in J. R. Hale (ed.), *Renaissance Venice* (London, 1973), pp. 409–30.

Pullan, B., *Rich and Poor in Renaissance Venice: The Social Institutions of a Catholic State, to 1620* (Oxford, 1971).

———, "The Occupations and Investments of the Venetian Nobility in the

Middle and Late Sixteenth Century," in J. R. Hale (ed.), *Renaissance Venice* (London, 1973), pp. 379–408.

Queller, D. E., *The Venetian Patriciate: Reality versus Myth* (Urbana, 1986).

—— and T. F. Madden, "Father of the Bride: Fathers, Daughters, and Dowries in Late Medieval and Early Renaissance Venice," *Renaissance Quarterly* 46 (1993), pp. 685–711.

Radke, G. M., "Nuns and Their Art: The Case of San Zaccaria in Renaissance Venice," *Renaissance Quarterly* 54 (2001), pp. 430–59.

Ranft, P., *Women and the Religious Life* (London, 1996).

Ravid, B., "Curfew Time in the Ghetto of Venice," in E. E. Kittell and T. F. Madden (eds.), *Medieval and Renaissance Venice* (Urbana, 1999), pp. 237–75.

Romano, D., *Patricians and Popolani: The Social Foundations of the Venetian Renaissance State* (Baltimore, 1987).

Roper, L., *The Holy Household: Women and Morals in Reformation Augsburg* (Oxford, 1989).

——, *Oedipus and the Devil: Witchcraft, Sexuality and Religion in Early Modern Europe* (London, 1994).

Rosa, M., "The Nun," in R. Villari (ed.), *Baroque Personae* (Chicago, 1995), pp. 195–238.

Rosi, M., "Le monache nella vita genovese dal secolo XV al XVII," *Atti d. soc. Ligure di storia patria* 27 (1895), pp. 5–205.

Ruggiero, G., *Violence in Early Renaissance Venice* (New Brunswick, 1980).

——, *The Boundaries of Eros: Sex Crime and Sexuality in Renaissance Venice* (New York, 1985).

——, *Binding Passions: Tales of Magic, Marriage and Power at the End of the Renaissance* (New York, 1993).

Russo, C., *I monasteri femminili di clausura a Napoli nel secolo XVII* (Naples, 1970).

Santschi, E., "L'obituaire de San Daniele (1577–1804): Etude démographique," *Studi veneziani* 13 (1971), pp. 655–64.

Scaraffia, L., and G. Zarri, *Donne e fede: Santità a vita religiosa in Italia* (Rome, 1994).

Schulenburg, J. T., "Strict Active Enclosure and its Effects on the Female Monastic Experience (c. 500–1100)," in J. A. Nichols and L. T. Shank (eds.), *Distant Echoes: Medieval Religious Women* (Kalamazoo, 1984), pp. 51–86.

Schutte, A. J., "Tra Scilla e Cariddi: Giorgio Polacco, donne e disciplina nella Venezia del Seicento," in G. Zarri (ed.), *Donne, disciplina, creanza cristiana dal XV al XVII secolo* (Rome, 1996), pp. 215–36.

Sedgwick, A., "The Nuns of Port-Royal: A Study of Female Spirituality in Seventeenth-Century France," in L. L. Coon et al. (eds.), *That Gentle Strength: Historical Perspectives on Women in Christianity* (Charlottesville, 1990), pp. 176–89.

Sennett, R., *Flesh and Stone: The Body and the City in Western Civilization* (London, 1994).

Sperling, J. G., *Convents and the Body Politic in Late Renaissance Venice* (Chicago, 1999).

Spinelli, G., "I religiosi e le religiose," in B. Bertoli (ed.), *La chiesa di Venezia nel seicento* (Venice, 1992), pp. 173–209.

Strasser, U. " 'Aut murus aut maritus?' Women's Lives in Counter-Reformation Munich" (unpublished doctoral dissertation, University of Minnesota, 1997).

——, "Bones of Contention: Cloistered Nuns, Decorated Relics, and the Contest over Women's Place in the Public Sphere of Counter-Reformation Munich," *Archiv für Reformationsgeschichte* (1999).

Tacchi-Venturi, P., *Storia della compagnia di Gesù in Italia* (Rome, 1930).

Thornton, D., *The Scholar in His Study: Ownership and Experience in Renaissance Italy* (Yale, 1997).

Tramontin, S., "La visita apostolica del 1581 a Venezia," *Studi veneziani* 9 (1967), pp. 453–533.

——, "La diocesi nelle relazioni dei patriarchi alla Santa Sede," in ed. Bruno Bertoli, *La chiesa di Venezia nel seicento* (Venice, 1992), pp. 55–90.

Trexler, R., "Le Célibat à la fin du moyen âge: Les religieuses de Florence," *Annales: ESC* 27 (1972), pp. 1329–50.

Walker, J., "Gambling and Venetian Noblemen, c. 1500–1700," *Past and Present* 162 (1999), pp. 28–69.

Weaver, E., "Spiritual Fun: A Study of Sixteenth-Century Tuscan Convent Theater," in M. B. Rose (ed.), *Women in the Middle Ages and the Renaissance* (Syracuse, 1986), pp. 173–205.

——, "The Convent Wall in Tuscan Convent Drama," in C. Monson (ed.), *The Crannied Wall* (Michigan, 1992), pp. 73–86.

Weissman, R.F.E., *Ritual Brotherhood in Renaissance Florence* (New York, 1982).

Wiesner, M. E., "Nuns, Wives and Mothers: Women and the Reformation in Germany," in S. Marshall (ed.), *Women in Reformation and Counter-Reformation Europe* (Bloomington, 1989), pp. 8–28.

——, *Women and Gender in Early Modern Europe* (Cambridge, 1993).

——, *Gender, Church and State in Early Modern Germany* (London, 1998).

————, *Christianity and Sexuality in the Early Modern World: Regulating Desire, Reforming Practice* (London, 1999).

Winkelmes, M. A., "Taking Part: Benedictine Nuns as Patrons of Art and Architecture," in G. A. Johnson and S. F. Matthews Grieco (eds.), *Picturing Women in Renaissance and Baroque Italy* (Cambridge, 1997), pp. 91–110.

Wootton, D., *Paolo Sarpi: Between Renaissance and Enlightenment* (Cambridge, 1983).

————, "Ulysses Bound? Venice and the Idea of Liberty from Howell to Hume," in idem (ed.), *Republicanism, Liberty, and Commercial Society, 1649–1776* (Stanford, 1994), pp. 341–67.

Wright, A. D., "The Venetian View of Church and State: Catholic Erastianism?", *Studi secenteschi* 19 (1978), pp. 75–106.

————, *The Counter-Reformation* (London, 1982).

Zanette, E., *Suor Arcangela: Monaca del seicento veneziano* (Venice, 1960).

Zarri, G., "I monasteri femminili a Bologna tra il XIII e il XVII secolo," *Atti e memorie della deputazione di storia patria per le province di Romagna* n.s. 24 (1973), pp. 133–220.

————, "Monasteri femminili e città (secoli XV–XVIII), in G. Chittolini and G. Miccoli (eds.), *Storia d'Italia: La Chiesa e il potere politico* (Turin, 1986), pp. 359–429.

————, "Monasteri femminili in Italia nel secolo XVI," *Rivista di storia e letteratura religiosa* 33 (1997), pp. 643–69.

Zorzi, A., *Venezia scomparsa,* 2 vols. (Milan, 1972).

————, *La monaca di Venezia: Una storia d'amore e di libertà* (Milan, 1996).

Index